# Alexander Milne

# Manual of Materia Medica and Therapeutics

Salzwasser

**Alexander Milne**

# Manual of Materia Medica and Therapeutics

1. Auflage | ISBN: 978-3-84605-576-2

Erscheinungsort: Frankfurt, Deutschland

Erscheinungsjahr: 2020

Salzwasser Verlag GmbH

Reprint of the original, first published in 1869.

# MANUAL

## OF

## MATERIA MEDICA AND THERAPEUTICS

### EMBRACING ALL THE

### MEDICINES OF THE BRITISH PHARMACOPŒIA

&c. &c.

BY

## ALEXANDER MILNE, M.D.,

# BY THE SAME AUTHOR.

1. ON THE COMPARATIVE VALUE OF THE LONG FORCEPS AND TURNING IN CASES OF CONTRACTED PELVIC BRIM.

2. ON PLACENTA PRÆVIA.

3. CRANIOTOMY AND CEPHALOTRIPSY CONTRASTED.

4. ON RETROVERSION OF THE GRAVID UTERUS.

# PREFACE TO THE FIRST EDITION.

THIS volume appears at the request of some of my Pupils at the Dispensary, who, on the publication of the British Pharmacopœia, felt greatly disappointed with that, in many respects, excellent work; perhaps owing to their anticipating too much from it, and what is only to be found in a commentary. It was begun not without misgivings, and carried on somewhat hurriedly amid not a few interruptions, and may therefore be chargeable with many imperfections; but if it serve to revive forgotten facts, or refresh the memory of the Student when time is awanting for the study of more elaborate works (such as the learned treatise of Professor Christison, and others), I shall feel abundantly satisfied.

With regard to the arrangement of the book, I have followed in part that of the B. Pharmacopœia; but I have preferred placing the officinal formulæ immediately below the drug from which they derive their title, as best adapted for easy reference, and in order that the various preparations of the medicines might be seen at a glance. I have frequently adopted the excellent descriptions of the characters of drugs given in the B. P.; in other cases, I have modified them or given my own. In conclusion, I have to express my regret that its appearance has been delayed several weeks after the appointed time.

A. M.

9 TEVIOT ROW, EDINBURGH, *May 1864.*

# PREFACE TO THE SECOND EDITION.

THE First Edition of this work has been " out of print " for a considerable time, and I have been often urged by pupils, publishers, and even practitioners, to prepare a Second. Various engagements, and the fact of other excellent works being extant on the same subject, have hitherto prevented me ; but I now yield to renewed solicitations. The book was chiefly intended for Students (pupils and others), and no attempt was made to obtrude it on the notice of the profession, but I am happy to find that it has travelled much beyond the former circle, and found a kindly welcome and appreciation among medical men in remote parts of the kingdom. Various members of the profession have written me spontaneously, testifying to its utility, and thanking me for hints found in it which they found new to them, but which I had hardly reckoned novel. For such testimonies, unexpected, I am not more surprised than highly gratified : at the same time I cannot flatter myself that anything more than brevity has been the soul of its merit, and the cause of its success. In this age of activity, there is little time for circumlocution ; and the deeply absorbed practitioner, above all men, desiderates condensation. The " mighty tome," therefore, however valuable a mine it may be, is more rarely explored, and the handy-book gets thumb-worn, and carries the day.

In reference to the arrangement of the Manual no alteration has been made ; but there are considerable additions, and it has also been subjected to careful revision. Some drugs rising into renown have been more largely touched upon, and others of growing reputation introduced. The more potent poisons, with their tests and antidotes, have been briefly treated of separately. For faults and shortcomings, I have again to plead much sadly broken time— an evil known by dire experience to most members of our common profession. A. M.

EDINBURGH, *March 1869.*

# CONTENTS.

# MATERIA MEDICA.

### Acaciæ Gummi. Gum Arabic.

One or more undetermined species of Acacia Linn. A gummy exudation from the stem ; collected chiefly in Cordofan in Eastern Africa, and imported from Alexandria. N. F. Leguminosæ.

*Charact.*—In whitish spheroidal tears, from the size of a pea to that of a nutmeg : transparent, brittle, with a bland taste ; soluble in water.

*Analysis.*—Arabin, a soluble gum, and water. The inferior sorts contain bassorin, an insoluble gum.

*Actions and uses.*—Nutritive, emollient, demulcent. As a demulcent it is much employed in the form of mucilage, to allay the acrimony of inflamed mucous membranes, as in sore throat, catarrh of the bladder, gonorrhœa, and that produced by irritant poisons. It is used for suspending rather insoluble substances, such as bismuth, in mixtures, and for giving tenacity and plasticity to pill-masses, but is inferior to the confection of roses where the pills are to be kept for any length of time. Dose, gr. xxx. to gr. lx., allowed to dissolve slowly in the mouth.

Mucilago Acaciæ. Take of gum arabic ℥iv. ; dist. water f℥vi. M.

### Acetum. Vinegar.

An acid liquid prepared from malt and unmalted grain by the acetous fermentation.

*Charact.*—A liquid of a straw colour and acetous odour.

*Actions and uses.*—Refrigerant, used externally in fevers, but in no way superior to cold water. Internally, diluted with water, as a drink, in the colliquative sweating of hectic, but inferior to dilute sulphuric acid. Employed also as an astringent in gargles, and as a fumigator in sick-rooms. In poisoning with the alkalies, or alkaline carbonates, it is one of the best antidotes. Dose, f$\mathfrak{z}$ij. to f$\mathfrak{z}$ss.

### Acidum Aceticum. Acetic Acid.

An acid liquid prepared from wood by destructive distillation, and containing 28 per cent of anhydrous acetic acid.

*Charact.*—A colourless liquid with a strong acid reaction, and odour of vinegar.

*Acidum Dilutum.*—Take of acetic acid Oj. ; dist. water Ovij. Mix. Dose, f$\mathfrak{z}$j. to f$\mathfrak{z}$ij.

### Acidum Aceticum Glaciale. Glacial Acetic Acid.

Concentrated acetic acid, $HO, C^4 H^3 O^3$ or $C_4 H_6 O_3$.

*Charact.*—A colourless fluid with a pungent acetous odour, converted when cooled to nearly $32^0$, into colourless prismatic crystals. Specific gravity 1·065, which is increased by adding to the acid 10 per cent of water.

*Uses.*—Acetic acid is a speedy and powerful vesicant, but seldom used as a counterirritant. It is one of the best caustics for destroying corns and warts, especially of a syphilitic origin.

### Acidum Arseniosum. Arsenious Acid.

Synonym.—Arsenicum Album, Ed. $As, O^3$ or $As_2 O_3$.

*Charact.*—A heavy white powder, which, when slowly sublimed in a glass tube, forms minute brilliant and transparent octa-hedral crystals. It is sparingly soluble in water, and its solution gives, with ammonio-nitrate of silver, a canary yellow precipitate, insoluble in water, but readily dissolved by ammonia and nitric acid.

*Actions and uses.*—Caustic, irritant, tonic, alterative, anti-periodic. As a caustic it was formerly employed in cancerous and malignant ulcerations, such as lupus, noli-me-tangere, cancer, fungus hœmatodes ; but it has now given place to other remedies free from the risk of poisoning by absorption. As an irritant it is a very potent poison, three

or four grains having occasioned death. Its most conspicuous effects are inflammation of the alimentary mucous membrane : at other times the most marked symptom is intense
depression of the circulation, death taking place from mortal
faintness ; or, as Orfila observes, " the vital properties of
the heart being destroyed." Secondary affections, such as
epileptic convulsions, partial palsy, dyspepsia, and emaciation are also witnessed. In poisoning, the stomach-pump
should be used, or failing it, an emetic of sulphate of zinc,
vomiting being aided by demulcent drinks. The hydrated
sesquioxide of iron, and magnesia in the gelatinous condition, or calcined, are important antidotes.

*Medicinal actions.*—In small doses it is a tonic, and perhaps in virtue of this, alterative, getting rid of various
morbid conditions of the system, on which the atony
depends. It is widely given as an antiperiodic, but in ague
it is inferior to quinia, in neuralgia to iron, in epilepsy to
zinc, silver, or digitalis. Arsenic is often of great service in
chronic cutaneous diseases, such as lepra and psoriasis, its
action being favoured by combination with iodide of potassium. Chronic rheumatism has sometimes been benefited
by it. We need hardly say that so powerful a remedy
must be carefully watched. The physiological effects are,
increased pulse, tenderness of the eyes, puffiness of the
eyelids, whiteness of the tongue, heat and dull pain along
the alimentary canal. When these occur it is time to in-
termit its use. Dose, from $\frac{1}{80}$ to $\frac{1}{12}$ of a grain, in the form of
pill with bread-crumb ; but the liquor is by far the pre-
ferable way of prescribing it.

*Liquor Arsenicalis.*—Take of arsenious acid gr. lxxx. ;
carbonate of potash gr. lxxx. ; comp. tinct. lavender f℥v. ;
distilled water a sufficiency. Place the As, $O^3$ and the KO,
$CO^2$ in a flask with f℥x. of the water, and apply heat until
a clear solution is obtained. Allow this to cool, then add
the lavender and as much dist. water as will make the
bulk of one pint. The specific gravity of this preparation
is 1·009. Dose, min. iij., gradually increased to min. viij.
twice-a-day, or so. In min. v. there is $\frac{1}{24}$ grain of arsenious

acid. *Formula.* ℞ Liquoris arsenicalis fℨj. ; potassii iodidi gr. xxiv. ; infusi calumbæ ad fℨvi. misce. Sumat fℨss. ter in die. Tonic and alterative, in cutaneous diseases.

### Liquor Arsenici Hydrochloricus. Hydrochloric Solution of Arsenic.

Take of arsenious acid in powder 80 grains ; hydrochloric acid 2 fluid drachms. Distilled water a sufficiency. Boil the arsenious acid with the hydrochloric acid, and 4 ounces of the water until it is dissolved, then add distilled water to make the bulk up to one pint. This is of the same strength as the Liq. arsenicalis.

### Acidum Benzoicum. Benzoic acid.

An acid, HO, $C^{14} H^5 O^3$, or $HC_7 H_5 O_2$, obtained from benzoin by sublimation.

*Charact.*—In light feathery crystalline plates, nearly white, with a strong odour of benzoin : sparingly soluble in water, but freely in rectified spt.

*Action and uses.*—Expectorant, but of little efficacy. Formerly given as an antilithic. Dose, gr. v. to gr. xxx. dissolved in large quantity of water.

### Acidum Carbolicum. Carbolic Acid.

Synonym.—Phenic acid, HO, $C_{12} H_5 O$, or $HC_6 H_5 O$. An acid obtained from coal-tar oil by fractional distillation and subsequent purification.

*Charact.*—In colourless acicular crystals, which at a temp. of 95° become an oily fluid, having an odour and taste resembling creasote. Sp. g. 1·065.

*Uses.*—Caustic, stimulant, and antiseptic. This article has of late received a very great impulse from the researches of M. Pasteur, and the experiments of Mr Lister ; and surgeons are employing it extensively in wounds and bruises, in abscesses and compound fractures. In such cases it seems to do good in its threefold capacity of caustic, stimulant, and antiseptic. For example, it represses granulations where they are exuberant, invigorates weak and unhealthy sores, and averts the tendency to suppuration.

The theory of its action in the latter is, that it combats and destroys those minute organisms—spores of infusoria, &c., (discovered by Pasteur), floating in the air, especially of crowded cities, and which are believed to operate injuriously on breaches of continuity—exciting and promoting suppuration and unhealthy action. Ample evidence has already been afforded of its value in such cases, suppuration having been, if not averted, at least much diminished ; and irritative fever, and the risks of hectic and pyæmia averted. Did the drug do nothing more than this it would stamp it as the most invaluable of modern times, barring the wondrous chloroform. But it has a wider range of useful application. It is of service in burns ; in ulcers ; in skin diseases, such as lepra, psoriasis, porrigo, and scabies ; and even in lupus it fails not to leave a beneficial mark. As an injection (gr. j. to fʒiv. Aq.) it corrects fœtor of the bowel or bladder ; and foul breath is combated well by a gargle of the strength of gr. j. to the fʒi. Internally it is of service in chronic vomiting, and in worms. Dose, gr. j. to ij. in Aq. Cinnam, or Tinct. Cardam, Co. and Aq. The others are made thus—For compound fractures and abscesses, 1 part to 4 or 5 of boiled linseed oil. Weaker solutions answer for less serious cases, such as 1 to 10 ; and for skin diseases even more dilute. The paste is made by mixing the acid and oil with carbonate of lime.

Glycerinum acidi carbolici. Carbolic acid 1, glycerine 4, rub well till dissolved. Dose, min. v. to x. Applied somewhat diluted in skin diseases, &c.

### Acidum Citricum. Citric Acid.

An acid, 3 HO, $C_{12}$ $H_5$ $O_{11}$, +2 HO, or $H_3$ $C_6$ $H_5$ $O_7$. $H_2$ O, obtained from lemon juice, or from the juice of the fruit of citrus limetta, Risso, the Lime.

*Charact.*—In colourless right rhombic prisms, with a strong acid taste ; soluble in water.

*Actions and uses.*—Refrigerant, but not much employed. Does not possess the antiscorbutic virtues of the lemon juice. May be used for effervescing drinks, but tartaric acid, which is cheaper, is generally employed. Dose, gr. x. to gr. xxx. For artificial lemon juice, dissolve ten drachms in a pint of water.

### Acidum Gallicum. Gallic Acid.

An acid, 3 HO, $C^{14}$ $H^3$ $O^7$ +2 HO, or $H_3$ $C_7$ $H_3$ $O_5$. $H_2$ O, prepared from galls.

*Charact.*—In whitish, or pale fawn, acicular prisms, very sparingly soluble in cold, but freely so in boiling water, rectified spt. and ether. Gives a bluish-black precipitate with a persalt of iron.

*Preparation.*—Galls are exposed under the influence of air and moisture for six weeks, at a temp. of $60^0$ to $70^0$; when the tannin in them is decomposed, and converted into gallic acid.

*Actions and uses.*—An astringent of great power. It is of considerable value in hemorrhage from the lungs, stomach, kidney, bladder, and uterus. In Albuminuria, and fatty kidney, it often arrests, temporarily at least, the secretion of fat and albumen. In hæmoptysis beneficial results are seldom obtained, until the dose is increased to gr. xl. or gr. lx. per diem. The night sweating of phthisis is often mitigated by it. Dose, gr. v. to gr. xx.

*Formula.*—℞. acidi gallici gr. lx.; pulveris opii gr. iij.; pulveris aromatici gr. xii. Misce. Divide in pulveres sex, quorum capiat unum sextis horis. Useful in most kinds of hemorrhage; and augmented discharges, diarrhœa, &c. Incompatibles—the sesquisalts of iron.

Glycerinum acidi gallici, 1 part in 6 by weight.

### Acidum Hydrochloricum. Hydrochloric Acid.

Synonym.—Acidum muriaticum purum, Ed. Dub. Hydrochloric acid gas, HCl dissolved in water.

*Charact.*—A colourless and strongly acid liquid, emitting at ordinary temperatures white vapours, having a pungent odour. Gives with nitrate of silver a curdy white precipitate, soluble in excess of ammonia, but not in nitric acid.

*Actions and uses.*—A very powerful corrosive and irritant poison, dissolving the living animal textures with which it comes into contact. Antidotes—chalk, magnesia, and demulcent drinks. Used as a caustic in phagedenic ulcers, to arrest the extension of mortification in cancrum oris, and as an external application in hospital gangrene. It has been used also to destroy the plastic exudation of diphtheria, and, in the form of gargle, in the. sore throat of scarlatina.

*Acidum Hydrochloricum Dilutum.*—Take of hydrochloric acid 8 fluid ounces. Distilled water a sufficiency. Dilute the acid with 16 ounces of the water, then add more water, so that at a temp. of 60⁰ it shall measure 26½ fluid ounces.

*Actions and uses.*—Tonic. Given in diphtheria, malignant scarlatina, continued fevers. Also in debility of digestive organs, attended with a deposit of phosphates from the urine. A useful addition to gargles. Dose, min. x. to xl.

*Acidum Nitro-hydrochloricum Dilutum.*—Take of nitric acid f℥ijj. ; hydrochloric acid f℥iv. ; dist. wat. f℥xxv. Add to the water first the nitric, and then the hydrochloric acid. Mix.

*Actions and uses.*—Tonic and alterative. Given combined generally with a bitter infusion in secondary syphilis, and in sluggish action, and chronic induration, or abscess of the liver. Dose, min. x. to xxx. A foot-bath of the strength of f℥iv. ss. of the strong acid to three gallons of water—in a wooden vessel—is said to have a very palliative influence during the passage of biliary calculi through the duct.


**Acidum Hydrocyanicum Dilutum.** Dilute Hydrocyanic Acid.

Hydrocyanic acid, $HC^2 N$, or $HCN$, dissolved in water, and constituting 2 per cent by weight of the solution.

*Charact.*—A colourless fluid with a peculiar odour, only slightly and transiently reddening litmus. Treated with a minute quantity of a mixed solution of sulphate and persulphate of iron, and afterwards with potash, and finally acidulated with hydrochloric acid, it forms prussian blue. Specific gravity 0·997.

This acid contains rather more than half as much anhydrous acid as acidum hydrocyanicum, Ed.

*Preparation.*—Take of ferrocyanide of Potassium ʒij¼ ; sulphuric acid fʒj. ; dist. water fʒxxx. or a sufficiency. Dissolve the ferrocyanide in fʒx. of the water, then add the acid. sulph. previously diluted with fʒiv. of the water and cooled. Put them into a retort, and adapt this to a receiver containing fʒviij. of the water, which must be kept carefully cold. Distil with a gentle heat by the aid of a sand-bath, until the fluid in the receiver measures fʒxvij. Add to this fʒiij. of the water, or as much as may be sufficient to bring the acid to the required strength, so that 100 grains (or 110 minims) of it, precipitated with a solution of nitrite of silver shall yield ten grains of dry cyanide of silver.

*Actions and uses.*—One of the strongest poisons we possess, death having been caused by a mixture containing less than a grain of the anhydrous acid. In general, it has killed rapidly, death being preceded by spasmodic breathing, convulsions, and insensibility. If seen in time, the victim should be subjected to cold affusion, water being showered on the head and chest in steady streams, and ammonia inhaled at the same time. A mixture of a proto and a persalt of iron, with an alkaline carbonate, is also an antidote. In medicinal doses it is sedative, calmative, anodyne, and antispasmodic. It abates the force of the circulation, diminishes the sensibility of the nervous system, alleviates pain, and lessens spasm. Employed as a palliative in the cough of catarrh, pneumonia, pertussis, spasmodic asthma, phthisis, cynanche laryngea, and in the spasmodic cough of nervous and hysterical females. Benefit has accrued from it in the excited action of the heart in pericarditis ; and it seldom fails to relieve the painful spasm of the stomach in gastrodynia, enterodynia, and some cases of pyrosis. Externally it has been employed in the form of lotion for allaying the itching and irritation of some skin diseases, such as prurigo and lichen. Though not a cumulative poison, it should be well watched until the proper dose for the particular patient is ascertained. Those taking it complain at times of irritation about the fauces, and a feeling of enlargement of the tongue, with nausea.

*Dose.*—Min. ij. to viij. in syrup, and in the form of draughts.

*Formula for external use.*—℞ Acidi hydrocyanici diluti f℥ij. ; glycerini f℥j. ; aquæ ad f℥viij. Mix.

*Incompatibles.*—Strychnia, all sulphurets, nitrate of silver, sulphate of copper, and sulphate of iron, if along with an alkali.

### Acidum Nitricum. Nitric Acid.

*Charact.*—A strongly acid and corrosive liquid. Specific gravity 1·42. Prepared from nitrate of potash, or nitrate of soda by distillation with sulphuric acid and water, and containing 70 per cent by weight of the nitric acid, HO, $NO_5$, or $HNO_3$, corresponding to 60 per cent of anhydrous nitric acid, $NO_5$, or $N_2 O_5$.

*Actions and uses.*—A powerful corrosive and irritant, killing quickly form pain and exhaustion, resulting from organic injury of the alimentary canal. Antidotes same as for hydrochloric acid. As a caustic used as an application to poisoned wounds, parts bitten by rabid animals, venereal and phagedenic ulcers, and certain forms of hemorrhoids. The contiguous parts must be covered by plaster, or ung. resinæ.

### Acidum Nitricum Dilutum.

*Prep.*—Nitric acid, 6 fluid ounces ; distilled water, a sufficiency. Dilute the acid with 24 fluid ounces of the water, then add more water, so that, at a temp. of 60°, it shall measure 31 fluid ounces.

Tonic, but of no great power. Given in chronic hepatitis, phosphatic gravel, and by some as an antisyphilitic. It seems to have done good in secondary syphilis allied to a strumous habit. As an application to the callous edges of indolent ulcers it is inferior to pressure or a blister. Dose min. x. to xxx.

### Acidum Phosphoricum Dilutum.

Dilute Phosphoric Acid. Phosphoric acid, 3HO, PO$^5$, or H$_3$ PO$_4$, dissolved in water, and corresponding to 10 per cent by weight of anhydrous phosphoric acid, PO$_5$, or P$_2$ O$_5$.

*Charact.*—A colourless liquid with a sour taste, and strong acid reaction. With ammonio-nitrate of silver it gives a canary-yellow precipitate, soluble in ammonia and nitric acid. Specific gravity, 1·08.

*Actions and uses.*—A somewhat feeble tonic, given chiefly where there is a deposit of phosphates from the urine. Said to be a stimulant of the generative system, but experience does not give it a high standing as an aphrodisiac. As a drink, diluted, in diabetes it does little good, and the same, we fear, may be said in regard to its use in exostosis and other osseous tumours.

*Dose.*—Min. x. to xxx. well diluted.

### Acidum Sulphuricum. Sulphuric Acid.

Monohydrated sulphuric acid, HO, SO$^3$, or H$_2$ SO$_4$, contains 96·8 per cent by weight of the sulphuric acid, HO, SO$_3$.

*Charact.*—A colourless fluid of oily appearance, intensely acid and corrosive, evolving much heat on the addition of water. Specific gravity, 1·843.

*Actions and uses.*—A powerful corrosive, rapidly destroying animal tissue. Antidote, chalk and magnesia. It is not much used in practice as a counterirritant. It has been used as a caustic to the conjunctiva for curing ectropium or eversion of the lid, and to the skin of the eye-lid, for entropium or inversion.—In France, a caustic paste for malignant and cancerous ulcerations, is made by mixing 2 parts of acid with one of saffron. In this country sawdust—a much cheaper article—has been substituted for the saffron.

*Acidum Aromaticum.*—Take of sulphuric acid f℥iij. ; rectified spt. Oij. ; cinnamon in coarse powder ℥ij. ; ginger in coarse powder ℥j¼. Mix the acid gradually with f℥xxxv. of the spt., then add the cinnamon and the ginger, and digest for 7 days, agitating frequently ; filter and add enough spt. to make up to Oij.

*Acidum Sulphuricum Dilutum.*—Take of sulphuric acid 7 fluid ounces ; distilled water, a sufficiency. Dilute the acid with 77 fluid ounces of the water, and when the mixture has cooled to 60⁰ add more water, so that it shall measure 83¼ fluid ounces.

*Actions and uses.*—Tonic, refrigerant, astringent, and diuretic. Useful as a tonic and refrigerant in continued fevers ; as an astringent in hæmoptysis, epistaxis, and bleedings from the uterus, stomach, and intestines, and in diarrhœa. Excellent in the nocturnal sweating of phthisis, or the perspirations of hectic. It is by no means a trustworthy diuretic ; yet, singularly, it will succeed in some few cases where more powerful diuretics fail.

*Dose.*—Min. x. to xxx. in an ounce or so of simple syrup, or infusion of calumba or gentian.

*Incompatibles.*—Most metals and their oxides ; alkalies and their carbonates ; acetate of lead, nitrates, organic substances, essential oils ; tinctures and astringent infusions.

### Acidum Sulphurosum. Sulphurous Acid.

Sulphurous acid gas, $SO_2$, dissolved in water and constituting 9·2 per cent by weight of the solution.

*Charact.*—A colourless liquid with a strong, suffocating, sulphurous odour, sp. gr. 1·04.

*Uses.*—Antiseptic, disinfectant ; a powerful deoxidizer, and destroyer of vegetable life. This is one of those drugs which have been suddenly pitch-forked into vast, but we fear scarcely permanent, eminence, by the sensational pamphlets of one or two gentlemen. It was at one time used chiefly as a lotion (℥j. to ℥viij. of Aq.) in tinea, but is now recommended for almost every ailment under the sun ! It seems to do some good in inflamed fauces, and affections of the mucous membrane, especially the respiratory tract, in which cases it is used in the form of spray, or inhalation. Also in the form of gargle, 1 to 6 or so of water. The ugly patches of diphtheria were expected to recede on its approach, but we have not found them do so. Our own experience, in fact, is this, that we get fully more good in such cases from the nitrate of silver. Mixed with an equal part of glycerine, it is employed in various skin diseases, such as lupus, lichen, &c., with benefit ; and also where fungi exist. In neuralgia we have not found it reliable ; but (internally) in sarcina it does good. Dose, min. xxx. to lx., well diluted with water.

### Acidum Tannicum. Tannic Acid.

An acid, $C^{54} H^{22} O^{34}$, or $C_{22} H_{27} O_{17}$, obtained from galls.

*Charact.*—A pale-yellow amorphous powder, with a strong astringent taste and acid reaction, readily soluble in water and rectified spt., but sparingly in ether. Dissolved in water it precipitates a solution of gelatine yellowish-white, and the persalts of iron of a bluish-black colour. Test : leaves no residue when burned with free access of air.

*Prep.*—Galls in coarse powder ℥viij. ; ether Oiij. ; dist. water f℥vj. On percolating the tannin is separated by means of the ether ; two distinct fluid strata are seen ; the heavier containing the tannin is evaporated on a water bath, and the residue dried in a hot-air chamber, temp. not exceeding 212°.

*Actions and uses.*—An astringent of great power, well adapted for the various hemorrhages for which gallic acid is given ; and for chronic mucous discharges, and the diarrhœa and perspirations of hectic. From its chemical action on gelatine, it has been proposed as an anthelmintic, but it has not proved very successful ; at least, we have not seen it so. It is more apt to induce derangement of the stomach than gallic acid, and it certainly aggravates dyspepsia. Extensively used in the form of gargle, gr. v. to x. to the ounce of water ; and as an injection in mucous and muco-purulent discharges from the vagina and urethra. In the form of ointment, it has done good in eczema and herpes ; and combined with a little opium, I have frequently known it beneficial in piles. Dose, gr. ij. to x.

Formula for hemorrhoids, ℞ Acidi tannici gr. xx. ; sulphuris sublimati gr. x. ; pulveris opii gr. vj. ; unguenti cetacei 3j. Misce.—For chapped nipples and ulcerated sore-throat the following will be found useful : ℞ Acidi tannici gr. xx. ; glycerini f3j. M.

Glycerinum Acidi Tannici.

Tannin 3j. Glycerinum 3v. Mix. Useful for chapped nipples.

*Suppositoria.*—Tannic acid. Benzoated lard, white wax, and oil of theobroma. There are 2 grs. tannin in each.

*Trochisci.*—Tannin, tolu, sugar, gum, water. Each lozenge contains gr. ¼ tannic acid.

*Incompatibles.*—Alkalies and their carbonates; the mineral acids, acetate of lead, nitrate of silver, lime water, tartar emetic, the persalts of iron.

### Acidum Tartaricum. Tartaric Acid.

An acid, 2 HO, $C_8 H_4 O_{10}$, or $H_2 C_4 H_4 O_6$, obtained from the acid tartrate of potash.

*Charact.*—In colourless oblique rhombic prisms, strong acid taste, readily soluble in water.

*Actions and uses.*—Refrigerant ; used chiefly for making effervescing powders. Dose, gr. x. to xxx. in a good deal of water. For effervescing draughts the bicarbonate of soda is given a little in excess of the acid ; and for seidlitz powders, from gr. xxx. to gr. cxx. of sodæ et potassæ tartras with a little sugar and essence of lemon, are added.

### Aconiti Radix. Aconite Root.

Aconitum napellus Linn. The root, dried ; imported from Germany, or cultivated in Britain, and collected in the winter or early spring, before the leaves have appeared. N. F. Ranunculaceæ.

*Charact.*—From one to three inches long, not thicker than the finger at the crown, tapering, wrinkled, blackish-brown, internally whitish. A minute portion cautiously chewed, causes prolonged tingling and numbness.

*Analysis*—An alkaloid named aconitia, combined with aconitic acid, an acrid volatile principle, albumen, different salts, &c.

*Actions and uses.*—Sedative and a powerful poison. A minute portion causes a tingling sensation and numbness, while larger quantities induce depression of the vital powers, the effects being confusion, loss of sight and of common sensation, paralysis of the voluntary muscles, death taking place from paralysis of the respiratory muscles. This drug was once lauded as an anodyne in acute rheumatism, but experience does not warrant us in joining in the panegyric. As a deobstruent in diseased mesenteric glands, scrofulous tumours (external), scirrhus, &c., it has proved quite a failure. Internally, then, we do not look with confidence to this drug. As an external application its efficacy is undoubted in neuralgic pains, as tic douloureux and lumbago. Dose.—Powder of the root, gr. ij. to v. gradually increased.

*Linimentum.*—Aconite root, powder, ℥xx. ; camphor ℥j. ; rectified spt. f℥xxx. Macerate 7 days, and percolate, the product should be Oj. Useful in rheumatism and neuralgia.

*Tinctura.*—Aconite root, powder, ℥ij¼ ; rectified spt. Oj. Macerate 48 ho., then percolate, and add spt. to make a pint. Dose, min. v. to xv. gradually increased, and carefully watched.

### Aconitia. Aconitia.

An alkaloid, $C^{60} H^{47} NO^{14}$, obtained from aconite root.

*Charact.*—A white, usually amorphous solid, soluble in 150 parts of cold, and 50 of hot water ; much more soluble in alcohol and ether. Rubbed on the skin it causes tingling and protracted numbness.

*Actions and uses.*—A very active poison, possessing in a concentrated degree the properties of the other forms. Used for the ointment, not internally.

Unguentum. Aconitia gr. viij. ; rect. spt. f℥ss. ; prepared lard ℥j. A small portion (gr. xx. or so) may be applied over the seat of a neuralgic pain.

### Aconiti Folia. Aconite Leaves.

Aconitum napellus Linn. Monkshood. The fresh leaves and flowering tops, gathered when about one-third of the flowers are expanded, from plants in Britain.

*Charact.*—Leaves smooth, palmate, divided into five deeply cut wedge-shaped segments ; exciting, when chewed, a sensation of tingling ; flowers numerous, irregular, deep blue, in spikes. Used for the extract.

*Extractum.*—For prep. see British Pharm. Dose, gr. ss. to ij.

### Adeps Benzoatus. Benzoated Lard.

*Prep.*—Lard, 1 pound ; Benzoin, in coarse powder, 160 grs. Melt the lard, add the benzoin, stirring frequently ; remove the residual benzoin by straining. A useful healing ointment, slightly stimulant, and used in the preparation of ung. gallæ, ung. zinci, &c.

### Adeps Præparatus. Prepared Lard.

*Synonym.*—Axungia, Ed. Hog's fat, deprived of its membranes, and purified by heat.

*Charact.*—A soft white fatty substance, melting at about 100°.

*Uses.*—A simple dressing for excoriations, and a basis for ointments.

Unguentum simplex. White wax $\text{З}$ij. ; lard $\text{З}$iij. ; almond oil f$\text{З}$iij. A simple dressing after blisters, and for excoriations.

### Æther. Ether.

*Synonym.*—Æther sulphuricus, Ed. Dub. Oxide of ethyl, $C^4 H^5 O$, or $C_4 H_{10} O$, with about 8 per cent by volume of alcohol.

*Charact.*—A colourless very volatile and inflammable liquid, emitting a pungent odour, and boiling below 105°. Poured on the hand it evaporates rapidly, producing a sensation of cold. Sp. gravity, 0·735.

*Actions and uses.*—Narcotic, antispasmodic, stimulant, anæsthetic, and an external refrigerant. In large doses, or inhaled for a long time, it is a poison, causing intense excitement, various affections of the mental state, delirium, insensibility, suspension of voluntary motion. Its property of inducing stupefaction led to its being used as an anæsthetic in America in 1846 ; but the happy discovery of the virtues of chloroform by Dr Simpson, soon after, led to its immediate abandonment. It is given as a stimulant in asphyxia, fainting, and the adynamic stages of various fevers, but the short-lived nature of its action renders it inferior to alcoholic fluids. It is of most service as an antispasmodic, combined with opium, in stomach-cramp, hiccup, and flatulent colic ; and in asthma and hysterical aphonia. It acts as a carminative by its vapour attracting the gases evolved in the stomach ; and it is a powerful external refrigerant owing to its rapid evaporation, often relieving headache of various kinds. Dose, f℥ss. to f℥i. in a little cinnamon water or tinct. cardam. co.

*Spiritus.*—Ether f℥x. ; rect. spt. Oj. M. Dose, min. xxx. to xc. It is more miscible in mixtures than the Æther.

### Æther Purus. Pure Ether.

Ether free from alcohol and water.

### Albumen Ovi. Egg Albumen.

The liquid white of the egg of Gallus domesticus.

### Alcohol Amylicum. Amylic Alcohol.

Synonym.—Fousel oil.
*Uses.*—Unimportant ; used in the preparation of the valerianate of Soda.

### Aloe Barbadensis. Barbadoes Aloes.

Aloe Vulgaris Lam. Encycl. The juice of the leaf, inspissated ; imported from Barbadoes. N. F. Liliaceæ.
*Charact.*—In dark-brown opaque masses, breaking with a dull conchoidal fracture ; has a nauseous bitter taste, and a disagreeable odour, usually imported in gourds.
*Analysis.*—Aloine (a bitter extractive matter), two peculiar acids, resin, &c.
*Preparations.*—Enema, Aloes gr. xl. ; carb. potash gr. xv. ; mucilage of starch f℥x. M.
Extractum. Dose, gr. ij. to v.
Pilula. B. aloes ℥ij. ; hard soap ℥j. ; oil carraway f℥j. ; conf. roses ℥j. M. Divide into 5 grain pills. Dose, gr. v. to x.

Pilula Aloes et Ferri. Sulphate of iron Ʒiss. ; Barb.
Aloes, Ʒii. ; Comp. Powd. of cinnamon Ʒiii. ; Conf. Ros. Ʒiv.
Mix. An excellent cathartic and emmenagogue, in Amen-
orrhœa. Dose, gr. v. to x.

Pilula Cambogiæ composita.—See Cambogia.

Pilula Colocynthidis composita.—See Colocynthis.

Pilula Colocynthidis et hyoscyami.—See Colocynthis.

### Aloe Socotrina. Socotrine Aloes.

Inspissated juice of the leaf of one or more undetermined
species of aloes, Linn, procured from Socotra.

*Charact.*—In reddish-brown masses, opaque or translucent at the edges ; breaks with an irregular or smooth and
resinous fracture ; has a bitter taste, and a strong but fragrant odour ; dissolves entirely in proof spirit, and during
solution exhibits under the microscope numerous minute
crystals.

*Preparation.*—Enema.—See preceding enema.

Decoctum Aloes compositum. Extract of Soc. ; aloes, gr.
cxx. ; myrrh, saffron, of each gr. xc. ; carb. potash, gr.
lx. ; ext. liquorice, Ʒi. ; compd. tinct. cardam, Ʒviii. Dist.
water enough to make up to Ʒxxx. For prep. see Brit. P.
Dose, Ʒss. to Ʒii.

Extractum Colocynthidis compositum.—See Brit. Pharm.

Pilula aloes et assafœtidæ. Aloes, assafœtida, hard soap,
confect. roses, of each one ounce. M. Divide into 5 gr.
pills. Dose, gr. v. to x.

Pilula aloes socotrina. Soc. aloes Ʒii. ; hard soap, in
powder Ʒi. ; vol. oil of nutmeg Ʒj. ; conf. roses Ʒi. Mix.
Dose, gr. v. to x.

Pilula aloes et myrrhæ. Aloes Ʒij. ; myrrh Ʒj. ; saffron,
dried Ʒss. ; confect. roses Ʒijss. M. Divide into 5 gr.
pills. Dose, gr. v. to x.

Pilula rhei composita. Rhubarb Ʒiij. ; soc. aloes Ʒij¼. ;
myrrh Ʒjss. ; hard soap Ʒjss. ; English oil peppermint Ʒjss. ;
treacle Ʒiv. M. Make into 5 gr. pills. Dose, gr. v. to x.

Tinctura aloes. Aloes soc. Ʒss. ; ext. liquorice Ʒiss. ;
proof spt. 1 pint. Dose, Ʒi. to Ʒij.

Vinum aloes.   Soc. aloes ℥iss. ; cardamon seeds (bruised and freed from their pericarps), and ginger in coarse powder, of each gr. lxxx. ; sherry Oij. ; macerate for seven days. A useful laxative, the card. and ginger preventing griping.   Dose, ʒi. to ʒij.

*Actions and uses.*—Cathartic, and, in very small doses, perhaps slightly tonic.   It acts by exciting the peristaltic action of the bowel, and appears to have a preference for the large intestine, and more so for the rectum.   It seems, however, to affect the duodenum, or the mouths of the biliary ducts,-an increased flow of bile resulting ; and thus it is beneficial in some cases of jaundice.   It is one of the most extensively employed cathartics in constipation, with deficient bile ; and from its actions on the rectum, and by sympathy on the neighbouring uterus, it has done good as an emmenagogue.   Where hemorrhoids exist, and during pregnancy, it has been deemed inadmissible alone ; but combined with hyoscyamus, or sulphate of iron, its acrimony is lessened or modified, and it may be then safely given.   The iron seems also to increase the activity of the aloes.   Dose, gr. v. to x.   Barb. gr. ii. to v.

### Alumen.   Alum.

A sulphate of alumina and ammonia, crystallized from solution in water, $NH_4 O, SO_3 AL_2 O_3, 3 SO_3 + 24 HO$, or $NH_4 Al (SO_4)_2, 12H_2 O$.

*Charact.*—In colourless transparent crystalline masses, exhibiting the faces of the regular octahedron, with an acid, sweetish astringent taste.

*Actions and uses.*—An energetic astringent.   Useful in chronic diarrhœa, dysentery, menorrhagia, hæmoptysis, and hæmatemesis.   At times it does good in pyrosis ; and in colica pictonum it is found occasionally to allay the tormina and sickness of that ailment, when combined with a little opium.   Topically it is applied to arrest bleeding from small vessels.

*Dose.*—Gr. x. to xxx.   For pyrosis gr. x. to xx., thrice daily, in infus. calumbæ.   Formula for lead colic.   ℞  Al-

uminis ʒij. ; liquoris morphiæ hydrochloratis fʒij. ; syrupi
zingiberis fʒvj. ; infusi calumbæ fʒv.   Misce.   Capiat ʒss.
omnibus sextis horis.

*Alumen Exsiccatum.*—Alum heated in a porcelain capsule
until aqueous vapour ceases to be disengaged; dried and reduced to fine powder.   A little of this applied to the fauces,
by blowing it through a glass tube, has done good in the
early stages of inflammatory sore throat.   Dissolved in
water, it makes an excellent gargle, in relaxed uvula and
tonsils, in ulceration of the mouth and tongue, in spongy
gums, and excessive salivation.

*Incompatibles.*—Alkalies and their carbonates, lime, magnesia, acet. plumb., salts of mercury, and substances containing tannin.

### Ammoniacum.   Ammoniacum.

Dorema Ammoniacum Don Trans. Linn. Soc.   A gum-
resinous exudation from the stem ; collected in Persia and
the Punjaub.   N. F. Umbelliferæ.

*Charact.*—In pale cinnamon-brown tears or masses ; the
tears from two to eight lines diameter, breaking with a
smooth shining opaque white surface ; hard when cold ;
softening with heat ; a bitter, acrid, nauseous taste.

*Analysis.*—Resin, gum, and a trace of volatile oil.

*Actions and uses.*—A stimulating expectorant, and useful
along with squill, or tolu, in chronic bronchitis.   Externally, in the form of plaster, it is applied to chronic enlarged
glands, proving useful at times by its stimulating property ;
but it is inferior to iodine and others.   Dose, gr. x. to xx.,
made into emulsion with milk or water.

*Emplastrum Ammoniaci cum Hydrargyro.*—See Hydrargyrum.

*Emp. Galbani.*—See Galbanum.

*Mistura.*—Ammoniac ¼ ounce ; dist. water fʒviij.   Mix
well by trituration, and strain through muslin.   Dose, ʒss.
to ʒj.

*Pilula Scillæ Co.*—See Scilla.

**Ammoniæ Acetatis Liquor** (now *Liquor Ammoniæ Acetatis*).
Solution of Acetate of Ammonia.

Acetate of Ammonia, $NH^4$ O, $C^4$ $H^3$ $O^3$, dissolved in water.

*Charact.*—A transparent colourless liquid, with a saline taste.

*Prep.*—Acetic acid f℈x. ; carb. ammon. ℥iij¼, or a sufficiency ; dist. water Oijss. Reduce the carb. ammon. to powder, and add it gradually to the acid, until a neutral solution is formed, then add the water.

*Actions and uses.*—A very trustworthy diaphoretic, as a general rule not exciting the circulation much. Useful in catarrh, and slight febrile attacks. It seems peculiarly adapted for accelerating the elimination of alcohol from the system, and may thus be given in cases of stupefaction from " strong drink." Dose, f℈i. to f℈vi.

**Ammoniæ Benzoas.** Benzoate of Ammonia.

$NH_4$ O, $C_{14}$ $H_5$ $O_3$ + HO, or $NH_4$ $C_7$ $H_5$ $O_{2}$.

*Charact.*—In colourless laminar crystals, soluble in water and alcohol.

*Uses.*—Given in bronchitis with occasional benefit, in genito-urinary mucous discharges, and phosphatic deposits in the urine. Dose, gr. x. to gr. xxx.

**Ammoniæ Carbonas.** Carbonate of Ammonia.

Sesquicarbonate of Ammonia, 2 $NH^4$ O, 3 $CO^2$.

*Charact.*—In translucent crystalline masses, with a strong ammoniacal odour, and alkaline reaction; soluble in cold water, and sparingly in spirit.

*Actions and uses.*—Antacid and stimulant. Given to rouse the vital powers in the adynamic stage of continued fevers, and in chronic bronchitis attended with debility. Useful as " smelling salts " in fainting. Dose, gr. v. to xx.

*Spiritus Ammoniæ Aromaticus.*—Carb. ammon. ℥viij. ; strong solut. of ammon. f℥iv. ; volatile oil of nutmeg f℈iv. ; oil of lemon f℈vi. ; rectified spt. Ovj. ; water Oiij. Mix, and distil Ovij. Antacid, stimulant and antispasmodic.

Used in similar cases with the carbonate. Useful for correcting acidity in the stomach where it exists in the gaseous form ; and it does good by rousing (and otherwise) individuals from the stupor of alcoholic drinks. Dose, min. xv. to lx.

*Spiritus Ammoniæ Fœtidus.*—Assafœtida Ӡiss. ; strong solut. of ammon. fӠij.; rect. spt. Oj. M. Dose, Ӡss. to Ӡj.

**Ammonii Bromidum.** Bromide of Ammonium.

$NH_4$ Br. Colourless crystals, which become slightly yellow by exposure to the air. Have a pungent saline taste.

*Uses.*—Given in spasmodic coughs, such as pertussis, and others, when the neurotic element prevails. It is much less of a nerve-calmative than the K. Br. Dose, gr. ii. to xx.

**Ammonii Chloridum.** Chloride of Ammonium.

$NH_4$ Cl.

*Charact.*—In colourless translucent fibrous masses, tough and difficult to powder ; soluble in water and rect. spt.

*Actions and uses.*—Stimulant, deobstruant, diaphoretic, cholagogue, diuretic, and emmenagogue. It seems to have done good occasionally in amenorrhœa, and rarely in hooping-cough. Of late more used in cases of severe neuralgia, and does good where iron, iodide of potassium, arsenic, and quinia have failed. For such cases give 30-gr. doses thrice a day. Forms an excellent discutient application, along with spt. and vinegar, in ecchymosis, contusions, and sprains. Along with nitre it forms a refrigeratory mixture, useful for lessening the heat and pain of inflamed parts. Dose, gr. v. to xxx.

*Formula for Ecchymosis, &c.*—℞ Ammoniæ hydrochloratis Ӡj.; spiritus rectificati fӠij.; acidi acetici diluti Ӡxviij. Misce.

*Liquor Ammoniæ.*—Solution of ammonia. Strong solut. of ammon. Oj. ; dist. water Oij. Mix.

*Linimentum Ammoniæ.*—Liquor ammon. Ӡi. ; olive oil Ӡiij. Mix. A mild rubefacient, and useful in sore throat bronchitis, old sprains, &c.

**Ammoniæ Liquor Fortior.** Strong solution of Ammonia.

Ammoniacal gas $NH_3$, dissolved in water, and constituting 32·5 per cent of the solution.

*Charact.*—A colourless liquid, with an intensely pungent odour, and strong alkaline reaction. Sp. g. 0·891.

*Uses.*—A strong corrosive and narcotic poison, inflaming and corroding the parts with which it comes into contact, and occasioning tetanus and coma. Its antidotes are vinegar, lemon juice, tartaric acid. It is not given internally. Externally it produces irritation, redness, and vesication, hence it is used as a counterirritant in many affections. It forms a speedy blister, and may be employed for sudden attacks of internal inflammation, as in retrocedent gout. In the form of liniment mixed with oil, it forms an excellent rubefacient in sore throat, and over joints in chronic rheumatism.

*Linimentum Camphoræ Compositum.*—See Camphor.

**Ammoniæ Phosphas.** Phosphate of Ammonia.

$2NH^4 O, HO, PO_5$, or $(NH_4) 2HPO_4$.

*Charact.*—In colourless transparent prisms ; exposed to air, lose water and ammonia, becoming opaque ; soluble in water, insoluble in rectified spt.

*Uses.*—Recommended in gout and rheumatism, to help the solution of the urates of soda and lime. Dose, gr. v. to xx.

**Amygdala Amara.** Bitter Almond.

Seed of bitter almond tree, from Mogadore.

*Uses.*—Used only for obtaining the oleum amygdalæ.

**Amygdala Dulcis.** Sweet Almond.

The sweet almond tree. The seed ; from about Malaga. N. F. Rosaceæ.

*Charact.*—Above an inch in length, lanceolate, acute, with a clear cinnamon-brown seed-coat, and a bland, sweetish, nutty-flavoured kernel. Bruised with water, does not evolve the odour of bitter almonds.

*Uses.*—As a nutritive and emollient.

Mistura. Comp. powder of almonds ℥ijss.; dist. water Oj.
M. Strain through muslin. A vehicle for other medicines.

Pulvis. Amygdalæ Compositus. Sweet almonds ℥viij.;
refined sugar ℥iv.; gum arabic ℥j. Steep, and blanch the
almonds, dry them with a soft cloth, rub lightly in a mortar
to a smooth consistence. Mix the gum and sugar, and add
to the pulp gradually.

**Amygdalæ Oleum.** See *Oleum Amygdalæ.*

**Amylum.** Wheat Starch.

Tritricum vulgare. Common wheat. Starch procured
from the seed. N. F. Graminaceæ.

*Charact.*—In white columnar masses; rendered blue with
iodine.

*Uses.*—Demulcent. Used in the form of enema in
diarrhœa and dysentery. The powder is dusted on excoriations, incipient bed sores, and erythematous patches.

Glycerinum amyli. Starch ℥i.; glycerine ℥viij. Mix
intimately, then place in a porcelain dish, and apply heat
gradually to 240°, stirring until a translucent jelly is
formed.

Mucilago. Starch gr. cxx.; dist. water f℥x. Triturate,
then boil a few minutes.

**Anethi Oleum.** See *Oleum Anethi.*

**Anethi Fructus.** Dill. Fruit.

Anethum graveolens Linn. The fruit; cultivated in
England. N. F. Umbelliferæ.

*Charact.*—Oval, flat, about a line and a half in length,
with a pale membranous margin. Odour aromatic, taste
warm, and slightly bitter.

*Aqua Anethi.*—Dill. ℥xvi.; water cong. ij. Distil one
gallon.

*Uses.*—Carminative and slightly stimulant. Given in
the flatulence of infants. Dose, ℥ss. to ℥iij.

*Formula,* found useful in the griping flatulence of children.—℞ Magnesiæ levis ℥ss.; sacchari albi ℥j.; olei anisi

min. ij. ; aquæ calcis ʒij. ; aqua anethi ʒij.   Misce.   Capiat cochleare parvum, pro re nata.

**Anisi Oleum.**   See *Oleum Anisi.*

**Anthemidis Oleum.**   See *Oleum Anthemidis.*

**Anthemidis Flores.**   Chamomile Flowers.

Anthemis nobilis Linn.  Common chamomile.  The flower heads, single and double, dried; wild, and cultivated in Britain.   N. F. Compositæ.

*Actions and uses.*—Tonic, stimulant, carminative.  Useful in simple dyspepsia, and irritability of the stomach, with flatulence.   The fresh infusion is best.   A strong infusion at times proves emetic ; yet in the vomiting of pregnancy it has done good when sedatives have failed.   The oil dropped on a bit of sugar is a good carminative.

Extractum.   See Brit. Pharm.   Dose, gr. ij. to x.

Infusum.   Cham. flowers ʒss. ; dist. water fʒx.   Infuse fifteen minutes, and strain.   Dose, ʒj. to ʒiv.

**Antimonii Oxidum.**   Oxide of Antimony.

Sb O$^3$, or Sb$_2$ O$_3$.

*Charact.*—A white powder, fusible at a low red heat, insoluble in water, but readily dissolved by hydrochloric acid.

*Preparation.*—See Brit. Pharm.

*Actions and uses.*—Diaphoretic and sedative, but not much to be trusted.   Occasionally it has seemed to do good in catarrh and pneumonia.   Used for preparing pulv. antimonialis.   Dose, gr. i. to v.

*Pulvis Antimonialis.*—Oxide of antimony ʒj. ; precipitated phosphate of lime ʒij.   M.

*Actions and uses.*—Sedative and diaphoretic.   This compound was formerly very indefinite and irregular in its composition, and therefore annoyingly uncertain in its action. Now that we have got something definite, we may be able to place more reliance upon it ; although possessing the antim. tart., we can always have the same actions in an enhanced degree.   It may be given in the early stages of fevers, and inflammatory diseases, in catarrh, and, combined with opium, in acute rheumatism.   Dose, gr. iii. to x.

### Antimonii Chloridi Liquor. Solution of Chloride of Antimony.

Terchloride of antimony, Sb. $Cl^3$, dissolved in hydrochloric acid.

*Charact.*—A heavy liquid of a yellowish-red colour.

*Uses.*—Caustic ; rarely employed in practice in this country. Has been used by German oculists in staphyloma, the tumour being touched with a camel's hair pencil. Occasionally applied to malignant tumours. Never given internally.

### Antimonium Nigrum. Black Antimony.

Synom.—Prepared sulphuret of antimony. Native sulphide of antimony, $Sb S_3$, or $Sb_2 S_3$, purified from siliceous matter by fusion, and afterwards reduced to fine powder.

*Charact.*—A greyish-black crystalline powder. Dissolves almost entirely in boiling hydrochloric acid, giving sulphuretted hydrogen.

*Uses.*—Not employed in medicine ; but used for preparing antimon. sulphuratum and liquor antimonii chloridi.

### Antimonium Sulphuratum. Sulphurated Antimony.

Sulphide of antimony, $Sb S^3$, or $Sb_2 S_3$, with a small and variable amount of teroxide of antimony, $Sb O^3$.

*Charact.*—An orange-red powder, readily dissolved by caustic soda, also by hydrochloric acid with the evolution of sulphuretted hydrogen, and the separation of a little sulphur.

*Uses.*—Diaphoretic, of no great value. An ingredient of the comp. calomel pill.

*Pilula calomelanos composita.*—See Calomel.

### Antimonium Tartaratum. Tartarated Antimony.

A tartrate of potash and antimony, $KO, Sb O_3 C_8 H_4 O_{10} + 2 HO$, or $K Sb C_4 H_4 O_7. H_2 O$.

*Charact.*—In colourless transparent crystals, with triangular facets, soluble in water, and less so in proof spirit.

*Preparation.*—Oxide of antim. ℥v. ; acid. tart. potash ℥vi. ;

dist. water Oij. Mix the ox. antim and tart. potash with sufficient dist. water to form a paste, and set aside for 24 ho. ; then add the rest of the water, and boil $\frac{1}{4}$ ho., stirring frequently. Filter, and set aside the clear filtrate to crystallize. Pour off the mother liquor, and evaporate to one third, and set aside, that more crystals may form. Dry the crystals on filtering paper at the temperature of the air.

*Actions and uses.*—An important drug from its different actions and varied applications. It is an irritant poison in large doses ; in small, a diaphoretic, sedative, expectorant, and emetic. In poisoning, we have inflammation of the alimentary tract, &c. Antidotes.—Tannin, or astringent decoctions. As a sedative, it has been given to lower the frequency and force of the heart's action, and thus arrest local inflammation. Its sedative action has been sought in two ways. First (and what may be termed the heroic way), it has been given in one, two, or three grain doses every two hours or so ; and, second, in the milder and safer, nauseating dose of $\frac{1}{8}$ or $\frac{1}{4}$ grain. Experience, however, has shown, that in the presence of active inflammation, doses sufficient to develop the symptoms of poisoning in the healthy state are wonderfully borne ; and yet who cannot but plead guilty to a suspicion that, although during the bold contra-stimulant method, the more common physiological effects—such as faintness, vomiting, purging, sweating—are either not called into operation, or first called, and then, by a continuance of the plan, subdued, the system has received actual and unwarrantable injury ; in other words, the tolerance is more apparent than real. As a nauseating sedative, in doses of $\frac{1}{8}$ gr. or so, every hour or two, it has rendered great service in erysipelas, arachnitis, acute bronchitis, pneumonia, and pleuritis, and especially in the latter two diseases. The best results in these cases are obtained when nausea and diaphoresis are both kept up ; and the latter is best and most vigorously sustained when the former exists, and perhaps is dependent on it. As an expectorant, it may be given in small doses of $\frac{1}{12}$ gr. oft repeated, or in emetic doses. The former plan answers well in acute inflammation of the substance of the lungs, the latter in hooping-cough. As an emetic in doses of gr. ii. or so, it operates effectually in from twenty minutes to half-an-hour, causing nausea and depression. It is thus employed for the evacuation of the stomach, not in cases of poisoning, for it is too tardy and depressant for that, but in ordinary cases, and, above all, with the view of cutting short, or aborting at an early stage, acute inflammations, such as croup, pertussis, ophthalmia, hernia humoralis, and bubo. In continued fever, especially the type of the present time, it is not at all successful. Being a specific emetic, it acts when injected into the veins, and it has been thus employed to promote by vomiting the expulsion of solid bodies located in the œsophagus. As a relaxant in dislocations, strangulated hernia, and rigidity of the os uteri, it has been superseded by chloroform ; but I occasionally meet with cases of unyielding os, where, the anæsthetic completely failing, I obtain softness and pliability from this nauseating drug.

Catharsis is seldom sought from antim. tart., but along with sulph. magnes., it has done good as a cooling cathartic in acute inflammations and sthenic fevers. Externally, in the form of ointment, or on the face of a plaster, it raises a profuse crop of pustules ; and thus proves an excellent counterirritant in internal diseases of the head, thorax, abdomen, and medulla spinalis ; in muscular and neuralgic pains, and diseases of joints. Dose, emetic gr. j. to iij. ; expect. diaph. and sedative, gr. $\frac{1}{12}$ to $\frac{1}{4}$.

*Unguentum.*—Tart. antim. $\frac{1}{4}$ ounce. Simple oint. one ounce. Mix.

*Vinum antimoniale.*—Tart. antim gr. xl. Sherry Oj. Dissolve. Dose, emetic ℥ss. to ℥j. ; expect. diaph. and sed. min. v. to lx.

*Incompatibles.*—Alkalies and their carb. acids ; plumb. acet. ; hyd. corrosiv. sub. ; aq. calc. chlor. calc. earths ; some of the metallic oxides ; hydrosulphurets ; strong astringent infusions and decoctions.

### Aqua. Water.

Natural water, HO, the purest that can be obtained, cleared if necessary by filtration.

*Aqua Destillata.*—This answers best for most pharmaceutical purposes, and should be used in mixtures containing any of the following articles : Argent, nit. plumb. acet. ; ferri sulph. ; zinci. sulph. antim. ; tart. acid. ; sulphuric. Hydrarg. corrosiv. ; sub. liq. ; plumb. subacet.

*Mineral Waters* are an important class ; yet they possess no great healing virtues beyond many mineral and vegetable drugs which we can boast of. The benefits alleged to accrue from their use, are in many cases, no doubt, due to their surroundings and accessories—pure air, exercise, rural scenery, social pleasures, and exemption from the toils of business. The more common substances existing in them are sulphur, iron, acids, and various salts. They are cold and warm—the latter being termed *thermal.* They may be divided into 1. Chalybeate ; 2. Saline ; 3. Sulphureous ; 4. Acidulous.

*Chalybeate.* These contain iron in the form of carbonate, sulphate, &c. Their action is tonic, strengthening the pulse, augmenting muscular tone, and improving the colour of the blood, and are useful in debility, scrofula, amenorrhœa, &c. A few may be named : Hartfell, near Moffat, cold ; Tunbridge, in Kent, cold ; Bath, in Gloucestershire, thermal.

*Saline.* In these we have salts such as sulph.-soda, sulph.-magnesia, &c. They are mostly purgative. They are given in constipation, to restore the healthy action of the bowels, and help digestion. Examp. : Seidlitz, in Bohemia, cold ; Epsom, in Surrey, cold ; Leamington, in Gloucestershire, cold.

*Sulphureous.* These owe their character to hydro-sulphuric acid, free, and combined with soda, lime, &c. They have rather a disagreeable odour. Their action is stimulant and diaphoretic. They are given in chronic skin diseases, chronic rheumatism, chlorosis, amenorrhœa, secondary syphilis, and dyspepsia hinging on disordered

action of the liver.    Examp.: Moffat and Strathpeffer,
cold ; Aix-la-Chapelle, thermal ; Harrogate, cold.

*Acidulous.*    These are characterized by the presence of
carbonic acid gas, with various salts of soda, lime, &c.
They have an acid taste, and sparkle on being poured.    They
are stimulant and diuretic, and are given in dyspepsia, in
dropsy with debility, in chlorosis, and deposit of phosphate
in the urine.    They stimulate considerably, but transiently,
the nervous and vascular system.    Examp. : Seltzer, cold ;
Spa, cold ; Scarborough, cold ; Carlsbad, thermal.

There are a number of thermal springs which owe their
virtues apparently to their temperature ; for they contain
but an insignificant amount of solid matter.    Such are
Matlock, Buxton, Wildbad, Aix-en-Provence.

**Argenti Nitras.**    Nitrate of Silver.

Ag O, NO$^5$, or Ag NO$_3$.

*Charact.*—In colourless tabular right-rhombic prisms, or
in white cylindrical rods; soluble in dist. water, and in
rectified spt.

*Actions and uses.*—Caustic and tonic.    It is a corrosive
poison, but its action is prevented considerably by the chloride of sodium, and mucus of the stomach, which decompose
it.    The antidote is chloride of sodium.    It is an excellent
caustic, its corrosive action being mild, yet effectual, and
not attended with protracted pain.    Used for corroding
warts, corns, and other small growths, and for keeping
down on sores their redundant granulations.    It has a
stimulant and alterative action ; hence it is found to improve or render more healthy various constitutional ulcers,
such as chancre, venereal ulceration of the throat, and
strumous or syphilitic ulcers of the cornea.    Applied either
in solution or the solid form to these, they more quickly
assume a healing bias.    Indolent ulcers also put on a more
healthy aspect after an acquaintanceship with it.    A strong
solution, or the solid rod, painted over the involved part,
and a little beyond, has at times arrested external spread-
ing inflammation, such as erysipelas and erythema, and at

other times failed. In relaxed sore throat with enlarged tonsils and uvula, in purulent and gonorrhœal ophthalmia, a rather strong solution, gr. v. to x. to the ounce, is of signal service ; and a weaker solution, gr. ij. to v. to the ounce, is equally beneficial in acute conjunctivitis. Skin diseases, such as ringworm, eczema, impetigo, are sometimes benefited by it, and good results flow from its use, in the form of injection, in purulent discharges from the urethra and vagina. Its utility is doubtful in stricture of the œsophagus, and that of the urethra. Good has been done in croup (early stages), and inflammation of the mucous membrane of the larynx, by a solution applied with a piece of spunge on a curved flexible rod ; but the practice of injecting it into the bronchial tubes, as has been done in chronic bronchitis, is open to various objections. As a tonic, nitrate of silver cannot be placed high. In gastrodynia it sometimes does a little good, in phthisis less, and in hysteria not more. In gastric ulcer, and ulceration of the ileum in typhoid fever, it is often of considerable service. In the convulsive disorders, epilepsy and chorea, it seems to act specifically, and with frequent benefit, but there is now a decided reluctance to its use, owing to the fact that ere success can be achieved, an unfading bluish-grey tint is imparted to the patient's skin, rendering him, as he walks abroad, an ugly spectacle, and the cynosure of many eager eyes. The period required to produce this colouration is sometimes variable ; but a few months have sufficed. There is no known method of prevention or cure as yet, the iodide of potassium, even in the large doses of the Brussels physician, having failed. Some recommend a protracted course of potass. bitart ; but we doubt whether it is of much service. Dose, gr. ¼ to 1.

*Formula for tonic purposes.*—℞ Argenti nitratis gr. ij. ; pulveris aromatici gr. xij. ; extracti taraxaci gr. xxx. M. Divide in pilulas duodecim, quarum capiat unum bis die.

*Incompatibles.*—Ordinary water ; lime water ; alkalies and their carb. ; most acids, including hydrocyanic ; iodid ; potassium ; astringent infusions.

### Argenti Oxidum.   Oxide of Silver.

$Ag\,O$, or $Ag_2\,O$.

*Charact.*—An olive-brown powder, which at a low red heat gives off O, and is reduced to the metallic state. Slightly soluble in water.

*Actions aud uses.*—Tonic, and may be given in the same diseases as the nitrate, but it is more inert.   Of considerable service in hæmorrhage from the bowels.   Dose, gr. ss. to ij. in pill.

### Argentum Purificatum.   Refined Silver.

Used only in preparing the nitrate.

### Armoraciæ Radix.   Horseradish Root.

Cochlearia Armoracia Linn.   The fresh root ; cultivated in Britain.   N. F. Cruciferæ.

*Charact.*—Long, cylindrical, white, sweetish, hot, acrid ; when scraped gives off a pungent odour.

*Actions and uses.*—A warm stimulant, given chiefly along with other drugs to modify their nauseating effect ; and in some cases of dyspepsia.   At one time employed as an antiscorbutic.   As a sialogogue in paralysis of the tongue it is next to worthless.   A rubefacient ; but we have better ones.

*Spiritus Armoraciæ Compositus.*—Horse-radish ℥xx. ; bitter orange peel ℥xx. ; nutmeg ℥ss. ; proof spt. cong. j. ; water Oij.   Mix and distil a gallon.   Dose, ℥j. to ℥iij.

### Arnicæ Radix.   Arnica Root.

Arnica montana Linn.   The root dried ; collected in middle and southern Europe.   N. F. compositæ.

*Charact.*—A contorted, cylindrical root-stock, 1 to 3 in. long, and 2 to 3 lines thick, rough from the scars of the coriaceous leaves, and furnished with many long slender fibres ; has a peppery taste.

*Actions and uses.*—Leopard's bane has been loudly and perhaps rather undeservedly panegyrized, especially by homœopathists, who have declared it to possess the most varied and wonderful properties. It has been given as a stimulant in low fevers, in chronic rheumatism, paralysis, amaurosis, amenorrhœa, and nervous headache; and it sometimes does good in the latter. Externally it is a useful stimulant in ecchymosis and sprains, promoting absorption of effused material. Dose, powder of the root, gr. x.

*Tinctura.*—Arnica root, powder ʒj.; rect. spt. Oj.; macerate 48 ho., then percolate, and add spt. to make Oj. Dose, ʒss. to ʒiij.

### Assafœtida.  Assafœtida.

Narthex Assafœtida. A gum resin, obtained by incision from the living root, in Affghanistan and the Punjaub. N. F. Umbelliferæ.

*Charact.*—In irregular masses and tears. Colour when fresh cut, opaque white, but gradually becoming purplish-pink, and then pinkish-brown. Taste bitter, acrid; odour fetid, alliaceous, and persistent. Dissolves almost entirely in rectified spt.

*Analysis.*—Resin and volatile oil (on which its properties depend), gum, bassorin, saline matter, &c.

*Actions and uses.*—A powerful stimulant and antispasmodic. It is a diffusible stimulant, exciting the nervous and vascular system, and pervading quickly the entire secretions. It is given chiefly in hysteria, where it is of great service, and in chorea, amenorrhœa, and dysmenorrhœa, but with more variable success. It should be given in pretty full doses in hysterical cases, both during the paroxysm and interval. As a carminative, whether by the mouth or rectum, it gets rid of flatulence very effectually. As a diuretic it is not much to be depended on; as an anthelmintic it is entitled to more confidence. A great bar to its wider employment is its abominable odour and taste; but this has been taken advantage of in the treatment of malingerers, and those more afflicted with whim than disease; mixtures well impregnated with it serving to stave them off for a time. Dose, gr. v. to gr. xx.

Enema. Assafœtidæ. Assaf. gr. xxx.; dist. water ʒiv. M. Highly useful in tympanites, and in the thread-worm.

*Pilula aloes et assafœtidœ.*—See Aloes.

Pilula. Assaf. co. Assaf. ℨij.; galbanum ℨij.; myrrh ℨij.; treacle ℨj. M. Divide in 5 gr. pills. Dose, gr. x. to xx.

*Tinctura.*—Assaf. ℨijss.; rectified spt. Oj.; macerate 7 days, filter, strain, and add spt. to make Oj. Dose, fℨss. to fℨij.

### Atropia. Atropia.

An alkaloid, $C_{34} H_{23} NO_{6}$, or $C_{17} H_{23} NO_{3}$, obtained from Belladonna root.

*Charact.*—In colourless acicular crystals, sparingly soluble in water, more readily in alcohol and ether. Its solution in water gives a citron-yellow precipitate with terchloride of gold, has a bitter taste, and powerfully dilates the pupil.

*Prep.*—See British Pharm.

*Actions and uses.*—An active poison, and, in consequence, not well adapted for internal use. It has been pretty extensively employed in diseases of the eye; a drop on the lower lid of a solution of the strength named below dilating the pupil extensively, in from ten to twenty minutes, and the enlargement abiding for two or three days. It possesses several advantages over the extract, such as greater efficacy, cleanliness, freedom from irritation and pain, and the absence of redness or eruption on the eyebrow. It should be cautiously used; for if the proper quantity be much exceeded, symptoms of poisoning might be set up. Antidotes same as for Belladonna.

*Solution of Atropia* for the eye. Atropia gr. j.; acid nitric dil. min. j.; sp. vini rect. min. iij.; aqua dest. fℨj. M. One drop with a camel's-hair pencil on the lid, or in the eye. Another formula is : ℞ Atropiæ sulph. gr. j.; aq. dest. fℨiv. M. A full drop in the eye, as before.

*Liquor.*—Atropia gr. iv.; spt. rect. fℨj.; dist. water fℨvij. Mix the spt. and water, and dissolve the atropia in the mixture. This may be also used for dilating the pupil. Dose, min. j.

*Unguentum.*—Atropia gr. viij.; rect. spt. fℨss.; prep. lard ℨj. M. 20 to 30 grs. of oint. may be used at a time. It is cleaner than the Belladonna.

### Atropiæ Sulphas. Sulphate of Atropia.

*Prep.*—See British Pharm.

Liquor atropiæ sulphatis. Sulph. atrop. gr. iv.; dist. water, fℨi. Dissolve. One minim contains $\frac{1}{110}$th gr. Dose, min. j. to ij. As it is free from spt. it is better adapted for the eye.

Atropine paper, and gelatine, invented by Mr Ernest Hart, and others, are much used by oculists. A small disc is placed between the eye and the lower lid, and it is a neat, clean, and effectual method.

### Aurantii Aqua Floris. Orange-flower Water.

Citrus bigaradia, the bitter orange tree, and citrus aurantium, the sweet orange tree. N. F. Aurantiaceæ.

The distilled water of the flowers; prepared mostly in France. Not in present Pharmacopœia.

*Charact.*—Nearly colourless, fragrant. Not coloured by sulphuretted hydrogen.

*Actions and uses.*—Used as an agreeable vehicle for other remedies. In France it is looked on as anodyne, and it seems occasionally to induce sleep in hysteria. Dose, ℨj. to ℨij.

*Syrupus Aurantii Floris.*—Orange-flower water, fℨviij.; refined sugar lb. iij.; dist. water, fℨxvi. Dissolve the sugar, with heat, in the water; add when nearly cold the orange-flower water; and make up to lb. ivss. with dist. water. Dose, fℨj. to fℨiv.

### Aurantii Cortex. Bitter Orange-Peel.

Critus Bigaradia Risso. The outer part of the rind, dried; from the ripe fruit imported from the south of Europe.

*Uses.*—Feeble tonic; used chiefly for its agreeable flavour.

*Infusum.*—Orange peel ℥ss.; boiling dist. water f℥x.; infuse 15 minutes. Dose, fʒj. to f℥ij.

*Infusum Aurantii Compositum.*—Bitter orange peel ℥¼; fresh lemon peel gr. lx.; cloves gr. xxx.; boiling dist. water f℥x. Infuse 15 minutes. Strain. Dose, fʒj. to ℥ij.

*Syrupus.*—Tinct. orange peel fʒj.; syrup f℥vij. M. Dose, ℈j. to ℥ij.

*Tinctura.*—Bitter orange peel ℥ij.; proof spt. Oj.; macerate 7 days, and strain. Dose, fʒj. to f℥iij.

**Balsamum Canadense.** See *Terebinthina Canadensis.*

**Balsamum Peruvianum.** Balsam of Peru.

A balsam obtained from Myroxylon Pereiræ. It exudes from the trunk after incision. From Salvador, in Central America.

*Charact.*—A reddish-brown treacle-like fluid, with a balsamic odour, and an acrid, slightly bitter taste; soluble in 5 parts of rect. spt.

*Actions and uses.*—A stimulating expectorant, but of little power. Given in chronic catarrh, bronchitis, humid asthma, &c. Used by some in gleet, but less reliable here than iron, buchu, and hygienic measures. Externally to sore nipples. Dose, min. x. to xv., in emulsion with mucilage.

**Balsamum Tolutanum.** Balsam of Tolu.

A balsam obtained from Myroxylon Toluifera. Exudes from the trunk of the tree after incision. From New Granada.

*Charact.*—A soft, tenacious solid, with a balsamic odour. Soluble in rect. spt.

*Uses.*—A stimulating expectorant, of more efficacy than the preceding balsam. Given in catarrh, bronchitis, and all chronic chest affections where expectoration is desiderated. Its agreeable flavour renders it also a useful adjunct to pectoral mixtures. Dose, gr. x. to xxx.

*Syrupus.*—Bals. tolu. ℥j¼; refined sugar lb. ij.; dist. water Oj. Boil the balsam in the water for half an hour. Filter the solution when cold, add the sugar, and dissolve with the aid of a steam or water-bath. The product should weigh lb. iij.  Dose, f3i. to 3ij.

*Tinctura.*—Bals. tolu. 3ijss.; rect. spt. Oj.  Macerate until the balsam is dissolved, and filter; add spt. to make Oj.  Dose, f3ss. to 3j.

### Beberiæ Sulphas.  Sulphate of Beberia.

$C_{35} H_{20} NO_6, HO, SO_3$, or $C_{35} H_{40} N_2 O_6. H_2 SO_4$.

The sulphate of an alkaloid prepared from Nectandra or Bebeeru bark.  Bark got from British Guiana.  N. F. Lauraceæ.  Bark in large, flat heavy pieces, 1 to 2 feet long, 2 to 6 inches broad, about ¼ inch thick.

*Characters of the Sulphate.*—Small, shining, reddish brown plates, with an intensely and persistently bitter taste, soluble in water, but more so on the addition of a little dilute sulphuric acid.

*Actions and uses.*—An excellent tonic and antiperiodic. As a tonic it is useful in dyspepsia, convalescence from acute diseases, and the debility attending phthisis, the colliquative sweating of which it helps to arrest.  As an antiperiodic it cannot be placed nearly so high as quinia, especially in intermittent fever, but it may be tried when the more valuable drug cannot be had.  Periodic headache, hemicrania, and various neuralgias are occasionally benefited by it; and if quinia, iron, arsenic, potass. iodid., or ammon. chlorid., fairly fail in the more obstinate cases, resort should be had to this drug.  In some few cases it will emulate these drugs strongly, and show itself the more powerful remedy.  Dose, gr. i. to x.

*Formula.*—℞ Beberiæ sulphatis gr. lx.; acidi sulphurici diluti f3i.; syrupi floris aurantii f3vj.; aquæ ad. f3vj. Misce.  Fiat mistura, capiat cochleare magnum ter in die.

### Belæ Fructus.  Bael Fruit.

Ægle Marmelos D. C.  N. F. Aurantiaceæ.

The half-ripe fruit, dried; from Malabar and Coromandel.

*Charact.*—Fruit roundish, about the size of a large orange, with a hard woody rind ; usually imported in dried slices. Rind about 1¼ lines thick, covered with a smooth greyish epidermis, and internally, as well as the dried pulp, of a brownish-orange or cherry-red colour.

*Actions and uses.*—Demulcent and astringent, and useful in diarrhœa and dysentery.

*Extractum Belæ Liquidum.*—See Brit. Ph.  Dose, f℥j. to f℥ij.


### Belladonnæ Folia.  Belladonna Leaves.

Atropa Belladonna.  Deadly nightshade.  N. F. Solanaceæ.  The leaves fresh and dried, and the fresh branches ; gathered when the fruit has begun to form, from wild or cultivated plants in Britain.

*Charact.*—Leaves alternate, 3 to 6 inches long, ovate, acute, entire, smooth, the uppermost in pairs and unequal. The expressed juice, dropped into the eye, dilates the pupil.

*Analysis.*—Atropia, malic acid, pseudotoxin and phytocolla, starch, wax, gum, salts, &c.

*Actions and uses.*—Narcotic, anodyne, calmative, antispasmodic.  In large doses it is an active poison, the effects being dryness and constriction of the throat, difficult deglutition, attempts at vomiting ; and then delirium, gay or acsurd, with dilatation of the pupil, and blunting or suspension of common sensibility, coma, and death.  The treatment is emetics, cold to the head, active cathartics, ammonia internally and externally, stimulants.  In small doses it has been employed as an anodyne in convulsive, spasmodic, and neuralgic diseases.  It has done good in tic-douloureux, in nervous irritability, muscular rheumatism, dysmenorrhœa, painful glandular swellings, spasm of the sphincter ani, and spasmodic stricture of the urethra ; but in epilepsy and hooping-cough it has not been very successful.  The grand idea, in our opinion, is, to carry on the internal and external use of the drug (as in neuralgia, rheumatism, spasm of the sphincter ani, stricture of the urethra) simultaneously. Not very long ago, it was deemed a prophylactic of scarlatina. This opinion is now completely exploded. Applied in the neighbourhood of the eye, belladonna produces dilatation of the pupil; hence it is useful in the operation for cataract, in iritis, to avert or break down adhesions between the iris and lens, and to facilitate the examination of the posterior chamber of the eye. Externally, in the form of ointment or plaster, it is an admirable application in external neuralgia, though not uniformly successful; and for chordee, orchitis, and hemorrhoids. Dose of the powdered leaves, gr. j. increased gradually.

*Emplastrum.*—Extract. bellad. ℥iij.; resin plaster ℥iij. rect. spt. f℥vi. For neuralgic and rheumatic pains; over the lumbar and sacral region in reflex uterine pains.

*Extractum.*—See Brit. Pharm. This is more used than the powder. Dose, gr. ¼ increased gradually to gr. j.

*Tinctura.*—Bellad. leaves ℥j.; proof spt. Oj. Macerate 48 ho. Percolate, and add spt. to make Oj. Dose, min. v. to xx.

*Unguentum.*—Extract. bellad. gr. lxxx.; prep. lard ℥j. M. Used over the perineum in irritation of the bladder, and on the penis in chordee.

### Belladonnæ Radix. Belladonna Root.

Atropa Belladonna Linn. The root, dried; imported from Germany, or cultivated in Britain.

*Charact.*—One to two feet long, and from one half inch to two inches thick; brownish white, branched and wrinkled. An infusion dropt into the eye dilates the pupil.

*Actions and uses.*—The root possesses the powerful narcotic properties of the leaves. It is used only for preparing atropia and the liniment.

*Atropia.*—See *Atropia.*

*Linimentum.*—Bellad. root, powder ℥xx.; camphor ℥j.; rect. spt. ℥xxx. Macerate with a portion of the spt. seven days, then percolate. The product should be a pint. Useful in neuralgic and rheumatic pains. A formula for this purpose is: R Linimenti belladonnæ f℥iij.; chloroformi f℥ij.; linimenti opii ad f℥ij. Misce.

### Benzoinum. Benzoin.

Styrax Benzoin, D. C. N. F. Ebenaceæ. A balsamic resinous exudation from the stem; imported from Siam and Sumatra.

*Charact.*—In lumps consisting of agglutinated tears, or of a brownish mottled mass, with or without white tears imbedded in it; gives off, when heated, fumes of benzoic acid; has little taste, but a pleasant odour, and is soluble in rectified spt.

*Actions and uses.*—Stimulant and expectorant. Has an old and extensive popular reputation in chronic coughs. The compound tincture named "Friar's Balsam," is what is usually employed; and it has a sort of name as an application to wounds and bruises. Dose, gr. x. to xxx.; but powder seldom given.

*Tinctura Benzoini Composita.*—Benzoin ℥ij.; prep. storax ℥jss.; balsam tolu ℥ss.; soc. aloes gr. clx.; rect. spt. Oj. Macerate seven days. Dose, f℥ss. to f℥j.

### Bismuthi Carbonas. Carbonate of Bismuth.

$2 (BiO_3, CO_2), HO$, or $2 (Bi_2 CO_5) . H_2O$.

*Charact.*—A white powder, blackened by sulphuretted hydrogen; insoluble in water, but soluble with effervescence in nitric acid.

*Uses.*—Similar to those of the subnitrate. Dose, gr. v. to xx.

### Bismuthi Subnitras. Subnitrate of Bismuth.

$BiO_3, NO_5, 2 HO$, or $BiNO_4. H_2 O$. (Synonym. Bismuthum album).

*Charact.*—A heavy white powder in minute crystalline scales, blackened by sulphuretted hydrogen, insoluble in water.

*Actions.*—Tonic; and perhaps possessing a slightly sedative effect on the nerves of the stomach. It is given, and often with considerable benefit, in dyspepsia, with irritability of the stomach, pain after meals, vomiting, and pyrosis, in the absence of organic disease. It should be given in pretty large doses, and its utility is increased by washing it down with an ounce or so of infusion of calumba or chamomile. It does less good in atonic dyspepsia, with deficient gastric secretion, seemingly not having so much of a tonic as of a soothing virtue. It occasionally does service in the diarrhœa of nervous females. Two drachms have produced the symptoms of inflammation of the alimentary canal ; but as some specimens have contained arsenic, this potent poison must have been the cause. Dose, gr. v. to xx. twice or thrice daily.

*Trochisci.*—Each lozenge contains gr. ij. bismuth subnit.

### Liquor Bismuthi et Ammoniæ Citratis. Solution of Citrate of Bismuth and Ammonia.

*Prep.*—See Brit. Pharm.

*Charact.*—A colourless solution with a saline and slightly metallic taste.

*Uses.*—Same as preceding one, and will be found more convenient than the subnitrate, which is insoluble in water. Ammonia, potash, soda, and their carbonates are incompatibles. Dose, f$\mathrecit{3}$js. to $\mathrecit{3}$ij.

### Bismuthum. Bismuth.

A crystalline metal. As met with in commerce, generally impure.

Used for preparing the Bism. Pur.

### Bismuthum Purificatum. Purified Bismuth.

A crystalline metal of greyish-white colour, with a distinct roseate tinge. Sp. g. 9·83.

Used only for the preparations of bismuth.

### Borax. Borax.

Biborate of Soda.    $NaO, 2 BO^3 + 10 HO$, or $Na_2 B_4 O_7$ 10 $H_2 O$.

*Charact.*—In transparent colourless crystals, sometimes slightly effloresced, with a weak alkaline reaction ; insoluble in rectified spt., soluble in water.

*Actions and uses.*—Astringent, antilithic, emmenagogue. As an astringent it is used externally in the shape of lotion, gargle, or electuary, for aphthous ulceration of the mouth and throat, chapped nipples, mercurial salivation, and some skin diseases, such as ringworm and pityriasis.  For these latter a solution in vinegar, gr. xxx. to the ounce, is employed.  The mel boracis is well adapted for the sore mouth of children.  As an antilithic it does not stand very high, but it does at times correct the uric acic deposit.  As an emmenagogue it often fails; but when it does stimulate the uterus, it is with considerable vigour.  Like ergot, to which, however, it is inferior, it exerts most power over the active uterus ; hence any good we obtain from it is got during labour, or about a menstrual period ; and given at this latter time we occasionally obtain fair results in scanty menstruation.  Dose, gr. v. to xl.

*Mel Boracis.*—Borax, powder, gr. lxiv. ; clarified honey ℥j.  M.  In aphthæ and ulcers of the mouth, and in ptyalism.

*Glycerinum Boracis.*—Borax ℥i. ; glycerine f℥iv.  M. Useful for sore nipples.

### Bromum. Bromine.

A liquid non-metallic element, obtained from sea-water, and from some saline springs.

*Charact.*—A dark, brownish-red, very volatile liquid, with a strong and disagreeable odour.  Sp. g. 2·966.  Gives off red vapours at the common temp. of the air, and boils at 117⁰.

Used only to prepare the ammon. bromid. and the potass. bromid.

### Buchu Folia. Buchu Leaves.

1. Barosma betulina ; 2. Barosma crenulata ; 3. Barosma serratifolia. N. F. Rutaceæ. The dried leaves ; imported from the Cape of Good Hope.

*Charact.*—Smooth, marked with pellucid dotes at the indentations and apex ; having a powerful odour, and a camphoraceous taste, and leave a sense of coldness in the mouth.

*Analysis.*—A yellowish-brown volatile oil (the active part), gum, resin, &c.

*Actions and uses.*—A stimulating and very diffusive diuretic. While exciting the kidneys to increased action, it has also a tonic effect on the genito-urinary mucous membrane. It is of service in chronic mucous discharges from the bladder, in incontinence resulting from prostatic disease, and in irritability of the bladder. The natives of the Cape use it in the form of a spirit for chronic rheumatism, and the powdered leaves as a vulnerary in wounds and other injuries. In catarrh of the bladder, I think most good will be obtained by a combination of buchu and uva ursi. Dose, powder, gr. xx. to xl.

*Infusum.*—Buchu ℨss. ; boiling dist. water f℥x. Infuse an hour, and strain. Dose, f℥j. to f℥iv.

*Tinctura.*—Buchu ℨijss. ; proof spt. Oj. Macerate 48 ho. ; percolate ; add proof spt. to make Oj. Dose, fℨj. to f℥ii.

### Cadmii Iodidum. Iodide of Cadmium.

CdI, or $CdI_2$.

*Charact.*—In flat micaceous crystals of a white, pearly lustre, melting at $600^0$ or so, and forming an amber-coloured fluid. Used for preparing the ung.

*Unguentum Cadmii Iodidi.*—Cadm. iodid. gr. lxij. ; simp. oint ℨi. Mix. Stimulating and resolvent.

### Calcii Chloridum. Chloride of Calcium.

CaCl, or $CaCl_2$.

*Charact.*—In white agglutinated masses, dry, but deliquescent. Seldom given internally. Dose, gr. x. to xx.

Muriate of lime, in crystal, consists of equal parts by weight of water and dried chloride of calcium. It is useful in sickness, and glandular diseases. Dose, gr. ij. to x.

**Calcis Carbonas Præcipitata.** Precipitated Carbonate of Lime.

CaO, $CO_2$, or $CaCO_3$.

*Charact.*—A white crystalline powder, insoluble in water, dissolving in HCl with effervescence.

*Actions and uses.*—Antacid, and, in virtue of this, astringent. Useful in acidity of the stomach, with diarrhœa, and well adapted for children. It is used externally in bed sores, erysipelas, and some simple cutaneous diseases. A solution in water by means of an excess of $CO^2$ (" Carrara water ") is very useful as a drink in dyspepsia, with acidity and flatulence. Preparations of lime should not be given where there is a tendency to deposit of phosphates in the urine. Dose, gr. x. to gr. lx.

**Calcis Hydras.** Slaked Lime. See under Calx.

**Calcis Phosphas.** Phosphate of Lime.

3 CaO, $PO^5$, or $Ca_3 P_2 O_8$.

*Charact.*—A light white amorphous powder, insoluble in water, but soluble without effervescence in dilute nitric acid.

*Uses.*—Given in mollities ossium, rickets, and un-united fractures, but with poor results. Dose, gr. x. to xl.

**Calumbæ Radix.** Calumba Root.

The root of the Jateorrhiza and Coculus Palmatus sliced transversely, and dried. From Mozambique. N. F. Menispermaceæ.

*Charact.*—Slices flat, somewhat circular, about 2 inches in diameter, and from 2 to 4 lines thick, softer and thinner towards the centre, greyish-yellow, bitter. A decoction, when cold is blackened by a solution of iodine.

*Analysis.*—A crystalline bitter neutral principle, calumbin starch, volatile oil, gum, wax, &c.

*Adulterations.*—The root of bryonia epigœa, and that of

Frasera Walteri (false calumba), have been sold for the true. The former has an acrid bitter taste; the latter is known by its infusion becoming dark-green, on the addition of a sesquisalt of iron, an infusion of the true root remaining unchanged.

*Actions and uses.*—An admirable bitter tonic, and free of astringency. Of service in dyspepsia, with defective tone, irritability, and diminished secretion. In vomiting, apart from inflammatory or organic disease, it is often very useful. This anti-emetic action is probably due to the calumbin, which possesses slightly sedative properties. In the advanced stages of diarrhœa and dysentery, with want of tone and debility, good results, at times, follow its use. Dose, gr. x. to xxx.

*Extractum.*—See Brit. Pharm. An excellent tonic. Dose, gr. ij. to x.

*Infusum.*—Calumba ℥ss.; cold dist. water f℥x. Macerate one hour, and strain. Dose, f℥j. to f℥ij.

*Tinctura.*—Calumba ℥ijss.; proof spt. Oj. Macerate 48 ho., percolate, add spt. to make up Oj. Dose, f℥j. to f℥ij.

*Incompatibles.*—Iodine, nitrate of silver, and acetate of lead.

### Calx. Lime. CaO.

*Charact.*—In light lumps, externally dirty-white colour, white within. Used for making officinal preparations.

*Calcis Hydras. Slaked Lime.*—Lime recently burned lb. ij.; dist. water Oj. Pour the water on it, and set aside to cool. Pass through an iron-wire sieve; keep in a well-stopped bottle. Used for the liquor calcis.

*Linimentum.*—Solution of lime f℥ij.; olive oil f℥ij. M. Commonly called carron oil. Very useful in recent scalds and burns.

*Liquor Calcis.*—Slaked lime ℥ij.; dist. water cong. j. Antacid, and serviceable in dyspepsia with heartburn and irritability of the stomach. In diarrhœa it will sometimes answer well when more powerful remedies fail. In the vomiting and irritability of the stomach of infants, a little often repeated during the day enables them to retain their milk better, promoting also its digestion. As an antilithic it does good by correcting acidity and forming the soluble lithate of lime. It may be given in poisoning with oxalic, hydrochloric, and nitric acids. Dose, f𝔷j. to 𝔷iv. The use of it should be occasionally suspended.

*Liquor saccharatus.*—Slaked lime 𝔷j.; refined sugar 𝔷ij.; dist. water Oj. This is a stronger solution, but in some constitutions it does not answer well, concretions of carbonate of lime forming in, and constipating the bowel. Dose, min. xv. to lx.

*Incompatibles.*—Vegetable and mineral acids; metallic and alkaline salts; ant. tart.; and most vegetable infusions and decoctions.

### Calx Chlorata. Chlorinated Lime.

Hypochlorite of lime, CaO, ClO, with chloride of calcium, and a variable amount of hydrate of lime (" Bleaching Powder ").

*Charact.*—A dull-white powder, with a feeble odour of chlorine ; partially soluble in water.

*Actions and uses.*—Irritant, astringent, stimulant, antiseptic. As an astringent it is used externally, in the form of solution, gr. x. to xv. to the ounce, in skin diseases, such as ringworm, lepra, psoriasis, and scabies, and with decided benefit in the latter. It is employed also as an astringent and stimulant in dysentery and continued fever ; but while good has been often obtained in the former (where it may also be given in the form of enema), the results in typhus have been extremely variable. As an antiseptic it possesses in a high degree the power of annihilating fetid effluvia, and arresting animal decay, a property depending on its power of decomposing the noxious gases generated and evolved during the process of decomposition. It is thus of great service in gangrenous and foul ulcers, in the fetid breath of mercurial salivation, venereal ulceration of the throat and mouth ; as an injection in the fetor of malignant disease of the uterus, and that from the bowel in dysentery. In the ulcerations referred to, it seems not only to correct their repulsive odour, but by its astringent action disposes them to heal. In the sick-room it is much employed as a disinfectant. Dose, gr. ij. to gr. v. in syrup. aurant., or simple syrup. For external use in solutions, varying from gr. x. to xxx. in f℥j. of water. These should be strained. A useful formula for a gargle is : ℞ Calcis chloratæ ℨiij.; aquæ ℥ix.; solve et cola, dein adde, syrupi florum aurantii f℥vj.; syrup zingiberis f℥ij. Misce. Fiat liquor, quo gingivas sæpè gargarizet.

*Liquor Calcis Chloratæ.*—Chlorinated lime lb.j.; dist. water cong. j. Mix well, and shake occasionally during three hours. Strain through a calico filter.

*Vapor Chlori.*—Inhalation of chlorine. Chlorinated lime ℨij.; water, a sufficiency. Put the powder into a suitable apparatus, moisten it with the water (cold), and let the vapour that arises be inhaled.

*Incompatibles.*—Sulphuric acid and its salts ; oxalates ; the alkalies, and all soluble carbonates.

In poisoning with it, give emetics and albuminous liquids.

### Cambogia. Gamboge.

Obtained from Garcinia Morella. N. F. Guttiferæ. The gum-resin ; imported from Siam.

*Charact.*—In tawny-coloured cylinders, breaking easily, with a smooth conchoidal fracture ; yellow when rubbed with moisture, taste acrid. Forms an emulsion with water.

*Analysis.*—From 68 to 75 per cent of resin (gambogic acid), soluble gum, and a trace of woody fibre.

*Actions and uses.*—Irritant, and drastic cathartic, and errhine. In doses of gr. lx. it has killed, the effects being inflammation and ulceration of the alimentary tract. In small doses it is a drastic and hydragogue cathartic, producing copious watery stools. Given alone, and especially if not in very fine powder, it occasions very severe tormina ; it is therefore better to combine with it other cathartics, such as scammony or jalap, when it will operate as a safe and effectual hydragogue, and may be given in anasarca and other dropsies. Along with an alkali, it is said to be diuretic ; but we possess better remedies than it for acting on the kidneys. Dose, grj. to jv.

*Pilula Cambogiæ Composita.*—Gamboge ʒj. ; barb. aloes ʒj. ; compound powder of cinnamon ʒj. ; hard soap ʒij. ; syrup, a sufficiency. M. Make into five gr. pills. Cathartic. Dose, gr. v. to gr. x.

In poisoning with gamboge, give demulcent drinks, and enemeta ; small doses of opium and warm bath.

### Camphora. Camphor.

Camphora officinarum. N: F. Lauraceæ. A concrete volatile oil, obtained from the wood by sublimation, and re-sublimed in bell-shaped masses ; imported from China and Japan.

*Charact.*—White, translucent, tough, and crystalline ; has a powerful, penetrating odour, and a pungent taste, followed by a sensation of cold ; floats on water ; volatilizes slowly at ordinary temperatures ; is slightly soluble in water, but readily soluble in rectified spirit and in ether.

*Actions and uses.*—Narcotic and irritant, sedative, expectorant, antispasmodic, diaphoretic, stimulant. There is considerable contrariety of opinion in regard to the actions of this drug, but its most notable effect is, that of a diffusible stimulant. Large quantities have a kind of intoxicating effect, occasioning giddiness, dimness of vision, confusion of ideas, and delirium, with increased frequency of the pulse, stupor, and convulsions. The amount necessary for the production of these effects varies very much in different individuals ; and it is this variable and fluctuating action, due perhaps to a widely-prevailing idiosyncrasy, which has given rise to the dubiety that exists in regard to its operation. As a stimulant, it is given with benefit in the advanced stages of continued fever, when nervous symptoms, such as subsultus tendinum, watchfulness, and delirium exist ; where it seems also to exercise a sedative influence.  It is given, but with poor results, as an expectorant in catarrh ; as an anodyne or sedative, with fair results, in gout and rheumatism, and in painful diseases of the urinary organs, and dysmenorrhœa. Decided benefit is obtained in the nervousness and irritability following some cases of labour, especially combined with an opiate.  Externally, in the form of the liniment, camphor is useful as a stimulant and anodyne application in rheumatic pains, enlarged glands, and bruises ; and the spirit is one of the best remedies for allaying the heat and itching of chilblains.  Two other virtues are popularly assigned to camphor when attached in a bag to the person, namely, that of warding off contagious diseases, and checking the secretion of milk !  There is reason to fear that such a belief is destitute of foundation.  Dose, gr. ij. to x. in the form of pill ; or it may be given suspended in water with mucilage or syrup.

*Aqua.*—Camphor ℥ss. ; dist. water cong. j.  Enclose the camphor in a muslin bag in the water, invert the jar, and stand for 2 days.  Dose, ℥i. to ℥ii.  Useful for filling up stimulant mixtures.

*Linimentum.*—Camphor ℥j. ; olive oil, f℥iv.  M.

*Lin. Camph. Co.*—Camphor ℥ijss. ; English oil, lavend. f℈j. ; strong. sol. ammon. f℥xv. ; rect. spt. f℥xv.  M. Stimulant.  Useful in neuralgia, rheumatism, and enlarged glands.

*Spiritus.*—Camphor ℥j. ; rect. spt. f℥ix.  M.  Dose, min. x. to xxx.

*Tinct. Camph. Composita.* — Opium in coarse powder gr. xl. ; benzoic acid gr. xl. ; camphor gr. xxx. ; oil anise f℈ss. ; proof spt. Oj.  Macerate 7 days ; filter, and add proof spt. to make Oj.  Paregoric Elixir.—Anodyne and expectorant in bronchitis.  Dose, min. xxx. to f℥ij.

### Canellæ Albæ Cortex.   White Canella Bark.

The bark of Canella Alba.  From the West Indies.

*Charact.*—In hard quills of a yellowish-white or pale orange colour.  Has a clove-like odour, and peppery taste.

*Uses.*—An aromatic tonic, and usually given along with other bitter tonics. Dose, gr. x. to xxx. An ingredient also of the Vinum Rhei.

### Cannabis Indica. Indian Hemp.

Cannabis Sativa Linn. N. F. Urticaceæ. The flowering tops of the female plant from which the resin has not been removed, dried ; cultivated in India.

*Charact.* — Tops consisting of one or more alternate branches, bearing the remains of the flowers and smaller leaves, and a few ripe fruits, pressed together in masses which are about two inches long, harsh, of a dusky-green colour, and a characteristic odour. Different parts of the plant are known in India, under the names Gunjah, Bhang, and Hachish.

*Analysis.*—Cannabin, a resin on which its properties depend, and developed only in warm countries ; a small quantity of volatile oil, extractive, &c.

*Actions and uses.*—Narcotic, antispasmodic. Long used in India as an intoxicant, but introduced into practice in this country only twenty-five years ago, after a notice of its alleged virtues by a Calcutta physician. It has now become better known. Like alcohol, it produces a variety of effects on different individuals : in one a dull heavy state of pleasant reverie, with a rapid succession of unconnected ideas ; in another a cheerful activity, with giddiness, and a tendency to talk, sing, laugh, or dance. It alleviates pain and subdues spasm, and for this purpose it has been given, but with extremely· variable results (it may be owing to inert specimens of it), in neuralgia, chronic rheumatism, painful menstruation, infantile convulsions, hydrophobia, and tetanus. In the latter disease a few striking cures have been achieved, but in other cases it has failed. Spasm and spasmodic coughs are frequently relieved by it ; and some obtain sleep from it, who are debarred the more certain soporific opium, owing to its evil effects. In uterine hæmorrhage it often arrests the flooding, and it relieves the pain in dysmenorrhœa.

*Extractum.*—Indian hemp lb.j.; rect. spt. Oiv. Macerate 7 days, press out the tincture; distil off the spirit, and evaporate by a water bath to a proper consistence. Dose, gr. ¼ to gr. j.

*Tinctura.*—Ext. Indian hemp ℥j.; rect. spt. Oj. Dissolve. Each f℥j. contains rather more than gr. ij. of ext. Dose, min. v. to xxx. gradually increased; and in mucilage or syrup, not in water.

### Cantharis. Cantharides.

Cantharis vesicatoria. Class, insecta; order, coleoptera. The beetle, dried; collected in Russia, Sicily, and Hungary.

*Charact.*—From eight to ten lines long, furnished with two wing-covers of a shining metallic-green colour, under which are two membranous transparent wings; odour strong and disagreeable; powder greyish-brown, containing shining green particles. Test.—Should be free from mites.

*Analysis.*—Cantharidine (a white crystalline substance, on which the activity of the article depends); a yellow fat oil, a green concrete oil; uric, acetic, and phosphoric acids; salts, &c.

*Actions and uses.*—A stimulating diuretic, and in some cases aphrodisiac. In large doses it is a dangerous poison, producing inflammation of the alimentary canal, and of the urinary organs (with strangury, bloody urine, priapism); delirium, convulsions, and coma. About gr. xx. have proved fatal. These bad effects are to be met by emetics, mucilaginous drinks, blood-letting, opiates, by the mouth, and in the form of enema. Benefit is derived from it, in cautious doses, in leucorrhœa; in gleet it is not so successful; and more barren still are the results in amenorrhœa, paralysis of the bladder, and incontinence of urine. In dropsy depending on cardiac disease we will frequently obtain benefit from it; in chronic skin diseases it is next to a failure. For external use it is a consequential drug, owing to its excellent vesicating power. Applied to the skin it occasions, in the course of from four to ten hours, an effusion of serum between the cuticle and the true skin, or, in briefer terms, a blister.   This effect is produced with considerable uniformity, and without  inducing much pain. Where the skin, as in  a  few cases, resists its action, a sina-pism before, or  a  poultice after, will promote it.   Blisters are used as derivatives, or counter-irritants, in  a number of diseases ; such as inflammation of the brain and medulla spinalis, acute and chronic ; in diseases of the chest and abdomen ; in tic douloureux, and sciatica.   As a vascular stimulant, too, much benefit is derived from blisters over indolent and specific tumours, such as buboes, dropsical effusions, effusions into joints, strumous abscesses, and over the surface of old and indolent ulcers, and chronic pustular eruptions.   They are in frequent use also as excitants in the coma of typhoid fever, cholera, and apoplexy.   Lastly, they are in daily use for maintaining a  continuous dis-charge from issues, and for removing the cuticle for ender-mic applications.   They should be used with caution in young persons, or in the old, and those attenuated and exhausted by disease, as dangerous sloughing is apt to be induced.   Dose, gr. ss. to j. ; but the powder is not given.

*Acetum.*—Cantharid ℥ij. ; glacial acetic acid ℥ij. ; acetic acid ℥xviij.   Prepared by percolation.

*Uses.*—Vesicant.

*Charta Epispastica.*—Blistering paper, a clean vesicant preparation, suitable for the young, as less likely to occasion strangury, &c.

*Emplastrum Cantharidis.*—Cantharides in fine powder ℥xij. ; yellow wax ℥vijss. ; prepared suet ℥vijss. ; resin ℥iij. ; prepared lard ℥vj.   Liquefy the wax, suet, and lard together, by a water bath, and add the resin previously melted ; then remove them from the bath, and a little before they solidify, sprinkle in the cantharides, and mix thoroughly.   This is used for producing a blister ; it is spread with a cold spatula, or the thumb, on leather, or adhesive plaster.   It will act with more vigour and cer-tainty if a small portion of the flies is dusted on the surface, and then rubbed or pressed in with a spatula, or the thumb, as before.   Ten hours generally suffices to produce vesication ; and on removal of the blister the elevated cuticle may be cut : the inflamed part should then be dressed with a little ung. simp. and a layer of raw cotton ; a speedy healing being thus insured. If wished, the surface may be kept raw by a dressing of ung. sabinæ, or ung. cantharid.

*Emplastrum Calefaciens.*—Cantharid. ℥iv. ; boiling water Oj. ; expressed oil of nutmeg ℥iv. ; yellow wax ℥iv. ; resin ℥iv. ; soap plaster lb.iij¼. ; resin plaster lb.ij. Infuse the canth. in the boiling water six hours ; squeeze through calico, and evaporate the expressed liquid by a water bath till reduced to one-third ; then add the other ingredients, and melt in a water bath, stirring well until all is thoroughly mixed. A rubefacient plaster ; useful in chronic bronchitis.

*Liquor Epispasticus.*—Canth. ℥xviij. ; acetic acid ℥iv. ; ether, a sufficiency. Prepare by percolation ; fill up to ℥xx. with ether. A speedy blister. Applied with a brush or lint.

*Tinctura.*—Cantharides in coarse powder ℥¼. ; proof spt. Oj. Macerate 7 days ; filter, and add spt. to make Oj. This is the preparation chiefly employed internally. Dose, min. v. to xx.

*Unguentum.*—Canth. ℥j. ; yellow wax ℥j. ; olive oil f℥vj. M. Rubefacient, and for keeping issues open.

Strangury occasionally results from the external use of flies ; when it does so, small doses of pu. ipecac. cum. op., in barley water, is of service.

### Capsici Fructus. Capsicum Fruit.

Capsicum fastigiatum. N. F. Solanaceæ. The ripe fruit dried ; imported from the coast of Guinea, and from the East and West Indies.

*Charact.*—Pod membranous, 5 to 8 lines long, 2 lines broad, conical, orange-red, corrugated, intensely hot in taste.

*Actions and uses.*—This aromatic and hot condiment is stimulant, tonic, and an epispastic. Given occasionally in dyspepsia with want of appetite, and defective secretion. Seldom used as a counterirritant, but at times in coma.

Most commonly employed in gargles, for relaxed sore-throat, and cynanche maligna. Doze, gr. ss. to ij. in pill.

*Tinctura.*—Capsicum, bruised, ℥¾ ; rect. spt. Oj. Macerate 48 ho. ; percolate, filter ; add spt. to make Oj. Dose, min. x. to xx.

### Carbo Animalis. Bone Black.

Used for prep. of the pure.

### Carbo Animalis Purificatus. Purified Animal Charcoal.

Bone black, deprived of its earthy salts.
*Charact.*—A black pulverulent substance.
*Uses.*—A useful decolorizing agent, and of service in many chemical processes; but little used in medical practice. Said to counteract the poisonous effects of morphia, aconitia, and strychnia. Dose, gr. xx. to lx.

### Carbo Ligni. Wood Charcoal.

Wood charred by exposure to a red heat without access of air.
*Charact.*—In black, brittle, porous masses, tasteless, odourless, very light, and retaining the form and texture of the wood whence it was obtained ; insoluble in water.
*Uses.*—Antiseptic. Employed chiefly in the form of poultice to destroy the fetor of gangrenous sores and phagedenic ulcers; and as a dentifrice it corrects the odour from carious teeth, and fetid breath. Internally it has been given in dysentery to improve offensive evacuations; and to correct the fetid eructations, and flatulence of some cases of dyspepsia. Here, along with a tonic and aperient, it is often beneficial, and is perhaps entitled to increased consideration. Dose, gr. x. to xxx.

*Cataplasma.*—Wood charcoal, powder, ℥ss. ; bread ℥ij. ; linseed meal ℥jss. ; boiling water f℥x. For foul sores.

Formula for dyspepsia, with flatulence and fetid eructations. ℞ Pulveris cinchonæ. F. gr. lx. pulveris calumbæ gr. lx. ; pulveris rhei gr. xxxvi. ; pulveris carbonis ligni gr. cxx. Misce. Divide in pulveres duodecim, quarum sumatur una ter in die.

### Cardamomum. Cardamoms.

Elettaria Cardamomum. The Malabar Cardamom. N. F. Zingiberaceæ. The seeds, contained in their capsules, which are to be removed when the seeds are employed; cultivated in Malabar.

*Charact.*—Seeds obtusely angular, corrugated, reddish-brown, internally white, with a warm aromatic taste and odour.

*Uses.*—An agreeable aromatic stimulant and carminative. Chiefly employed as an adjunct to, and corrective of, other medicines, such as the griping of cathartics.

*Pulvis Aromaticus.*—See Cinnamon.

*Tinctura Cardamomi Composita.*—Cardamoms, bruised, ℥ss; caraway bruised ℥ss; raisins freed from their seeds ℥ij.; cinnamon, bruised, ℥ss.; cochineal in powder gr. lx.; proof spt. Oj. Proceed in the usual way. Dose, f℥j. to ℥ij.

### Carui Fructus. Caraway Fruit.

Carum Carui Linn. N. F. Umbelliferæ. The fruit, dried; cultivated in England.

*Uses.*—An aromatic carminative. A corrective of other medicines.

*Aqua.*—Caraway, bruised, ℥xvj.; water cong. ij.; distil one gallon. Dose, f℥j. to ℥ij. Given in the flatulent colic of children.

### Carui Oleum. See *Oleum Carui.*

### Caryophylli Oleum. See *Oleum Caryophylli.*

### Caryophyllum. Cloves.

Caryophyllus aromaticus Linn. N. F. Myrtaceæ. The unexpanded flower-bud, dried; cultivated in Penang, Bencoolen, and Amboyna.

*Uses.*—Stimulant, and in large doses irritant, especially the oil. Used in medicine chiefly as a corrective of other drugs, as in the griping of some of the gum-resins. A drop of the oil in the cavity of a carious tooth sometimes relieves toothache.

*Infusum.*—Cloves, bruised, ʒꜱꜱ. ; boiling dist. water fʒx. Infuse ¼ ho. and strain.   Dose, fʒj. to ʒiv.

*Pulvis Aromaticus.*—See Cinnamon.

### Cascarillæ Cortex.   Cascarilla Bark.

ˉ Croton Eluteria.   N. F. Euphorbiaceæ.   The bark ; from the Bahama Islands.

*Charact.*—In quills 2 to 3 in. long, 2 to 5 lines in diameter, dull-brown, but coated with white crustaceous lichens ; warm and bitter to the taste ; emitting a fragrant odour when burned.

*Analysis.*—A bitter neutral crystalline principle cascarillin ; tannin, albumen, fatty matter, gum, volatile oil, resin, pectic acid, salts, &c.

*Adulterations.*—Copalchi bark, from the croton pseudochina, a native of Mexico, has been substituted for it. The quills are much longer than those of the true, are more covered with white lichens, and have no transverse cracks.

*Actions and uses.*—An aromatic tonic, but of no great power.   It is used chiefly, along with other tonics, in chronic diarrhœa and dyspepsia.   As a febrifuge it is not successful, and cannot be relied on in intermittent fever. Dose, gr. xx. to xl.

*Infusum.*—Cascarilla ʒj. ; boiling dist. water fʒx.   Infuse an hour.   Dose, fʒj. to fʒij.

*Tinctura.*—Cascarilla ʒijss. ; proof spt. Oj.   Proceed as usual.   Dose, fʒj. to fʒij.

### Cassiæ Pulpa.   Cassia Pulp.

Cassia Fistula Linn.   Purging Cassia.   N. F. Leguminosæ.   The pulp of the pods ; imported from the East Indies.

*Uses.*—A laxative, and an ingredient of the conf. sennæ. Dose, ʒss. to ʒi.

### Castoreum.   Castor.

Castor Fiber Linn.   The Beaver.   Class Mammalia, order Rodentia.   The preputial follicles and their secretion, dried, separated from the somewhat shorter and smaller oil-sacs which are frequently attached to them ; from the Hudson's Bay Territory.

*Charact.*—Follicles in pairs about 3 in. long, fig-shaped, brownish, containing a dry resinous reddish-brown odorous secretion, in great part soluble in rectified spt. and ether.

*Actions and uses.*—Antispasmodic, but of no great power. Some believe it useful in the milder forms of hysteria, and in the nervous symptoms of adynamic fever.

*Tinctura.*—Castor ℥i. ; rect. spt. Oj. Macerate 7 days and filter. Dose, f℥ss. to f℥ij.

### Cataplasmata.

These are placed under the substances whence they derive their name.

### Catechu Pallidum. Pale Catechu.

Uncaria Gambir. An extract of the leaves and young shoots ; prepared at Singapore, and in the Eastern Archipelago. N. F. Leguminosæ.

*Charact.*—In cubes, or masses formed of coherent cubes ; the former about an inch in diameter, externally brown, internally pale brick-red ; breaking easily with a dull earthy fracture. Taste bitter, very astringent.

*Analysis.*—Tannin and catechuic acid.

*Actions and uses.*—An excellent astringent. Employed with benefit to check increased mucous discharges; such as chronic diarrhœa, dysentery, chronic catarrh, cystirrhœa, leucorrhœa, and gleet. It is perhaps fully more beneficial in the former, than in the latter four affections; and in the two first named it is often usefully combined with a little opium. Relaxed mucous membranes get firmer under its use, and passive hemorrhage from the intestines is checked. For most, if not all, of the foregoing complaints, however, we will obtain better results from either tannin or gallic acid. As a topical application it is useful in chapped nipples, aphthous ulcerations of the mouth, chronic cynanche tonsillaris, elongated uvula, congestion, and sponginess of the gums. For these purposes it may be applied in the form of lotion, gargle, or powder.  Dose, gr. x. to gr. xl. in powder.

*Infusum.*—Catechu gr. clx. ; cinnamon gr. xxx. ; boiling dist. water f℥x.  Infuse half-an-hour.  Dose, f℥j. to f℥ij.

*Pulvis Catechu Compositus.*—Catechu ℥iv. ; kino ℥ij. ; rhatany ℥ij. ; cinnamon ℥j. ; nutmeg ℥j.  Mix well, and pass through a fine sieve.  Dose, gr. xx. to gr. xl.

*Tinctura.*—Catechu ℥ijss. ; cinnamon ℥j. ; proof spt. Oj.  Proceed as usual.  Dose, f℥ss. to f℥ij.

*Trochisci.*—Catechu, sugar, gum tinct. capsic., and water. A useful astringent for clearing the voice of public speakers and singers ; gr. l, in each lozenge.

### Cera Alba.  White Wax.

Yellow Wax, bleached by exposure to moisture, air, and light.  British, and imported.

### Cera Flava.  Yellow Wax.

Apis Mellifica Linn.  The hive bee.  The prepared honeycomb.  British, and imported.

*Uses.*—Emollient.  Used chiefly for making ointments, plasters, and suppositories.

*Unguentum simplex.*—White wax ℥ij. ; prep. lard ℥iij. ; almond oil f℥iij.  M.  A simple, cooling dressing.

### Cerevisiæ Fermentum.  Beer Yeast.

The ferment obtained in brewing beer.

*Uses.*—Has been recommended as a stimulant in typhoid fever, but appears to do little good.  There are better carminatives for tympanitis ; and it is not equal to the charcoal poultice as an application to foul sores.  As an application to recent bruises, spread on lint, it does seem to promote restoration.  Dose, f℥ss. every three or four hours, in a little camphor water.

*Cataplasma Fermenti.*—Beer yeast f℥vi. ; flour ℥xiv. ; water, heated to 100⁰, f℥vi.  Mix the yeast with the water, and stir in the flour.  Place the mass near the fire till it rises.  For foul sores ; rather a painful poultice.

**Cerii Oxalas.   Oxalate of Cerium.**

$$2\ CeO,\ C_4\ O_6\ +\ 6\ HO,\ \text{or}\ Ce\ C_2\ O_4.\ 3\ H_2\ O.$$

A salt which may be obtained as a precipitate by adding solution of oxalate of ammonia to a soluble salt of cerium.

*Charact.*—A white granular powder, insoluble in water, decomposed at a dull red heat into a reddish-brown powder.

*Actions and uses.*—Sedative and tonic, of considerable service in chronic vomiting, and the vomiting of pregnancy. Given also in irritable stomach, and pyrosis, but with less benefit.   Has been tried in chorea and epilepsy, but with unsatisfactory results.   Dose, gr. j. to gr. ij. two or three times a-day.

**Cetaceum.   Spermaceti.**

Physeter macrocephalus Linn.   The sperm whale, inhabiting the Pacific and Indian Oceans.   Nearly pure cetine, separated by purification from the oil contained in the head.

*Charact.*—Crystalline, pearly-white, glistening, little taste or odour; reducible to power by addition of a little rect. spt.

*Uses.*—Demulcent, but seldom used internally; chiefly for ointments.

*Unguentum Cetacei.*—Spermaceti ℥v.; white wax ℥ij.; almond oil Oj.   Melt with a gentle heat, and stir till it solidifies.   A cool and emollient dressing for raw surfaces.

**Cetraria.   Iceland Moss.**

Cetraria Islandica.   N. F. Lichenaceæ.   The entire lichen; native of the north of Europe.

*Charact.*—Foliaceous, lobed, crisp, cartilaginous, brownish-white, paler beneath, bitter, and mucilaginous.   A strong decoction gelatinizes on cooling.

*Analysis.*—Two starchy matters, lichenin and inulin, a bitter principle, cetrarin; two acids, lichestearic and lichenic acids, sugar, gum, salts, &c.

*Actions and uses.*—A feeble tonic, possessing also nutritive properties.   Formerly had rather a high reputation as a tonic and restorative in exhausting diseases, such as phthisis, but experience has led many to doubt or deny this. Its tonic property depends on the cetrarin, which is said to have done good in ague. As an antiscorbutic, it is not very much confided in.

*Decoctum Cetrariæ.*—Iceland moss ℥j.; dist. water Oj.; wash the moss to remove impurities ; boil it with the dist. water for ten minutes in a covered vessel, and strain while hot. The product should measure about a pint. Dose, f℥j. to f℥iv.

### Chirata. Chiretta.

Ophelia Chirata D. C. N. F. Gentianaceæ. The entire plant; collected in Northern India, when the fruit begins to form.

*Charact.*—Stems about three feet long, of the thickness of a goose-quill, round, smooth, pale-brown, branched ; branches opposite; flowers small, numerous panicled ; the whole plant intensely bitter.

*Actions and uses.*—An extremely bitter tonic. Useful in dyspepsia with constipation, owing to its possessing also slightly laxative properties, and an influence on the biliary secretion. As a febrifuge it may be employed where quinia cannot be had.

*Infusum Chiratæ.*—Chiretta ℥¼.; dist. water at 120°, f℥x. Infuse half an hour. Dose, f℥j. to f℥ij.

*Tinctura.*—Chiretta ℥ijss.; proof spt. Oj. Make in the usual way. Dose, f℥ss. to f℥ij.

### Chlori Liquor. Solution of Chlorine.

Chlorine gas dissolved in half its volume of water, and constituting 0·006 of the weight of the solution.

*Charact.*—A yellowish-green liquid, smelling strongly of chlorine, and immediately discharging the colour of a dilute solution of sulphate of indigo. Sp. gr. 1·003.

*Actions and uses.*—Irritant, stimulant, astringent, and a disinfectant. In large quantities it is an irritant poison, exciting inflammation of the alimentary canal. As a stimulant—some say tonic—it has been given in typhus and typhoid fever; failing in some types, and achieving fair results in others. As an astringent, it has been extensively employed in the form of inhalation in phthisis and chronic bronchitis; in many cases diminishing, and in a few others entirely drying up the sputa, especially in the latter disease. Water weakly impregnated with chlorine, and kept at a temp. of about 100°, is used for this purpose. The results obtained, we think, quite warrant a revival of the practice, which has fallen into desuetude in this quarter. Externally, in a dilute form, chlorine water has been applied to foul ulcers, chronic skin diseases, and as a gargle in cynanche maligna. It is alleged to have the power of counteracting the poison of rabies, but this is open to doubt. As a disinfectant, we have spoken of it under Chlor. Lime. Dose, min. x. to xxx.

*Incompatibles.*—Nitrate of silver; acetate of lead.

In poisoning, give albumen and milk.

### Chloroformum. Chloroform.

$C^2 HCl^3$, or $CHCl_3$.

*Charact.*—A limpid colourless liquid, of an agreeable ethereal odour, and sweet taste. Mixes with alcohol and ether in all proportions; and dissolves slightly in water, communicating to it a sweetish taste. Burns, though not readily, with a green and smoky flame.

*Prep.*—Chlorinated lime lb. x.; rect. spt. f℥xxx.; slaked lime a sufficiency; water cong. iij.; sulphuric acid a sufficiency; chloride of calcium, in small fragments, ℥ij.; dist. water f℥jx. Place the water and spt. in a capacious still, and raise the mixture to the temp. of 100°. Add the chlor. lime, and lb. v. of the slaked lime, mixing thoroughly. Connect the still with a condensing worm encompassed by cold water, and terminating in a narrow-necked receiver; and apply heat, so as to cause distillation, taking care to withdraw the fire the moment that the process is well established. When the distilled product measures ℥l., the receiver is to be withdrawn. Pour its contents into a gallon bottle, half filled with water, mix well by shaking, and set at rest for a few minutes, when the mixture will separate into two strata of different densities. Let the lower stratum, which constitutes crude chloroform, be washed by agitating it in a bottle with ℥iij. of the dist. water. Allow the chloroform to subside, withdraw the water, and repeat the washing with the rest of the dist. water in successive quantities of ℥iij. at a time. Agitate the washed chloroform for five minutes in a bottle, with an equal volume of sulphuric acid; allow the mixture to settle, and transfer the upper stratum of liquor to a flask containing the chlor. calc., mixed with ℥ss. of slaked lime, which should be perfectly dry. Mix well by agitation. After the lapse of an hour, connect the flask with a Liebig's condenser, and distil over the pure chloroform by means of a water bath. Preserve the product in a cool place, in a bottle with an accurately ground stopper.

*Actions and uses.*—Narcotic, stimulant, sedative, antispasmodic, anæsthetic. In large doses it is a narcotic poison, producing profound coma, and death from syncope, or from asphyxia. In medicinal doses it is sedative and antispasmodic, and has been given in tetanus, hydrophobia, hysteria, cancerous diseases, painful digestion, chronic vomiting, neuralgia, asthma, and spasmodic cough. In all of these diseases, with the exception of the second, excellent results will often be obtained. In irritable cough especially, and some cases of hysteria, decided benefit almost invariably accrues. As an external application, well diluted, chloroform is useful in neuralgia and muscular rheumatism; but far inferior to opium, belladonna, or aconite; and it subdues the itching, if it does not promote the cure, of some skin diseases, such as lichen, prurigo, and urticaria. Such are some of the uses and applications of chloroform, and if we were to stop here, it would occupy but a comparatively humble position in the category of sedative drugs; but it has another property of a higher kind, which has won for it a name and unrivalled fame throughout the civilized world, namely, that of inducing insensibility to pain. For its introduction for this purpose, we are indebted to the distinguished Professor of

Midwifery in the University of this city, whose early labours and experiments in connection with it, entitle him to the gratitude of mankind. As an anæsthetic, it stands *per se*, and unequalled; no previou or subsequent one being so safe, speedy, or effectual. When inhaled in doses of from fʒss. to fʒss. coma is produced, generally in a few minutes, with stertorous respiration, upturning and fixing of the eyes, muscular relaxation, unconsciousness, and insensibility to pain. The pulse is sometimes stronger, at other times weaker and quicker. This comatose condition is preceded by a variety of feelings, sensations, and manifestations on the part of the patient, such as ringing in the ears, fulness in the head, dizziness, agreeable ideas and sights, change in the colour of objects. In some there is a tendency to laughter and calm repose, in others, to sonorous talk and turbulence. The state of insensibility lasts, in general, about ten minutes, but may be prolonged much longer ; after this, there is a revival of consciousness and sensibility, with mayhap no recollection of what passed, and often neither sickness, headache, nor exhaustion. Some few do not tolerate it well, excessive depression of the heart's action resulting ; but it is not easy to say what are the conditions which contra-indicate it. I have administered it frequently without any apparent bad effects in phthisical patients, and some where there were suspicions, if not more, of cardiac disease, and I know that this is the experience of not a few. It is better, however, to be very chary and cautious in these cases, and the pulse and respiration — which in the soundest patient demand the strictest vigilance—should be observed with increased care. If the former become weak and the latter irregular, it is better to suspend its use. In some few, the tongue becoming powerless, falls backward, threatening asphyxia ; in these cases it is grasped, and pulled forwards, and the process of stupefaction may be carried on as before. When death is threatened, either from an overdose or constitutional peculiarity, a current of cold air should be directed across the face, cold water applied to the head and chest, ammonia held to the nostrils; and artificial respiration resorted to if required. On the partial revival of the patient, internal stimulants may be given. The therapeutical applications of chloroform, in the form of inhalation, may almost be inferred from the foregoing remarks; wherever a painful operation has to be borne, there will it be found a boon. For the prevention of pain, then, during surgical operations, it is in daily use; and there are some cases, such as dislocations, strangulated hernia, and catheterism in spasmodic stricture, where it serves a twofold purpose, namely, that of a relaxant, as well as a prophylactic of pain. The exceptions to its use during surgical operations are few; those about the mouth and nose are unfavourable to it, owing to the risk of blood flowing into the air passages while the patient is insensible. Further, in midwifery practice, chloroform has been of incalculable service, not more in the way of banishing the pain of natural labour, than of facilitating interference in that which is not natural. I need only name the forceps, version, craniotomy, and the Cæsarian section (which, however, is a rare thing in this part of the world), to show its utility and value. Dose, internally in the fluid form, min. iij. to x. in a glass of mucilage or syrup. For anæsthetic purposes, from fʒj. to ʒij. is poured on a handkerchief hollowed somewhat like a cup, and inhaled by the mouth and nostrils—the handkerchief being brought gradually into contact with the face, the patient lying on his back, with head slightly elevated.

*Linimentum.*—Chloroform fʒij.; liniment of camphor fʒij. Mix.

*Spiritus Chloroformi.*—Chloroform fʒj.; rectified spt. fʒxix. Dissolve. Dose, min. xx. to lx.

*Tinctura Chlorof. Co.*—Chlorof. fʒij.; rect. spt. fʒviii.; tinct. cardam. comp. fʒx. Mix. Dose, min. xx. to lx.

**Cinchonæ Flavæ Cortex.** Yellow Cinchona Bark.

Cinchona Calisaya. N. F. Cinchonaceæ. The bark; collected in Bolivia and Southern Peru.

*Charact.*—In flat pieces, deprived of the periderm, rarely in coated quills, from 6 to 18 in. long; 1 to 3 in. wide; 2 to 4 lines thick, compact and heavy; outer surface brown, marked by broad shallow irregular longitudinal depressions; inner surface tawny-yellow, fibrous. Powder, cinnamon-brown, somewhat aromatic, and persistently bitter.

100 grains yield about two gr. quinia, or more than the other two.

### Cinchonæ Pallidæ Cortex.   Pale Cinchona Bark.

Cinchona Condaminea. The bark; collected about Loxa, in Ecuador.

*Charact.*—From half a line to a line thick, in single or double quills, from 6 to 15 inches long, 2 to 8 lines diam.; outer surface brown and wrinkled, or grey and speckled with adherent lichens, with or without numerous transverse cracks; inner surface bright orange or cinnamon-brown. Powder, pale brown, slightly bitter, very astringent.

200 grains yield two gr. of alkaloids.

### Cinchonæ Rubræ Cortex.   Red Cinchona Bark.

Cinchona Succirubra. The bark; collected on the western slopes of Chimborazo.

*Charact.*—In flat or incurved pieces, less frequently in quills, coated with the periderm, from a few inches to 2 feet long, 1 to 3 in. wide, 2 to 6 lines thick; outer surface reddish-brown, rarely whitened by lichens, wrinkled longitudinally, often warty, and crossed by deep transverse cracks; inner surface redder. Powder, red brown; taste bitter and astringent.

100 grs. yield about 2 grs. of alkaloids.

*Analysis.*—Four alkaloids, viz., quinia, cinchonia, quinidinia, and aricinia, in union with three acids, kinic, or cinchonic, kinovic, and tannic; with two colouring matters, cinchonic yellow and red; fatty matter, kinate of lime, a trace of volatile oil, starch, gum, &c. The medicinal virtues of the bark are owing to the first three alkaloids, and especially the quinia.

*Adulterations.*—Bark is mixed with inferior, yet true kinds, and with various false barks. Three are named,—Piton bark, Caribean, and Pitaya ; the last only being encountered in British commerce. They have all a mawkish bitter taste, non-aromatic. The Pitaya bark is in thin quills, greyish-yellow externally, blackish-brown internally. Red saunders-wood is sometimes mixed with the powdered barks; it may be discovered by agitating the doubtful sample with ether; if adulterated, the ether will acquire a saffron colour, but not if the bark be pure. Various tests are employed to discover the most efficacious and valuable barks. According to Berzelius, the most efficient happen to contain most tannin; therefore, those which in infusion give the largest precipitate with solution of gelatine, and with antim. tart., ought to be preferred.

*Actions and uses.*—Astringent, antiseptic, and a powerful tonic and antiperiodic. As an astringent and antiseptic, it is employed topically to correct the discharge and fetid odour of foul ulcers and gangrenous sores, but is inferior to charcoal or the preparations of chlorine. As a tonic it is very widely used for imparting tone, and aiding digestion in functional disorders of the stomach, and to restore nervous tone and muscular strength where these have been undermined by protracted disease or exhausting discharges. There are some cases of dyspepsia attended with pain, feeling of weight at the stomach, and irritability, yet not based on organic disease, which, so far from improving under it, seem rather to be aggravated. They are soon found out; for almost the first dose, as well as successive ones, intensifies these symptoms. Cinchona cannot be called a febrifuge, having no power in the way of arresting continued or eruptive fevers ; it possesses, however, an unfailing influence in periodic fevers, and therefore antiperiodic is the more correct title. It will destroy the condition, or chain of conditions, on which ague and remittent fever depend, almost as certainly as opium will induce sleep, or croton oil catharsis. It is given in full doses during the stage of intermission or remission. In periodic neuralgia, headache, and rheumatism, it is also of great service; but here, the sulphate of beberia, or iron, will answer equally well. As a constitutional remedy in gangrene or erysipelas it is not now much trusted in. The therapeutic virtues of the bark exist unimpaired in the alkaloid quinia; but where a tonic effect merely is desiderated, it is better to abide by the former. Dose of the powder, which, however, is not often prescribed; tonic, gr. x. to lx.; anti-periodic, gr. lx. to cxx. every two or three hours.

*Decoctum Cinchonæ Flavæ.*—Yellow cinchona bark ℥jʒ.; dist. water Oj. Boil ten minutes in a covered vessel. Strain, when cold, through calico; add dist. water to make up to f℥xvi. Dose, f℥ss. to ℥ij.

*Extractum Cinchonæ Flavæ Liquidum.*—See Brit. Pharm. Dose, min. x. to xxx.

*Infusum Cinchonæ Flavæ.*—Yellow bark ℥ss.; boiling dist. water f℥x. Infuse two hours, and filter through paper. Dose, f℥j. to ℥ij.

*Tinctura Cinc. Flav.*—Yellow bark ℥iv.; proof spt. Oj. Macerate 48 ho.; percolate and add spt. to make Oj. Dose, f℥ss. to f℥ii.

*Tinct. Cinch. Co.*—Pale bark ℥ij.; bitter orange peel ℥j.; serpentary ℥ss.; saffron gr. lx.; cochineal gr. xxx.; proof spt. Oj. Proceed as before. Formerly called Huxham's tincture. Dose, f℥ss. to ℥ij.

**Cinnamomi Oleum.** See *Oleum Cinnamomi.*

**Cinnamomi Cortex.** Cinnamon Bark.

Cinnamomum Zeylanicum. N. F. Lauraceæ. The inner bark of shoots from the truncated stock; imported from Ceylon.

*Charact.*—In closely rolled yellowish-brown quills, ¼ line thick, 4 line diameter.

*Uses.*—An aromatic stimulant; used chiefly as an agreeable addition to more active drugs. Dose, powder, gr. x. to xxx.

*Aqua.*—Cinnamon, bruised, ℥xx.; water cong. ij.; distil cong. j. Useful for filling up mixtures.

*Pulvis Cinnamomi Compositus.*—Cinnamon Cardamon seeds, and ginger, of each, ℥j. Powder, and mix well, and pass through a fine sieve. A corrective of, and agreeable addition to, other medicines, such as cathartic and tonic powders. Dose, gr. v. to x. Formerly called aromatic powder.

*Tinctura.*—Cinnamon ℥ijss.; proof spt. Oj.; make in the usual manner. Dose, fℨss. to fℨii.

### Coccus. Cochineal.

Coccus Cacti Linn. Class Insecta, order Hemiptera.

The female insect, dried; reared in Mexico and Teneriffe.

*Charact.*—Ovate, plano-convex, about 2 lines long, wrinkled, black or greyish-white; yields, when crushed, a puce-coloured powder. The greyish-white insect quickly becomes black when warmed before the fire.

*Uses.*—Said to be an antispasmodic and anodyne, and popularly employed as such in hooping-cough; but it seems somewhat ineffectual. In neuralgia, for which it has been recommended by some, I have not seen it of the slightest service.

*Tinctura Cocci.*—Cochineal ℥ijss.; proof spt. Oj.; Macerate 7 days. Dose, fℨss. to fℨiss. Useful for colouring mixtures, &c.

### Colchici Cormus. Colchicum Corm.

Colchicum Autumnale Linn. N. F. Melanthaceæ. Meadow Saffron. The fresh corm; collected about the end of June, and the same stripped of its coats, sliced transversely, and dried at a temp. not exceeding 150°. Indigenous.

*Charact.*—About the size of a chestnut, flattened on one side, where it has an undeveloped bud; furnished with an outer brown and an inner yellow coat; internally white; solid and fleshy; yielding, when cut, a milky acrid and bitter juice. Dried slices about a line thick, moderately indented on one side, rarely on both, firm, flat, whitish, amylaceous.

**Colchici Semina.**   Colchicum Seeds.

Colchicum Autumnale Linn.   The seeds, fully ripe.

*Charact.*—About the size of black mustard seed, very hard, reddish-brown.

*Analysis.*—The cormus contains an uncrystallizable alkaloid called veratria, combined with gallic acid, starch, gum, &c.   The seeds contain a compound, brown resinous-looking mass, named colchicia, from which a neutral crystalline principle, colchicerine, has more lately been obtained.

*Actions and uses.*—Irritant, cathartic, diuretic.   In large doses, gives rise to vomiting, purging, burning pain of the throat, pain, sensation of fulness, and heat about the abdomen ; thirst, and intense depression of the circulation, death taking place from exhaustion, the result of inflammation of the intestines, and preceded occasionally by delirium, stupor, and insensibility.   When these effects are present, they are to be met by demulcent drinks and tannic acid ; and for the coma, if present, brandy, ammonia, and other stimulants.   In medicinal doses, one of the most tangible effects is catharsis, yet colchicum is never given as a cathartic, owing to the other disagreeable concomitants.   It has also a sedative effect on the circulation, yet we seldom seek its aid in this way, and for a similar reason.   It is a diuretic, too, but uncertain, and not to be trusted.   Despite of these drawbacks, it is an indispensable drug, and that owing to its influence over gout and gouty rheumatism.   Here again, then, we have a drug on which we can depend : we know that, almost as certainly as chloroform will produce anæsthesia, colchicum will alleviate the paroxysm, and abbreviate the fit of gout.   Its use, however, is not unattended with evil.   In some, not by any means in all cases, the employment of it induces irregular or atonic gout—a serious matter indeed !   The kind of rheumatism in which it is beneficial, is that supposed to be blended with gout, and jumping about from one small joint to another. It may be given during the paroxysm or after the fit; during its operation the quantity of urea in the urine is increased. Small doses should be begun with, owing to its variable effect on different individuals; it ought then to be gradually pushed on until its physiological action is developed; this, in the majority of instances, but assuredly not in all, being necessary for successful therapeutic action. Dose, powder of the corm gr. i. to v. ter quaterve die.

*Extractum Colchici.*—See Brit. Pharm. Dose, gr. ss. to gr. ij. frequently.

*Extractum Colchici Acetecum.*—See Brit. Pharm. Dose, gr. ss. to gr. ij.

*Vinum Colchici.*—Colchicum corm ℥iv.; sherry Oj. Macerate 7 days, strain through calico; pour on the marc sufficient sherry to make Oj.; press, strain, and mix the fluids. Dose, min. x. gradually increased to min. xl.

*Tinctura Colchici Seminum.*—Colchicum seed ℥ijss.; proof spt. Oj. Make in the usual way. Dose, min. x. carefully increased to min. xxx.

### Collodium. Collodion.

Pyroxylin $C^{36}, 8 \left.\begin{array}{l} H^{22} \\ NO^4 \end{array}\right\} O^{30},$ dissolved in ether, mixed with $\frac{1}{3}$ of its volume of rect. spt.

*Charact.*—A colourless highly inflammable liquid with ethereal odour, which dries rapidly on exposure to air, and leaves a thin transparent film; insoluble in water or rect. spt.

*Uses.*—Has been applied over recent wounds to facilitate union by the exclusion of dirt and air. It is of little use as an application to burns, skin diseases, and small-pox pustules.

### Collodium Flexile.

Collodion f℥vj.; Canada balsam gr. cxx.; castor oil f℈i Mix. Used as a protecting coat for wounds, &c.

### Colocynthidis Pulpa. Colocynth Pulp.

Citrullus Colocynthis. N. F. Cucurbitaceæ. The dried

decorticated fruit, freed from the seeds ; imported chiefly from Smyrna, France, and Spain.

*Charact.*—Light spongy, yellowish-white, intensely bitter.

*Analysis.*—A bitter principle colocynthin, to which it owes its purgative property; resin, gum, salts, &c.

*Actions and uses.*—Irritant and cathartic. The effect of a poisonous dose of " bitter apple," is inflammation of the mucous membrane of the intestines. It is a powerful hydragogue cathartic, but owing to its severity, it is invariably combined with other medicines, as in the compound pill, the form most commonly prescribed. The extract of hyoscyamus is an excellent corrective of its griping tendency, preventing it also from irritating the rectum. It may be usefully given in habitual constipation, passive dropsies, and as a revulsant in cerebral congestion. The powder sprinkled on a raw surface will induce cantharis. Dose, powder, gr. ij. to viij., but rarely given.

*Extractum Colocynthidis Compositum.*—See Brit. Pharm. Dose, gr. iij. to x.

*Pilula Colocynthidis Composita et Hyoscyami.*—Compound pill of colocynth ℨii. ; ext. hyoscyamus ℨj. Mix. Divide into 5 gr. pills. Dose, g. v. to x.

*Pilula Colocynthidis Composita.* —Colocynth ℨj., barb. aloes ℨij.; scammony ℨij.; sulph. potash ℨ¼.; oil of cloves fℨij.; dist. water, a sufficiency. M. Divide into 5 gr. pills. Dose, gr. v. to x.

**Confectiones.** These are all under the drugs from which they derive their name.

**Conii Fructus.** Hemlock Fruit.

Conium Maculatum Linn. Spotted Hemlock. N. F. Umbelliferæ. The ripe fruit; dried.

*Charact.* —Broadly ovate, compressed laterally; half-fruit, with five waved or crenated ridges.

**Conii Folia.** Hemlock Leaves.

Conium Maculatum. N. F. Umbelliferæ. The fresh leaves and branches of wild British plants, gathered when the fruit begins to form ; and the leaves dried in the sun, or at a temp. not exceeding 120⁰.

*Charact.*—Fresh leaves tripinnate, smooth, arising from a smooth stem with dark purple spots; dried leaves of a full green colour and characteristic odour. The leaf rubbed with caustic potash gives out strongly the odour of conia.

*Analysis.*—The leaves and fruit contain an alkaloid conia, which is the active principle. It is a colourless oily liquid, sp. gr. 0·89, and possessing a penetrating, disagreeable odour, and very acrid taste. It is a very energetic poison. It may be obtained by distilling the leaves with caustic potash. There is also present albumen, resin, a volatile odorous principle, salts, &c.

*Actions and uses.*—Sedative and hypnotic. It is a poison in large doses, exhausting the nervous force of the spinal cord and voluntary muscles, and giving rise to general paralysis of the muscles, and arrestment of respiration. Slight twitches and tremors of the muscles have been observed, but no convulsions nor coma. The treatment in cases of poisoning is the administration of emetics, stimulants internally and externally, and tannin. Hemlock is not very much used in practice now. As a sedative and anodyne in neuralgia, gangrene, scirrhous uterus, asthma, chronic catarrh, and hooping-cough, it seems hardly equal to opium, belladonna, &c.; and as a deobstruant and alterative, for which it was recommended in enlarged glands, enlarged liver and spleen, malignant ulcers, secondary syphilis, and chronic skin diseases, it has proved very much a failure. Externally, in the form of poultice, however, it alleviates the pain of cancerous and other ulcerations. Dose of the powdered leaves (not a good form), gr. ij. to x.

*Tinctura.*—Hemlock fruit ℥ijss.; proof sp. Oj. Macerate 48 hours, then percolate, and add sp. to make Oj. Dose, min. xx. to lx.

*Cataplasma Conii.*—Hemlock leaf, powder, ℥j.; linseed meal ℥iij.; boiling water f℥x. Mix the hemlock and meal, add them to the water gradually, constantly stirring.

*Extractum Conii.*—See Brit. Ph. Dose, gr. ij. to vj.

*Pilula Conii Co.*—Ext. hemlock ℥ijss; ipecac. powder, ℥ss.; treacle, a sufficiency. Mix. Dose, gr. v. to x. A useful pill in bronchitis.

*Succus Conii.*—Bruise hemlock leaves in a stone mortar; press out the juice, and to every three measures of juice add one of rect. spt. Set aside for seven days; filter, and keep in a cool place. One of the best preparations of hemlock. Dose, min. xx. to lx., increased carefully.

*Conia* is not in the Brit. Ph. It is a very powerful sedative, $\frac{1}{60}$ to $\frac{1}{30}$ of a gr. being the dose. If one gr. be dissolved in f℥ij. of water, the dose would be min. iij.

*Formula in Spasmodic Cough.*—℞ Succi conii f℥iij.; liquoris morphiæ hydrochloratis f℥iij.; spiritus chloroformi f℥ss.; syrupi f℥vi. Misce. Fiat mistura, cujus capiat cochleare parvum ter in die.

### Copaiba. Copaiva.

Copaifera multijuga; and other species of copaifera. N. F. Leguminosæ. The oleo-resin, obtained from the trunk by incision; chiefly from the province of Para, in Brazil.

*Charact.*—About the consistence of olive oil, clear, light-yellow, with a peculiar odour, and an acrid aromatic taste.

*Analysis.*—41 per cent of volatile oil, 51 per cent of hard yellow resin (copaivic acid), 2 of brown soft resin, and about 5 of water.

*Adulterations.*—Oil of turpentine, distilled oil of the gurjun balsam, castor oil, rape oil, poppy-seed oil. The pure is perfectly soluble in rect. spt. Dissolves ¼ of its weight of carb. magnesia, by the aid of heat, and remains transparent. Heating on a spatula will detect the odour of turpentine. The presence of fixed oil is detected by "a greasy areola surrounding the spot of resin, left on gently evaporating, over the flame of a lamp, a drop or two of the doubtful balsam on unsized paper."

*Actions and uses.*—Diuretic, cathartic, and a special stimulant or tonic to the mucous membranes, and especially the genito-urinary membrane. It is never given as a cathartic or as a diuretic, because it possesses a disagreeable taste and odour, and we have better ones at hand. It stands pre-eminent, however, as a remedy in urethral inflammation, with muco-purulent discharge, gonorrhœa being almost infallibly cured by it. Some believe it to be contra-indicated in the acute stage, but this is not altogether correct; it is only when the inflammation is unusually intense that it ought to be withheld. Leucorrhœa is not much benefited by copaiva, and chronic bronchitis less. In chronic catarrh of the bladder, however, it has done good, and also in chronic dysentery. In not a few cases it occasions considerable vomiting and purging, and a cutaneous eruption, resembling urticaria. During its use, the urine of the patient, when heated, presents a milky aspect, resembling albuminous urine; but the copaiva does not subside to the bottom as does the albumen. Dose, min. xx. to f℥j. Owing to its nauseous taste, it should be given floating on a glass of aq. camph. with a few drops of tinct. cardam co.

*Formula for Gonorrhœa.*—Copaibæ f℥ij.; pulveris cubebæ ℥j.; acidii gallici gr. lx.; pulveris aromatici gr. cxx. Misce. Fiat electuarium. Capiat cochleare parvum ter quaterve die.

**Copaibæ Oleum.**—See *Oleum Copaibæ.*

**Coriandri Oleum.**—See *Oleum Coriandri.*

**Coriandri Fructus.** Coriander Fruit.

Coriandrum Sativum Lind. N. F. Umbelliferæ. The ripe fruit, dried; cultivated in Britain.

*Charact.*—Globular, yellowish-brown, nearly as large as white pepper, beaked, finely ribbed; agreeable odour and flavour.

*Uses.*—Aromatic and carminative. A pleasant corrective of other drugs, such as senna.

**Creasotum.** Creasote.

A product of the distillation of wood tar.

*Charact.*—A colourless liquid, with a strong empyreumatic odour; sparingly dissolved by water, but freely by alcohol, ether, and acetic acid. Coagulates albumen. Sp. gravity, 1·071.

*Adulterations.*—Fixed and volatile oils. Its purity may be known by its being colourless, by its entire solubility in acetic acid, and by leaving no translucent stain on white filtering-paper when dropped on it, and exposed for ten minutes to a temp. of $212^0$.

*Actions and uses.*—Irritant, styptic, sedative, and antiseptic. In large doses it occasions giddiness, dimness of vision, depression of the heart's action, convulsions, and coma. Half a fluid dr. will kill a rabbit in a few minutes. When introduced into a vein, it kills by paralyzing the heart. As a styptic it arrests hæmorrhage, but is not much used in this way. As a stimulant and astringent, externally in the form of lotion or ointment, it has been of service in skin diseases, such as lepra, psoriasis, porrigo, &c. ; and indolent ulcers, and those arising from burns, assume a more healthy appearance under it. Caries of the bones, cancer, and noli-me-tangere, seem also to be arrested somewhat by it. It is one of the most successful topical remedies for toothache, a drop or two into the cavity—previously cleaned—seldom failing to give relief. Internally, creasote is a valuable sedative, standing almost *per se* in the vomiting of pregnancy, of hysteria, of sea-sickness, and even often allaying for a time that depending on organic disease. In diabetes it has been given to allay excessive thirst, but often fails ; and its alleged specific influence in phthisis and neuralgia is open to well-founded doubt. Dose, min. j. to ij. gradually increased, and given in a full wine-glassful of some aromatic water. As its action is transient, it should be repeated frequently.

*Mistura Creasoti.*—Creasote min. xvi. ; glacial acetic acid min. xvi. ; spt. of juniper f℥ss. ; syrup f℥j. ; dist. water f℥xv. Mix the creasote with the acid, gradually add the water, and lastly the syrup and spt. of juniper. Dose, f℥j. to f℥ij.

*Unguentum Creasoti.*—Creasote f℥j. ; simple oint. ℥j. M. For porrigo, tinea, &c.

*Vapor Creasoti.*—Creasoti min. xij.; boiling water f℥viii. For inhalation.

## Creta. Chalk.

Native friable carbonate of Lime. Used for the creta prep., and for producing carbonic acid gas.

## Creta Præparata. Prepared Chalk.

Carbonate of Lime, CaO, $CO^2$, nearly pure.

*Charact.*—A white amorphous powder, effervescing with acids, and dissolving perfectly, or with a mere trace of residue, in dilute hydrochloric acid.

*Actions and uses.*—Antacid and astringent.—See Calcis Carb. Præcip. Dose, gr. x. to lx.

Mistura Cretæ. Chalk Mixture.

*Prep.*—Chalk ℥ss; gum acacia, powder, ℥ss; syrup f℥ss.; cinnam. water f℥vijss. M. Useful in simple diarrhœa. Dose, f℥i. to f℥ij.

Pulvis Cretæ Aromaticus. Synonym Confectio Aromatica.

Cinnam. powd. ℥iv.; nutmeg and saffron in powder, of each ℥iij.; cloves ℥iss.; cardamom seeds ℥j.; refined sugar ℥xxv.; prepared chalk ℥xj. Mix thoroughly, and pass through a fine sieve. Antacid and aromatic. Dose, gr. x. to lx.

*Pulvis Cretæ Aromaticus Cum Opio.*—Aromatic powder of chalk ℥jxss.; opium powder ℥ss. Mix thoroughly, and pass through fine sieve; finally rub it lightly in a mortar. 1 of opium in 40. Excellent in diarrhœa of adults; attended with pain. Dose, gr. x. to xl.

## Crocus. Saffron.

Crocus Sativus Linn. N. F. Iridaceæ. The stigma, and part of the style, dried; imported from France and Spain.

*Charact.*—A thread-like style, terminated by 3 long orange-brown stigmas, which are broadest at their summit; has a powerful aromatic odour. When rubbed on the moistened finger, it tinges it intensely orange-yellow.

*Analysis.*—Albumen, mucilage, a colouring extractive matter, named polychroite, volatile oil, &c.

*Adulterations.*—The petals of the carthamus tinctorius, and of the calendula arvensis ; and fibres of smoked beef, with pomegranate blossoms. The flowers are detected by the thickness of their structure when soaked in water, and the beef by the odour emitted on burning it.

*Actions and uses.*—Stimulant, but of little power. Said to exert an influence over the uterus, but as an emmenagogue it is not trustworthy. It has been lauded by some as a remedy for the lumbar pains attendant on menstruation : I have never seen it of any service in such cases. Dose, gr. x. to lx.

*Tinctura Croci.*—Saffron ℥j. ; proof spt. Oj. ; make in the usual way. For improving the colour of mixtures, &c. Dose, f℥j. to f℥ij.

**Crotonis Oleum.** See *Oleum Crotonis.*

**Cubeba.** Cubebs.

Cubeba Officinalis. N. F. Piperaceæ. The unripe fruit, dried ; cultivated in Java.

*Charact.*—The size of black pepper, globular, wrinkled, blackish, supported on a stalk of rather more than its own length ; has a warm camphoraceous taste.

*Analysis.*—About 2 per ct. of green volatile oil ; 1 of yellow volatile oil ; 4 of a principle named cubebin ; balsamic resin, wax, &c.

*Actions and uses.*—A special stimulant like copaiva, acting on the urinary organs, and arresting urethral discharges. It is used solely for gonorrhœa, and is nearly equal to copaiva. In leucorrhœa and catarrh of the bladder, it sometimes does good, but often fails. As a carminative it is seldom given. Dose, gr. xxx. to cxx., three or four times a-day.

*Tinctura Cubebæ.*—Cubebs ℥ijss. ; rect. spt. Oj. Dose, f℥ss. to f℥ij.

**Cubebæ Oleum.**—See *Oleum Cubebæ.*

### Cupri Sulphas.  Sulphate of Copper.

$CuO, SO_3 + 5 HO$, or $CuSO_4. 5 H^2O$.  " Blue Vitriol."

*Charact.*—In oblique prismatic crystals, of a clear blue colour, soluble in water, and reddening litmus.  Its solution gives, with chloride of barium, a white precip. insoluble in hydrochloric acid, and a maroon-red precipitate with ferrocyanide of potassium.

*Actions and uses.*—Irritant, astringent, tonic, emetic.  It is a strong poison, occasioning inflammation of the parts with which it comes into contact, but influencing also, remotely, the brain and nervous system, inducing death with coma and convulsions.  In doses of gr. vi. to x. in several ounces of water, it is a reliable and speedy emetic, and thus adapted for narcotic poisoning ; but because, if retained in the stomach, it is more of an irritant than the sulphate of zinc, it has almost been abandoned for the latter.  As an astringent, it is of great service in chronic diarrhœa and dysentery, succeeding occasionally when vegetable astringents fail.  As a tonic, it by no means holds a high place, little benefit being obtained by it in chorea and epilepsy, the two diseases for which it has been recommended.  Its specific influence in croup may be strongly disputed.  Externally, solid, or in the form of solution, it is an excellent stimulating astringent in indolent and ill-conditioned ulcers, altering their action, improving their appearance, and disposing them to heal.  It is also serviceable in ophthalmia, and as an injection in gonorrhœa.  In the solid form, it reduces redundant granulations, destroys venereal warts, and improves the condition of chancres at an early stage.  Dose, gr. ss. to ij. tonic ; gr. vi. to xij. emetic.  Formula for chronic diarrhœa and dysentery.—℞ Cupri sulphatis gr. vi.; pulveris calumbæ gr. xxiv.; pulveris ipecacuanhæ gr. vi.; extracti taraxaci, quantum sufficiat.  Misce.  Divide in pilulas duodecim ; sumat unam sextis horis.

*Incompatibles.*—The alkalies and their carb.; lime water ; acetate of lead ; nitrate of silver ; iodide of potassium ; corrosive sublimate ; the salts of iron, except the sulphate ;

most astringent vegetables.  In poisoning give albumen,
and in its absence sugar and wheaten flour.

### Cuprum.  Copper.

Fine copper wire, about No. 25.
Used in the preparation of spt. ether. nit.

### Cusparia Cortex.  Cusparia Bark.

Galipea Cusparia.  N. F. Rutaceæ.  The bark, from tropical South America.

*Charact.*—In straight pieces, more or less incurved at the
sides, from half a line thick, pared away at the edges ; epidermis mottled, brown or yellowish-grey ; inner surface
yellowish-brown, flaky ; breaks with a short fracture ; bitter,
and slightly aromatic.  The cut surface examined with a
lens, usually exhibits numerous white points or minute
lines.

*Test.*—The inner surface touched with nitric acid does
not become blood-red.

*Analysis.*—About 3 per ct. of a bitter crystalline principle
named cusparin ; small portions of hard resin, soft resin,
volatile oil, gum, &c.

*Adulterations.*—The bark of strychnos nux-vomica, which
is highly poisonous, has sometimes been substituted for it.
This false bark is in thicker, heavier, and more perfectly
quilled pieces, with its epidermis thickly mottled with
greyish spots, and its taste is intensely and persistently
bitter.  But it is best detected by the test given above, viz.,
nitric acid.  This, when applied to the transverse fracture of
the false bark, gives a bright red colour, merely deepening
the colour of the true.

*Actions and uses.*—Tonic, but not so much employed,
owing to its adulteration with the poisonous bark, the confidence of practitioners being thus blasted.  It is held in high
repute in South America as a febrifuge in the malignant
bilious fevers of marshy districts, in which cases cinchona
would seem to be almost powerless.  It is serviceable in
atonic dyspepsia, improving the appetite, and obviating
constipation slightly ; and in the advanced stages of diarrhœa

and dysentery, especially in warm climates, its use is attended with great benefit.   Dose, gr. x. to xxx.

*Infusum Cuspariæ.*—Cusparia ʒss.; distilled water at 120°
fʒx.   Infuse 2 ho. and strain.   Dose, fʒj. to fʒij.

**Cusso.   Kousso.**

Brayera Anthelmintica.   N. F. Rosaceæ.   The flowers;
collected in Abyssinia.

*Charact.*—Flowers small, reddish-brown, on hairy stalks;
outer limb of calyx five-parted, the segments ovate reticulated.

*Analysis.*—A bitter acrid resin, a tasteless resin, tannin,
a fatty oil, chlorophylle, sugar, gum, &c.

*Adulterations.*—Powder of jalap and powdered pomegranate bark.   The dried flowers only should be obtained,
and tested by the above characters.

*Actions and uses.*—Anthelmintic.   Useful in tape-worm,
which is occasionally expelled by it, probably by being
poisoned.   It has a high reputation among the Abyssinians,
but it is hardly equal to the male shield fern.   It occasions
nausea and vomiting in some few cases, but its action on
the bowels is slight; it is therefore better to give a purgative a short time before, and after, if necessary.   From experiments made, it appears that tape-worms, immersed in an
infusion mixed with milk, are killed in about half an hour.
Though cusso leads to the expulsion of the worm, it seems
not to improve the morbid condition which favours its production.   A course of cinchona, and iron afterwards, is
beneficial.   Dose, from gr. cxx. to ʒss. for an adult; for
children, gr. xx. to gr. lx.

*Infusum Cusso.*—Kousso, in coarse powder, ʒɉ; boiling
dist. water fʒiv.   Infuse 15 minutes without straining.
This is the usual form for administration, the infusion and
powder along with it being swallowed.   Two such draughts
as the above may be given, and it is best in the morning
before the early meal.   A purgative may follow, in an hour
or two, as well as precede it.

**Decocta.**   Decoctions.   These will be found under the drugs
whence they derive their name.

### Digitalinum.

The active principle obtained from Digitalis.

*Charact.*—In porous mammillated masses, or small scales, white, inodorous, and intensely bitter; readily soluble in spirit, but almost insoluble in water and ether; dissolves in acids, but does not form with them neutral compounds. Its solution in hydrochloric acid is of a faint yellow colour, but rapidly becomes green. It powerfully irritates the nostrils, and is an active poison.

*Test.*—Leaves no residue when burned with free access of air.

*Prep.*—See Brit. Pharm.

*Actions and uses.*—Sedative, but a very active poison, possessing in a highly concentrated degree the properties of digitalis. It has a powerful effect on the pulse, reducing it in a few hours to about 40 beats per minute. It is not much employed here, as yet, owing to its potency, but in France it is said to have been serviceable in the treatment of intermittent fevers and spermatorrhœa. It has been applied endermically in painful cardiac disease with excited action of the heart; but this requires the greatest caution, the $\frac{1}{80}$ part of a grain having occasioned violent inflammation of the raw surface. The smallest over-dose has, moreover, given rise to protracted sickness and vomiting. Dose, $\frac{1}{80}$ to $\frac{1}{30}$ of a grain.

### Digitalis Folia. Digitalis Loaf.

Digitalis Purpurea Linn. Foxglove. N. F. Scrophulariaceæ. The dried leaf; from wild indigenous plants, gathered when about two-thirds of the flowers are expanded.

*Charact.*—Ovate-lanceolate, shortly petiolate, rugose, downy, paler on the under surface, crenate.

*Analysis.*—Digitaline, volatile oil, fatty matter, extractive, tannin, &c.

*Adulterations.*—The leaves of different species of verbascum. Attend to the characters given above.

*Actions and uses.*—Narcotico-irritant, diuretic, and sedative. In large doses it occasions vomiting, purging, cold sweats, stupor, a slow, weak, and irregular pulse, suppression of urine, and death, with coma and convulsions. In cases of poisoning, the stomach-pump should be used, and stimulating emetics, with powerful external and internal stimulants, administered. As a diuretic, digitalis deservedly stands high, great success attending its use in the various forms of dropsy. It succeeds best in those cases of effusion into the areolar membrane of the extremities and face depending on cardiac, renal, or hepatic disease, and it is more serviceable in cardiac dropsy than renal. Most good is achieved, too, in feeble constitutions : in robust individuals with inflammatory symptoms, antiphlogistic measures should precede it. In ascites it sometimes does good, but oftener fails; and in hydrothorax (simple), and hydrops pericardii, it will generally be found of little service. Its diuretic action is promoted by combination with others, such as squill, juniper, &c. When digitalis is administered for some time, in medicinal doses, it also operates as a sedative, influencing the heart and arterial system, diminishing the strength and frequency of the pulse, but inducing also irregularity. Nausea, giddiness, obscure vision, salivation, headache, and delirium, are also common effects ; and if the drug is continued, the symptoms of poisoning are developed. These symptoms may arise some days after it has been withdrawn, showing digitalis to be a cumulative medicine. Some affirm that the sedative and diuretic actions do not go on together, nay, that they are even incompatible: the truth appears to be that free diuresis lessens somewhat the sedative action. The narcotic and sedative actions are also occasioned when it is injected into a vein, or by clyster. As a sedative, then, digitalis is serviceable in diseases of the heart and large arteries, where we want to abate the force of the circulation ; as in simple hypertrophy, in increased action, not depending on organic disease, in some forms of functional palpitation, in aneurism of the aorta, and in active hæmorrhages, where the pulse is quick, full, and hard. It should not be used in hypertrophy (with or without dilatation), arising from obstruction or from regurgitation produced by valvular disease. As a deobstruant, digitalis has deservedly fallen into neglect; and as a tonic it is seldom employed. It has some advocates as a remedy in some forms of insanity; and in epilepsy, not dependent on organic disease, it has occasionally done good. In this latter disease it is perhaps entitled to further trial. The infusion (f℥ij. to f℥ss.) is given every night for four or five nights, and suspended for a time, to be renewed again in the same doses. The effects of digitalis should, of course, be observed with vigilance. Dose, powder, gr. ss. to ij.

*Infusum.*—Digitalis, dried, gr. xxx.; boiling dist. water f℥x. Infuse for an hour, and strain. Dose, f℥ss. to f℥j. This is an excellent preparation. As a diuretic, it should be given three times a-day. Some have recommended its external application (on spongio-piline, or flannel, covered with gutta-percha or oil-silk) to the legs in anasarca, and to the surface of the abdomen in ascites, and good has been done in this way. Dose, f℥ii. to ℥ss.

*Tinctura.*—Digitalis, bruised, ℥ijss. proof spt. Oj. Macerate 48 hours, and percolate, as usual. Dose, min. x. to xxx.

Formula in dropsies named above.—℞ Tinctura scillæ f℥iij.; infusi digitalis f℥iij.; decocti scoparii ad. f℥vj. Misce. Fiat mistura cujus capiat cochleare amplum ter die.

### Dulcamara.  Dulcamara.

Solanum Dulcamara Linn. Bitter-sweet. Woody nightshade. N. F. Solanaceæ.

The young branches, dried, from indigenous plants which have shed their leaves.

*Charact.*—Light, hollow, cylindrical, about the thickness of a goose-quill, bitter, and subsequently sweetish to the taste.

*Analysis.*—An alkaline principle solania (found also in the young shoots of the potato), salts of lime and potash, &c.

*Actions and uses.*—A feeble narcotic, and a diaphoretic. Formerly had a name as a remedy in cutaneous and other diseases, such as lepra, psoriasis, secondary syphilis, strumous and rheumatic swellings, ill-conditioned ulcers, &c., but not now much trusted. Some employ it as a vehicle for the preparations of iodine and arsenic, but it does not seem to promote their action much, if any.

*Infusum Dulcamaræ.*—Dulcamara, bruised, ℥j.; boiling distilled water f℥x. Infuse an hour, and strain. Dose, f℥j. to f℥ij.

### Ecbalii Fructus. Squirting Cucumber Fruit.

The fruit, very nearly ripe, of Ecbalium Officinarum. N. F. Cucurbitaceæ.

### Elaterium. Elaterium.

A sediment from the juice of the squirting cucumber fruit.

*Charact.*—In light friable, slightly incurved cakes, about one line thick, greenish-grey, acrid and bitter; fracture finely granular.

*Tests.*—Does not effervesce with acids; yields half its weight to boiling rectified spirit. This solution concentrated and added to warm solution of potash, yields on cooling not less than 20 per ct. of elaterine in colourless crystals.

*Analysis.*—A crystalline substance elaterin, the active principle of the drug; green resin, starch, &c.

*Actions and uses.*—An intensely irritant and acrid poison, and a drastic cathartic. A few grains of good elaterium will occasion inflammation of the alimentary canal, with severe griping pain, vomiting and purging. As a cathartic, it produces profuse watery stools, attended with depression of the circulation and nervous system. It is employed in dropsies, such as ascites and hydrothorax, and the fluid is sometimes lessened in these cases after the free evacuations which this drug occasions. It should be given with care in cases of debility. Dose, $\frac{1}{16}$th to $\frac{1}{4}$ grain, in pill. Formula. ℞ Elaterii granum; pulvis aromatici gr. xii.; extracti taraxaci gr. xxiv.; extracti gentianæ gr. xxiv.  Misce bene. Divide in pilulas xii.  Sumat unam bis die.  Watch their effects carefully.

Owing to the varying purity of the drug, *elaterine* has been proposed instead.  The dose is $\frac{1}{12}$th gr. to $\frac{1}{8}$th.

In poisoning with elaterium, give demulcent drinks, and enemata ; small doses of opium, and the warm bath.

### Elemi.  Elemi.

Botanical source undetermined, probably from canarium commune Linn.  A concrete resinous exudation ; chiefly imported from Manilla.

*Charact.*—A yellowish-white, soft unctuous adhesive mass, becoming harder by age, almost entirely soluble by rect. spt.

*Uses.*—Stimulant in the form of ointment to old and indolent ulcers and issues.

*Unguentum.*—Elemi ʒ¼.; simple oint. ʒj.  Melt, strain through flannel.

**Emplastra.**  Plasters.  The formulæ for the plasters will be found under the main drugs which give them their name.

**Enemata.**  Enemas.  These also found under the drugs from which they are prepared.

### Ergota.  Ergot.

Secale Cereale Linn.  Common Rye.  Ergot of Rye.  The grain diseased by the presence of an imperfect fungus.

*Charact.*—Subtriangular, curved, with a longitudinal furrow on the concave side, obtuse at the ends; from $\frac{1}{3}$d inch to an inch and half in length ; of a violet-brown colour on the surface, yellowish within ; solid, frangible, fracture short, odour faintly marked.

*Analysis.*—A reddish-brown extract, soluble in water, named ergotin, on which the emmenagogue properties of the drug depend ; a colourless fixed oil, soluble in ether, and which is poisonous ; fungin, gum, sugar, wax, &c.

*Adulterations.*—Plaster of Paris, and flour paste, carefully shaped and coloured. These are not very easily detected : the characters above given should be attended to.

*Actions and uses.*—Emmenagogue. In doses of gr. **xx.** or so, good ergot exerts a specific power over the uterus, causing contraction of the muscular fibres. It is the only drug on which we can rely for this purpose, borax being much less certain. It has little, if any, influence over the virgin uterus, unless when active, as at a menstrual period; but possesses great power over the pregnant uterus, especially when the expulsive contractions are begun. These it often recalls when in abeyance, and strengthens and quickens when weak or languid. It is extensively used in midwifery practice, to promote delivery when the uterine contractions are feeble. It should not be given if the os is not dilated, or if the soft parts are very rigid; nor in cases of obstruction from disproportion, deformity, or mal-presentation. Many also are against its being given in primiparous cases. It commonly operates in from five to twenty minutes ; and I have observed that a speedy and a vigorous action often concur. Ergot is given by some also to promote the expulsion of the placenta, to expel clots, polypi, and hydatids. In uterine hæmorrhage it is often of great service, and it does good occasionally in amenorrhœa; but it is not to be relied on in leucorrhœa. There is little doubt but that ergot endangers the life of the fœtus, but only when given in excessive doses. From some little experience, we should say that ʒj., though taken in doses of gr. lx. at a time, would almost certainly occasion the death of the child; the mother at one time being little the worse, at another experiencing nausea, headache, vertigo, pain and spasm of the stomach, and depression of the pulse. It probably kills both by arresting the utero-placental circulation, and by a specific influence on the circulation of the fœtus. When ergot is used for a lengthened period along with the food, as among rye-eating peoples, a singular disease called " ergotism " is supposed to be occasioned. There are two species of the disorder : 1. Convulsive ergotism, characterized by dimness of sight, giddiness, thirst, imperceptible pulse, cramp, pains in the chest and limbs, insensibility, convulsions, and death in a day or two.  2. Gangrenous ergotism, attended with languor, a sensation of a multitude of insects crawling over the body ; then, in a few days, cold, stiff, painful, benumbed limbs ; fever, with a tendency to hæmorrhage ; finally, dry gangrene of the limbs sets in ; the fingers or toes shrivel or drop off, and the patient either recovers by the setting in of healthy granulation, or sinks from exhaustion during the process of repair.   Dose, powder, gr. xx. to lx.

*Extractum Ergotæ Liquidum.*—See Brit. Pharm.   Dose, min. x. to min. xl.

*Infusum.*—Ergot ʒ¼. ; boiling dist. water fℨx.   Infuse half-an-hour.   Dose during parturition, fʒij. to fʒiij., renewed in half-an-hour, if necessary.   For other purposes, fʒss. to fʒj.

*Tinctura Ergotæ.*—Ergot, bruised, ℨv. ; proof spt. Oj. Make in the usual way.   Dose, min. xx. to lx.

### Essentia Anisi.   Essence of Anise.

Oil of anise fʒi. ; rect. spt. fℨiv.   Mix.   An excellent aromatic stimulant and carminative.   Employed in flatulent colic, and infantile diarrhœa.   Said to promote the secretion of human milk.   Dose, min. x. to xxx.

### Essentiæ Menthæ Piperitæ.   Essence of Peppermint.

Oil of peppermint fℨi. ; rect. spt. fℨiv.   Mix.

*Uses.*—Peppermint has an ancient reputation in flatulence, and it is probably one of the strongest aromatic stimulants of the Labiatæ.   Given in flatulent colic, and to cover the taste of nauseous medicines.   Dose, min. x. to min. xx.

### Extracta.   Extracts.

These are placed under the drugs from which they are made.

### Farina Tritici.   Wheaten Flour.

The grain of wheat, Triticum Vulgare, ground and sifted. Used only for cataplasma fermenti.

**Fel Bovinum Purificatum.  Purified Ox Bile.**

*Charact.*—A yellowish-green substance of pilular consistence, taste partly sweet and partly bitter ; soluble in water and in spt.

*Prep.*—Fresh ox bile Oj. ; rect. spt. Oij.  Mix the bile and the spt. by agitation in a bottle, and set aside for 12 hours, until the sediment subsides.  Decant the clear solution, and evaporate in a porcelain capsule, on a water-bath, until the residue acquires the consistence of a vegetable extract.

*Actions and uses.*—Tonic, and mildy laxative.  Given in dyspepsia with irritability of the stomach, and vomiting soon after meals, not resulting from organic disease.  Dose, gr. v. to x. thrice a-day, in the form of pills, with powder of calumba.

**Ferri Arsenias.  Arseniate of Iron.**

3 FeO, AsO$^5$, or Fe$_3$ As$_2$ O$_8$, partially oxidized.

*Charact.*—A tasteless amorphous powder, of a green colour, insoluble in water, but readily dissolved by hydrochloric acid.  This solution gives a copious light-blue precip. with the ferridcyanide of potassium, and a still more abundant one, of a deeper colour, with the ferrocyanide of potassium.

*Actions and uses.*—Tonic, and said to be useful in cutaneous diseases with anemia.  As an alterative, however, it is inferior to arsenious acid.  Dose, $\frac{1}{16}$th of a grain, gradually increased to $\frac{1}{4}$, in the form of pill.

**Ferri Carbonas Saccharata.  Saccharated Carbonate of Iron.**

Carbonate of iron, FeO, CO$^2$, or FeCO$_3$, mixed with peroxide of iron and sugar, and forming at least 57 per cent of the mixture.

*Charact.*—Small coherent lumps, of a grey-brown colour, with a sweet very feeble chalybeate taste.

*Prep.*—Sulphate of iron ℥ij. ; carbonate of soda ℥ijss. ; boiling dist. water, cong. ij. ; refined sugar ℥j.  Dissolve the sulphate of iron and the carb. of soda each in half a gallon of the water, and mix the solutions with brisk stirring in a deep cylindrical vessel, which is then to be covered as accurately as possible. Set the mixture by for 24 hours, and from the precip. which has subsided, separate the supernatant solution by a syphon. Pour on the remainder of the water, stir well, and after subsidence, again remove the clear solution. Collect the resulting carbonate on a calico filter, and having first subjected it to expression, rub it with the sugar in a porcelain mortar. Finally, dry the mixture at a temp. not exceeding 212⁰.

*Actions and uses.*—A chalybeate tonic, much superior to the ferri oxidum rubrum (otherwise named the carbonate, or sesquioxide), the sugar, as discovered by a German chemist, preventing the absorption of oxygen by the protoxide, and maintaining it in this latter form. It is of considerable service in anemia and neuralgia, and is very well suited as a tonic for delicate females and even children.. Dose, gr. v. to xx.

*Formula.*—℞ Ferri carbonatis saccharati gr. lx.; pulveris calumbæ gr. lx.; pulveris rhei gr. xxx.; pulveris aromatici gr. xxiv. Misce. Divide in pulveres xii., quarum sumatur una ter in die.

*Mistura Ferri Composita.*—Sulph. iron gr. xxv.; carb. potash gr. xxx.; myrrh, powder, gr. lx.; sugar gr. lx.; sp. of nutmeg fʒiv.; rose water fℨjxss. Triturate the myrrh and carb. potash with the sugar, the spt. nutmeg, and fℨvii. of the rose water, the latter being gradually added until a uniform mixture is obtained. To this add the sulphate of iron, previously dissolved in the remaining ounce of rose water, and enclose the mixture at once in a tightly corked bottle. Commonly known as " Griffith's Mixture." A very useful stimulant and tonic in amenorrhœa, with anemia. Dose, fℨj. to fℨij.

*Pilula Ferri Carbonatis.*—Saccharated carbonate of iron ℨj.; confect. roses ℨ¼. M. Divide into 5 gr. pills. Dose, one to four pills. A good tonic pill in anemia.

**Ferri et Ammoniæ Citras.** Citrate of Iron and Ammonia.

*Charact.*—In thin transparent scales of a hyacinth-red

colour, with tinge of olive-green, slightly sweetish and astringent in taste; feebly reddens litmus paper; is soluble in water.

*Preparation.*—See Brit. Pharm.

*Actions and uses.*—Feebly tonic, but may be given to delicate people, where, from irritability of the stomach, the stronger ferruginous preparations do not sit lightly. It is much less of an astringent, too, and therefore more suitable where there is a tendency to constipation. Dose, gr. v. to x.

*Vinum Ferri Citratis.*—Citrate of iron and ammonia gr. clx.; orange wine Oj. Dissolve. Dose, f3j. to f3iv.

### Ferri et Quiniæ Citras.  Citrate of Iron and Quinia.

Citric acid combined with peroxide of iron, protoxide of iron and quinia.

*Charact.*—Thin greenish golden-yellow scales, somewhat deliquescent, and entirely soluble in cold water. The solution is slightly acid, and is precipitated reddish-brown by solution of soda, white by solution of ammonia, blue by the ferrocyanide and ferridcyanide of potassium, and greyish-black by tannic acid.

*Actions and uses.*—An excellent tonic in debility after severe diseases, and in the less severe forms of neuralgia. Dose, gr. iij. to x. in water or a bitter infusion.

### Ferri Iodidum.  Iodide of Iron.

FeI, or FeI$_2$, with about 18 per cent of water of crystallization, and a little oxide of iron.

*Charact.*—Crystalline, green, with a tinge of brown, inodorous, deliquescent, soluble in water, forming a slightly green solution, which gradually deposits a rust-coloured sediment, and acquires a red colour.

*Prep.*—Fine iron wire ʒjss.; iodine ʒiij.; dist. water f3xv. Introduce the iodine, iron, and f3xij. of the water into a flask, and having heated the mixture gently for about ten minutes, raise the heat, and boil until the solution loses its red colour. Pass the solution through a small paper filter into a dish of polished iron, washing the filter with the remainder of the water, and boil down until a drop of the solution, taken out on the end of an iron wire, solidifies on cooling. The liquid should now be poured out on a porcelain dish, and as soon as it has solidified, should be broken into fragments, and enclosed in a stoppered bottle.

*Actions and uses.*—Tonic and deobstruant. Although its tonic property may be the strongest, it is by no means a feeble deobstruant. In enlarged and indurated cervical and mesenteric glands—strumous—it is often of decided benefit, softening and diminution resulting at times in a few days after its employment. Chronic rheumatism occasionally improves under it; but its success is by no means great in chlorosis, amenorrhœa, secondary syphilis, and cutaneous diseases. Along with cod liver oil, it does seem occasionally to arrest the progress of emaciation in some cases of phthisis. Dose, gr. ij. to v.; but it does not keep well, and the syrup is commonly employed.

*Pilula Ferri Iodidi.*—Fine iron wire gr. xl.; iodine gr. lxxx.; refined sugar gr. lxx.; liquorice root, powder, gr. cxl.; dist. water, min. i. Agitate the iron with the iodine and water in a strong stoppered ounce phial, until the froth becomes white. Pour the fluid upon the sugar in a mortar, triturate briskly, and gradually add the liquorice. Dose, gr. iij. to viij.

*Syrupus Ferri Iodidi.*—Fine iron wire ℥j.; iodine ℥ij.; refined sugar ℥xxviij.; dist. water f℥xiij. Prepare a syrup by dissolving the sugar in f℥x. of the water, with the aid of heat. Digest the iodine and the iron wire in a flask, at a gentle heat, with the remaining f℥iij. of the water, till the froth becomes white; then filter the liquid while still hot into the syrup, and mix. The product should weigh two pounds, eleven ounces, and should have the sp. gravity 1·385. Contains 4·3 grs. of iodide of iron in f℥j.

*Charact.*—A transparent almost colourless fluid, with a syrupy consistence, and a chalybeate taste.

*Uses.*—Given, same as the iodide, as a tonic and deobstruant in the varied manifestations of scrofula. Dose, children, min. x. to xx.; adults, min. xx. to f$\mathrecback{3}$j. three or four times a-day.

**Ferri Oxidum Magneticum.**   Magnetic Oxide of Iron.

Peroxide of Iron, Fe³ O⁴, or $Fe_3 O_4$, with about 9 per cent of peroxide of iron, and 20 per cent of water.

*Charact.*—Brownish-black, tasteless, strongly magnetic.

*Prep.*—See Brit. Pharm.

*Uses.*—Once highly esteemed as a chalybeate tonic, under the name æthiops martis, but lost ground, and fell into disuse, owing to its varying composition.   There is no reason now for not reviving its use, and it may yet emulate the saccharated carbonate.   Dose, gr. v. to x. thrice a-day, made into an electuary.

*Ferri Mistura Aromatica.*   Aromatic Mixture of Iron. Pale cinch. bark ℥i.; columba powder ℥ss.; cloves ℥¼.; fine iron wire ℥ss.; comp. tinct. card. f℥iii.; tinct. orange peel f℥ss.; peppermint water, sufficiency.   See Brit. Pharm. Aromatic Chalybeate in anemia and chlorosis.   Dose, f℥j. to f℥ij.

**Ferri Perchloridi Liquor Fortior.**   Strong Solution of
Perchloride of Iron.

Perchloride of Iron, Fe² Cl³, in solution in water.

*Charact.*—An orange-brown solution, without smell, but with a powerful styptic taste, miscible with water and alcohol in all proportions.   Sp. gravity 1·388.   Diluted with water, it is precipitated white by nitrate of silver, and blue by the ferrocyanide, but not by the ferridcyanide of potassium.

*Prep.*—Iron wire ℥ij.; hydrochloric acid f℥xij.; nitric acid f$\mathrm{3}$jx.; distilled water f℥viij.   Mix f℥viij. hydroch. acid with the water, and pour the mixture on the iron wire in successive portions, applying a gentle heat when the action becomes feeble, so that the whole of the metal may be dissolved.   Add to it the remainder of the HCl, and the HO NO₅ (after filtering), heat the mixture briskly till the liquid becomes orange-brown, then evaporate by means of a water-bath till it is reduced to f℥x.

*Uses.*—A powerful irritant poison. Used as a styptic, externally, for arresting hæmorrhage, and one of the most effectual we possess. Employed for making the solution.

*Liquor Ferri Perchloridi.*—Solution of perchloride of iron, f℥v.; rect. spt. f℥xv. Mix, and preserve in a stoppered bottle. Used in same cases as the next preparation. Dose, min. x. to xxx.

*Tinctura Ferri Perchloridi.*—Strong solution of perchloride of iron f℥v.; rect. spt. f℥xv. Same strength as the weaker liquor, which has been introduced to save the spt.

*Charact.*—Of a dark reddish-brown colour, and a slightly acrid, but strongly styptic, taste. Sp. gravity, 0·992.

*Actions and uses.*—In large doses irritant ; in smaller doses an excellent tonic and astringent. As a tonic it is useful in anemia, chlorosis, and simple amenorrhœa, in pale and weak females. As a tonic and astringent it is serviceable in chronic genito-urinary mucous discharges, in passive hæmorrhages from the kidneys and bladder, and in spasmodic stricture of the urethra. Its diuretic power is inconsiderable ; but, along with others, it does good in dropsies with debility. Some cases of erysipelas (not always those of leuco-phlegmatic persons) are benefited by it, but it is not by any means a sovereign remedy for this disease. It has become common for some years back to recommend it for a multitude of ailments of very varied character ; but it is a safe rule not to look to any one drug for the performance of widely opposite actions. Dose, min. x. to xxx., increasing it gradually ; in a full glass of water, or infusum calumbæ, and after meals.

*Incompatibles.*—Alkalies and their carb.; lime water; carbonate of lime, magnesia and carb.; and astringent vegetable preparations.

**Ferri Pernitratis Liquor.** Solution of Pernitrate of Iron.

Pernitrate of Iron, $Fe^2 O^3$, $3 NO^5$, in solution in water.

*Charact.*—A clear reddish-brown solution, slightly acrid and astringent to the taste; gives a blue precip. with the ferrocyanide of potassium. Sp. gravity, 1·107.

*Prep.*—Fine iron wire, free from rust, $\tilde{3}$j.; nitric acid f$\tilde{3}$ivss.; dist. water, a sufficiency. Dilute the nitric acid with $\tilde{3}$xvi. of the water, introduce the iron wire into the mixture, and leave them in contact until the metal is dissolved, taking care to moderate the action, should it become too violent, by the addition of a little more dist. water. Filter the solution, and add to it as much dist. water as will make its bulk one pint and a half.

*Actions and uses.*—Tonic, and an excellent astringent. It is found useful in chronic mucous diarrhœa, in the diarrhœa of feeble and nervous females, and in the colliquative diarrhœa of phthisis. In scrofulous children with enlarged glands, lienteric diarrhœa, and obstinate ophthalmia, it is also beneficial, especially along with cod-liver oil. It sits more lightly on the stomach in general than the previous preparation. Dose, for children, min. v. to x.; for adults, min. x. to xl., in water or syrup.

**Ferri Peroxidum Hydratum.** Hydrated Peroxide of Iron.

Formerly called Ferri Oxid., Ferri Sesquioxid., Ferrugo ; Red Oxide. $Fe_2 O_3 HO$, or $Fe_2 O_3. H_2O$.

*Charact.*—A reddish-brown powder, tasteless, odourless, and not magnetic.

*Uses.*—A chalybeate tonic, but not of much power. It was formerly a good deal employed in neuralgic affections, especially tic douloureux; for which, however, it often fails. As a palliative in cancerous diseases, it does little good. Dose, gr. xxx. to ccxl., in honey or jam.

*Emplastrum Ferri.*—Peroxide of iron $\tilde{3}$j.; Burgundy pitch $\tilde{3}$ij.; litharge plaster $\tilde{3}$viij. Add the peroxide to the Burgundy pitch and litharge plaster, previously melted together, and stir the mixture constantly till it stiffens on cooling. Affords mechanical support to a weak or relaxed part; and does good sometimes over the heart in nervous palpitation.

**Ferri Peroxidum Humidum.** Moist Peroxide of Iron.

Hydradrated Peroxide of Iron, $2 Fe^2 O_3$, $3 HO$, with about 86 per cent of uncombined water.

*Charact.*—A soft moist pasty mass, of a reddish-brown

colour; dissolves readily in dilute hydrochloric acid, without the aid of heat, forming a solution which gives a copious blue precip. with the ferrocyanide of potassium. A little of it dried at 212⁰ gives off moisture when further heated in a test tube.

*Prep.*—Solut. persulph. iron f℥iv.; solution of soda f℥xxxiij. or a sufficiency; dist. water Oj. Add the persulphate to the dist. water, and gradually pour the dilute solution into the solution of soda, stirring well for a few minutes; collect the precip. on a calico filter, and wash it with dist. water until the filtrate ceases to give a precip. with chloride of barium. Lastly, enclose the precip. without drying it in a porcelain pot, whose lid is made tight by a luting of lard.

This preparation should be recently made.

*Actions and uses.*—Chalybeate, and being more soluble, may be more efficient than the anhydrous peroxide. Its chief use, however, is as an antidote for arsenic, and it is the best. It should be given fresh and moist, and in the proportion of 12 to 1 of the arsenic swallowed. Dose, ℥ss to ℥ss.

### Ferri Phosphas. Phosphate of Iron.

Phosphate of Iron, $3 Fe O, PO^5$, partially oxidated.

*Charact.*—A slate-blue amorphous powder, insoluble in water, soluble in HCl.

*Actions and uses.*—Tonic, but not much employed. Given in simple amenorrhœa and chlorosis with occasional benefit. Recommended in rickets, but here has produced little good fruit. Said to diminish voracious appetite. Dose, gr. v. to x. in pill or powder.

*Syrupus Ferri Phosphatis.*—Tonic, and said by some to be wonderfully alterative, getting rid of cachectic conditions by enriching the blood, or in some other way. I have not obtained such good results from it as from other preparations of iron. Dose, f℥j to f℥iij.

### Ferri Sulphas. Sulphate of Iron.

$FeO\ SO_3 + 7\ HO$, or $FeSO_4 . 7\ H_2O$.

*Charact.*—In green-coloured oblique-rhombic prisms, with a styptic taste; soluble in water, insoluble in rectified spt. Gives a white precip. with chloride of barium, and a blue one with the ferridcyanide of potassium; and on exposure to the air gradually becomes turbid, depositing a reddish-brown sediment.

*Adulterations.*—The sesquioxide, known by the yellowish-brown colour of the crystals; and copper, which may be discovered by immersing a polished bit of iron in a solution of the salt, when the copper will adhere to it.

*Actions and uses.*—Irritant, astringent, and tonic. It is not a very strong irritant, but over-doses cause pain in the stomach, sickness, and vomiting; and a few drachms have proved fatal to a child. It is an excellent chalybeate tonic in dyspepsia, and anemic amenorrhœa, and an astringent in chronic mucous discharges, such as leucorrhœa. In solution some employ it topically in erysipelas, and for ill-conditioned ulcers, but it is not very successful in these cases. Dose, gr. j. to v. in pill.

*Formula.*—℞ Ferri sulphatis exsiccatæ gr. xij.; aloe Barbadensis gr. xii.; pulveris capsici gr. vj.; extracti taraxaci gr. xxiv. Misce. Divide in pilulas xij.; capiat unam bis die.

**Ferri Sulphas Exsiccata.** Dried Sulphate of Iron.

Sulphate of iron ℥iv. Expose it in a porcelain capsule to a moderate heat, which may be finally raised to $400^{\circ}$, until aqueous vapour ceases to be given off. Reduce the residue to a fine powder, and preserve in a stoppered bottle. Dose, gr. ss. to iij.

*Incompatibles.*—The alkalies and their carb.; nitric acid; lime water; nitrate and tartrate of potash; iodide of potassium; borax; acetate of lead; vegetable astringents.

**Ferri Sulphas Granulata.** Granulated Sulphate of Iron.

$FeO, SO^3 + 7 HO$, or $FeSO_4. 7 H_2O$.

*Charact.*—In small granular crystals of a pale-green

colour, and mildly styptic taste, soluble in water, insoluble in rectified spirit.

*Prep.*—See Brit. Pharm.

*Uses.*—Same as the foregoing, but purer. Dose, gr. iij. to v.

Liquor Ferri Persulphatis. Solution of persulphate of iron. Introduced for making various preparations of iron.

### Ferrum. Iron.

Wrought Iron in the form of wire or nails, free from oxide.

### Ferrum Redactum. Reduced Iron.

Metallic Iron, with a variable amount of Magnetic Oxide of Iron.

*Charact.*—A fine greyish-black powder, strongly attracted by the magnet, and exhibiting metallic streaks when rubbed with firm pressure in a mortar. It dissolves in hydrochloric acid with the evolution of hydrogen, and the solution gives a light-blue precipitate with the ferridcyanide of potassium.

Prepared by reducing the peroxide by means of a stream of dry hydrogen gas. See Brit. Pharm.

*Actions and uses.*—Iron in the metallic state exerts but little influence on the animal body, but it becomes oxidated in the stomach, and then acts as a tonic. When its use is continued for some time (and it does require to be continued for a considerable time), the pulse becomes quicker and fuller, the digestion improved, the secretions augmented, and the blood, and consequently the complexion, more florid. In the pathological condition of anemia, the blood is deficient in quantity and in the relative proportion of the red corpuscles, and that is the malady in which we look to iron for certain benefit. Whether the blood derives a direct accession of iron or not it is not easy to say, but the red corpuscles are very much increased under its use. In enlargement of the liver and spleen, we also often derive benefit from it, and probably because these are connected with a morbid condition of the blood.

In dyspepsia, with loss of tone or deficient secretion; in chlorosis, amenorrhœa, chronic dysentery, and neuralgia; in dropsical affections, valvular disease of the heart, and albuminuria, iron will often be found useful. But it should be borne in mind that it is in the anemic state, and in the disorders to which it gives birth, or with which it is associated, that we expect to obtain the best results. When iron or its preparations are pushed too far, or given to very plethoric people, headache, giddiness, and weight about the limbs, are apt to be occasioned; and they do not agree well where there is irritability of the digestive organs. They are tolerated, in general, best just after a meal. As their employment has to be continued for a good while, it is well to change the preparations, and it is very convenient to have so many to fall back upon. We might give the ferrum redactum for a week or two; then the carb. ferri. sacch.; now the tinct. perchlor.; then the liq. ferri. pernit. Or we may go from one to another just as they agree with the patient. Dose, gr. ii. to x. Trochisci Ferri Redacti. Dose, 1 to 6 lozenges.

### Ferrum Tartaratum. Tartarated Iron.

Tartrate of Iron and Potash, $Fe_2 O_3 KO C^8 H^4 O^{10} + HO$.

*Charact.*—Thin transparent scales of a deep garnet colour, slightly deliquescent, somewhat sweet, and rather astringent, soluble in water, and sparingly soluble in spirit.

*Prep.*—See Brit. Pharm.

*Actions and uses.*—A weak chalybeate tonic, said to be easily assimilated by the digestive organs. It is probably the least effectual of all the preparations of iron. Dose, gr. v. to xx.

### Ficus. Fig.

Ficus Carica Linn. N. F. Urticaceæ.

The dried fruit; imported from Smyrna.

*Uses.*—Nutritive and demulcent. Used in practice chiefly as suppuratives, or poultices to promote suppuration, especially in gum-boil.

### Filix Mas. Male Fern.

Aspidium Filix mas Swartz.   Indigenous.   N. F. Filices.
The Rhizome, dried; collected in summer.

*Charact.*—Tufted, scaly, greenish-brown; powder, greenish-yellow, with a disagreeable odour and a nauseous, bitter, somewhat astringent taste.

*Analysis.*—An odorous volatile oil, in very small proportion, to which its anthelmintic power is due; fixed oil, fecula, gum, sugar, woody fibre, &c.

*Actions and uses.*—Anthelmintic, and one of the most (if not the most) efficient and successful we possess for tapeworm.   That it occasionally fails, we think, is in great part owing to inert specimens or preparations, and this may be the reason why so old a vermifuge has been so long in again obtaining general confidence.   The liquid extract pretty recently prepared from the root collected in summer, is the best form, and it should be given soon after the bowels have been well evacuated by an energetic cathartic.   The best and most successful plan is to give min. xxx. of the extract in ʒij. to ʒiv. of a strong infusion of quassia or chiretta, following it up if necessary with a purgative.   Dose of the powdered root, ʒj. to ʒij.

*Formula.*—℞ Extracti filicis liquidi min. xxx.; olei anisi, minimum; infusi chiratæ fʒij.   Misce. fiat haustus.

*Extractum Filicis Liquidum.*—Fern root in coarse powder, lb. ij.; ether Oiv., or a sufficiency.   Mix the fern root with Oij. of the ether; pack closely in a percolator; and add the remainder of the ether at intervals, until it passes through colourless.   Let the ether evaporate on a water-bath, or recover it by distillation, and preserve the oily extract.   It is a dark-green oleo-resin, of the consistence of thick syrup, with an etherial and somewhat disagreeable odour.   Dose, min. xx. to lx.

### Fœniculi Fructus. Fennel Fruit.

Fœniculum dulce DC.   N. F. Umbelliferæ.   The fruit; imported from Malta.

*Charact.*—About 3 lines long and 1 broad, elliptical, beaked, having 8 pale-brown longitudinal ribs, the 2 lateral being double ; taste and odour aromatic.

*Uses.*—An aromatic stimulant and carminative like anise, but little employed.   Dose, gr. xxx. to lx.

*Aqua.*—Sweet fennel fruit ℥xvj. ; water cong. ij.   Distil one gallon.   A vehicle for other medicines.   Dose, ℥j. to ℥ij.

### Galbanum.  Galbanum.

A gum-resin, derived from an unascertained umbelliferous plant; imported from India and the Levant.

*Charact.*—In irregular tears, about the size of a pea, usually agglutinated into masses, of a greenish-yellow colour, translucent, with a strong disagreeable odour and an acrid bitter taste.

*Analysis.*—Resin, gum, a small portion of volatile oil, and malate of lime.

*Actions and uses.*—Antispasmodic, but inferior to assafœtida, an ingredient of the compound assafœtida pill. Dose, gr. x. to xx.

*Emplastrum Galbani.*—Galbanum ℥j.; ammoniac ℥j.; yellow wax ℥j.; litharge plaster ℥viij.   Melt the galb. and ammon. together, and strain.   Add the litharge plaster and wax, previously melted, together, and mix thoroughly.   A stimulating plaster.

### Galla.  Galls.

Excrescences on quercus infectoria Linn, caused by the punctures and deposited ova of diplolepis Gallæ tinctoriæ. N. F. Cupuliferæ.

*Charact.*—Hard, heavy, globular bodies, from ¼ in. to ¾ in. diam., tuberculated, the tubercules and intervening spaces smooth ; bluish-green on surface, yellowish-white within, with a small central cavity ; intensely astringent.

*Analysis.*—About 25 per cent of tannin, a trace of gallic acid, a compound of pectic acid and tannin, and tannates, and gallates of potash and lime, &c.

*Actions and uses.*—Powerfully astringent, but not very

much employed, tannin and gallic acid being preferable. It may, however, be used in the hæmorrhages and discharges for which these other are given. It is also an excellent antidote in cases of poisoning with tartarated antimony, ipecacuanha, and the vegetable alkaloids. Externally, galls have long been in repute as an astringent in hæmorrhoids, in relaxed uvula and tonsils, and in mucous discharges. I prefer going at once to the gallic acid or the tannin. Dose, in powder, gr. v. to xx.

*Acidum Tannicum.*—See *Tannic Acid.*

*Tinctura Gallæ.*—Galls ʒijss.; proof spt. Oj. Make in the usual way. Dose, fʒss. to fʒij.

*Unguentum Gallæ.*—Galls, in fine powder, gr. lxxx.; benzoated lard ʒj. M. Useful in piles. See formula under Tannic Acid. Another useful one is ℞ Acidi tannici gr. xx.; extracti belladonæ gr. xx.; olei olivæ ʒij.; adipis præparati ʒvi. Misce.

*Unguentum Gallæ Cum. Opio.*—Ointment of galls ʒj.; opium powder gr. xxxij. Mix. For painful hemorrhoids.

**Gentianæ Radix.** Gentian Root.

Gentiana Lutea Linn. N. F. Gentianaceæ. The root, dried; collected in the Alps, Apennines, and other mountains of Europe.

*Charact.*—From half-an-inch to one inch thick, several inches long, often twisted, much wrinkled, or marked with close transverse rings, brown externally, yellow within, tough and spongy; taste at first slightly sweetish, and afterwards very bitter.

*Analysis.*—An odorous volatile oil, a yellow, crystalline, bitter neutral principle, gentianin, said to be a compound of a colouring matter, a fatty matter, and a bitter principle; a green fixed oil, a free organic acid, sugar, gum, &c.

*Adulterations.*—Roots of other species of gentian; and, what is of more gravity, the roots of white hellebore, monkshood, and belladonna, occasionally. These are detected by their wanting the intense bitter taste, and the internal bright yellow colour.

*Actions and uses.*—An excellent bitter tonic. Useful in dyspepsia, with feeble digestion, and heartburn, but without irritability of the stomach. It possesses some little anthelmintic power; is somewhat of a febrifuge; but of little service in gout. Large doses are apt to prove emetic. Dose, powder, gr. x. to xxx., but seldom given.

*Extractum Gentianæ.*—Gentian lb. j.; boiling dist. water, cong. j. Macerate the gentian in the water for two hours; boil for 15 minutes; pour off, press, and strain; then evaporate by a water-bath to a proper consistence. Dose, gr. iij. to x.

*Infusum Gentianæ Compositum.*—Gentian ℥¼.; bitter orange peel ℥¼.; fresh lemon peel ℥ss.; boiling dist. water Oj. Infuse in a covered vessel 1 hour, and strain. Dose, ℥j. to ℥ij. Most commonly employed, and a good vehicle, for the alkaline bi-carbonates.

*Mistura Gentianæ.*—Gentian root ℥¼.; bitter orange peel, coriander fruit, of each gr. xxx.; proof spt. f℥ij.; dist. water f℥viij. Macerate the gent., orange peel, and coriander in the spt. for 2 ho. Add the water; macerate again for 2 ho.; strain. Dose, f℥ss. to f℥j.

*Tinctura Gentianæ Co.*—Gentian ℥jss.; bitter orange peel ℥¾.; cardamoms, bruised, ℥¼.; proof spt. Oj. Macerate 48 hours, and percolate, as before. Dose, ℥j. to ℥ij. Generally given along with the infusion.

### Glycerinum. Glycerine.

A sweet principle, $C_6 H_8 O_6$, obtained from fats and fixed oils, and containing a small percentage of water.

*Charact.*—A colourless, syrupy fluid, without odour, with a sweet taste; freely soluble in water or in alcohol. Spt. gravity, 1·25.

*Uses.*—Emollient. May be employed as a vehicle for various active medicines, such as tannin, iodine, &c. Externally, it is useful where we want to allay itching, or secure moistness of a part, as in some skin diseases. It has been used also to moisten cotton for insertion into the ear as a kind of artificial tympanum. Employed as a substi tute for cod liver oil in phthisis, but it is far inferior in nutrient power. Indeed, while the oil often shows early tangible restorative results, the other may be carried on long without doing any visible good. In the strumous diseases of children, too, it is equally unsatisfactory; for while they often improve under the cod liver oil, they gradually become attenuated under glycerine. Dose, from a few drachms to several ounces, being little more active than syrup.

### Glycyrrhizæ Radix. Liquorice Root.

Glycyrrhiza glabra Linn. Leguminosæ. The root, or underground stem, fresh and dried; cultivated in England.

*Charact.*—In long cylindrical branched pieces, an inch, or less, in diam.; greyish-brown externally, yellow internally, odourless, with a sweet mucilaginous and slightly acrid taste.

*Uses.*—Demulcent. Used in the form of decoction or extract in catarrhal affections. The powder is employed as a covering for pills. The root may be chewed at pleasure.

*Extractum.*—In the form of dark flattened sticks. A bit is usually put into the mouth, and allowed to dissolve gradually, in simple coughs.

### Gossypium. Cotton Wool.

The hairs of the seed of various species of gossypium, carded.

*Prep.*—Pyroxylin.

### Granati Radicis Cortex. Pomegranate Root Bark.

Punica Granatum Linn. N. F. Myrtaceæ. The bark of root, fresh or dried; chiefly imported dried from Germany.

*Charact.*—In quills or fragments of a greyish-yellow colour externally, yellow internally, having a short fracture, little odour, and an astringent, slightly bitter taste.

*Analysis.*—An acrid oleo-resinous principle, punicine, on which its anthelmintic properties depend; tannin, gallic acid, wax, and a sweetish substance resembling mannite.

*Adulterations.*—The root bark of the common barberry

(berberis vulgaris), and of buxus sempervivens, the box-tree are at times substituted. They are known by being devoid of astringency.

*Actions and uses.*—A good vermifuge in tapeworm, acting by killing the parasite. It is believed to act most effectively when joints of the worm are coming away naturally. It sometimes causes sickness and vomiting, probably owing to the movements of the worm excited by the drug. Dose, gr. xx. to xl. The decoction is the best.

*Decoctum Granati Radicis.*—Pomegranate root, fresh or dry, sliced, ℥ij.; dist. water Oij. Boil down to a pint, and strain. Dose, f℥j. to f℥ij.

### Guaiaci Lignum. Guaiac Wood.

Guaiacum officinale Linn. N. F. Zygophyllaceæ. The wood sliced or coarsely turned ; imported from St Domingo and Jamaica.

*Charact.*—Extremely hard; the young or outer wood is pale-brown, the old or central wood is greenish-brown.

*Test.*—Nitric acid applied to the bark produces a bluish-green colour.

### Guaiaci Resina. Guaiac Resin.

Guaiacum officinale Linn. The resin obtained from the stem, by natural exudation, by incisions, or by heat.

*Charact.*—In large masses of a greenish-brown colour ; fractured surface resinous, translucent at the edges.

*Test.*—A solution in rectified spt., strikes a clear blue colour when applied to the inner surface of the paring of raw potato.

*Analysis.*—The wood contains its own proper resin, which is a compound of guaiacic acid with a trace of gum, extractive matter, and woody fibre.

*Adulterations.*—The pine resins : they are soluble in hot oil of turpentine, while the true resin is not. The action of nitric acid, as above, will distinguish the guaiac from other woods.

*Actions and uses.*—A stimulating diaphoretic, very useful in chronic rheumatism, chronic tonsillitis, and at times in atonic gout. Benefit is occasionally obtained by it in chronic skin diseases, probably by its stimulating and reviving capillary action. It has long had a name in syphilitic affections, and though often rated much too high, secondary syphilis is sometimes benefited by it. If too long continued, it is apt to induce dyspepsia and torpidity of the bowels. The wood is not given alone, but is an ingredient of the compound decoction of sarsaparilla. Dose of the resin, gr. x. to xx., in treacle or preserve.

*Mistura Guaiaci.*—Guaiac resin ℥ss.; sugar ℥ss.; gum acacia powder ℥¼.; cinnamon water Oj. Triturate the guaiac with the sugar and the gum, adding gradually the cinnamon water. Dose, f℥ss. to f℥ij. two or three times a-day.

*Tinctura Guaiaci Ammoniata.*—Guaiac resin, in fine powder ℥iv.; aromatic spt. of ammonia Oj. Macerate 7 days, and filter. Dose, f℥ss. to f℥j. It is about the best preparation of guaiacum. It should be suspended in mixtures by means of mucilage or sugar, plain water decomposing it.

### Hæmatoxyli Lignum. Logwood.

Hæmatoxylum Campechianum Linn. N. F. Leguminosæ. The heart-wood sliced ; imported from Campeachy, in Central America, from Honduras and Jamaica.

*Charact.*—The logs are externally of a dark colour, internally, reddish-brown ; the chips have a feeble, agreeable odour, and a sweetish taste ; a small portion chewed imparts a dark pink colour to the saliva.

*Analysis.*—A red crystalline bitter principle, named hæmatin, or hæmatoxylin, resin, volatile oil, tannin, acetic acid, salts, &c.

*Actions and uses.*—An astringent. Given with benefit in chronic diarrhœa and dysentery, where it seems to arrest the discharges without occasioning constipation. It will be found useful also in the perspirations of hectic, and in diabetes.

*Decoctum Hæmatoxyli.*—Logwood chips Ʒj.; cinnamon powder gr. lx.; dist. water Oj. Boil the logwood in the water ten minutes, adding the cinnamon towards the end, and strain. The product should measure Ʒxvi. A good form. Dose, Ʒj. to Ʒij.

*Extractum.*—Logwood lb.j.; boiling dist. water cong. j. Macerate the logwood in the water 24 hours; boil down to one half, strain, and evaporate by a water-bath to a proper consistence, stirring with a wooden spatula. Iron vessels should not be used. Dose, gr. x. to xxx.

### Hemidesmi Radix. Hemidesmus Root.

Hemidesmus indicus D. C.  N. F. Asclepiadaceæ. The root, dried; imported from India.

*Charact.*—Yellowish-brown, cylindrical, tortuous, furrowed, and with annular cracks, with a fragrant odour and agreeable flavour.

*Uses.*—In repute in India as a tonic and diaphoretic, in the cachetic conditions for which sarsaparilla has been employed. It possesses no great efficacy, and is used in this country chiefly in the form of syrup, as an agreeable vehicle for other medicines.

*Syrupus Hemidesmi.*—Hemidesmus, bruised, Ʒiv.; refined sugar Ʒxxviij.; boiling dist. water Oj. Infuse the hemid. in the water, in a covered vessel, 4 hours, and strain. Set it by till the sediment subsides; then decant the clear liquor; add the sugar, and dissolve by a gentle heat. The product should weigh lb.ij. Ʒx. and have the sp. gr. 1·335. Dose, Ʒj. to Ʒiv.

### Hirudo. The Leech.

1. Sanguisuga Officinalis Savigny, the Speckled Leech; and 2. S. Medicinalis Sav., the Green Leech; imported chiefly from Hamburg. Class, vermes; order, annulata.

*Charact.*—Body elongated, two or three inches long, tapering to each end, wrinkled transversely; back olive-green, with six red longitudinal stripes. 1. Belly greenish-yellow, spotted with black; 2. Belly olive-green, not spotted. Spurious leeches are to be met with, a common one being the horse-leech. It is known by the absence of the rusty-red bands, or having only two. It is a popular, but unfounded belief, that this animal will bleed a person to death, the blood, as is said, discharging at the tail as fast as it is taken in by the mouth. The real truth is, that the leech is provided only with blunt teeth, and cannot properly perforate the human skin.

*Uses.*—They are useful for small local bleedings, and may be often applied where cupping-glasses cannot, and scarifications are inadmissible. Many persons, too, will admit of bleeding in this way, instead of by the lancet, which inspires considerable terror. Previous to their application, the part should be cleaned, and the leech (dried by rolling gently in a cloth) confined to the part by a glass or other receptacle. If they do not fasten, immersing them in porter, or besmearing the part with cream or blood, will sometimes overcome rebellion. But care should be exercised in their selection: those are most active which roll up into an oval ball on being lightly squeezed in the hand. They should not be applied where there is almost constant motion, as over the neck or costal cartilages; nor where the cellular tissue is lax, as in the eyelids, as erythema or œdema are apt to be occasioned. Large superficial veins, especially in the neck, in children, should be avoided, and the abdomen in general. The quantity of blood drawn by a leech is from ℨij. to ℥ss., but about thrice this amount may afterwards come away. Should the bleeding continue too long, compression, a red-hot wire, nitrate of silver, perchloride of iron, or transfixion with a needle, will, one or the other, arrest it. Leeches have occasionally been permitted to creep up the nostril, up the rectum, or even into the stomach. A strong solution of common salt sent after them will cause their death.

**Hordeum Decorticatum. Pearl Barley.**

Hordeum distichum Linn. Cultivated in Britain. N. F. Graminaceæ. The seeds deprived of their husks.

*Charact.*—White, rounded, retaining a trace of the longitudinal furrow.

*Uses.*—A nutritious food ; and in medicine useful as a demulcent drink in catarrh, dysentery, and inflammation of the bladder.

*Decoctum.*—Pearl barley $\bar{3}$ij.; dist. water Ojss. Wash the barley in cold water, and reject the washings ; boil with the dist. water for 20 minutes in a covered vessel, and strain. For soothing drinks and injections.

**Hydrargyri Iodidum Rubrum.** Red Iodide of Mercury.

$HgI$, or $HgI_2$.

*Charact.*—A crystalline powder, of a vermilion colour, becoming yellow when gently heated over a lamp on a sheet of paper ; almost insoluble in water, dissolves sparingly in alcohol, but freely in ether, or in an aqueous solution of iodide of potassium. When digested with solution of soda, it assumes a reddish-brown colour, and the fluid cleared by filtration, and mixed with solution of starch, gives a blue precipitate on being acidulated with nitric acid.

*Tests.*—Entirely volatilized by a heat under redness, and entirely soluble in ether.

*Actions and uses.*—Alterative and deobstruant, but possessing more of the actions of mercurials than of iodine. In not very large doses, it is an irritant poison, and it causes inflammation of the skin when left in contact with it. It may be given in secondary syphilis, and in various scrofulous disorders; and some have found it useful in valvular disease of the heart, permitting regurgitation. In the form of ointment, it may be topically applied in enlarged thyroid, and in chronic periostitic and glandular swellings, syphilitic. Dose, gr. $\frac{1}{16}$th to $\frac{1}{4}$th, made into pill with a little ext. gentian. and hyoscyam.

*Unguentum Hydrargyri Iodidi Rubri.*—Red iodide of mercury, in fine powder, gr. xvj.; simple oint. $\bar{3}$j. Mix. External stimulant and deobstruant.

**Hydrargyri Iodidum Viride.** Green Iodide of Mercury.

$Hg_2 I$, or $Hg I$.

*Charact.*—A dull green powder, insoluble in water, which darkens in colour on exposure to light. When gradually heated in a test tube, it yields a yellow sublimate, which upon friction becomes red, while a globule of metallic mercury is left in the bottom of the tube.

*Tests.*—Entirely volatilized by a heat under redness. When it is shaken in a tube with ether, nothing is dissolved.

*Actions and uses.*—Alterative, and much milder than the red iodide. May be employed with similar views, and for like purposes; and, being weaker, is adapted for the cutaneous diseases of children, especially those on the scalp; but here it should not be pushed far. Dose, gr. i. to iii., in pill, with extract as before; for children, gr. ⅛th to ½, with a little aromatic powder; magnesia being alternated occasionally.

### Hydrargyri Nitratis Liquor Acidus.    Acid Solution of Nitrate of Mercury.

Nitrate of Mercury, $HgO\ NO^5$, in solution in nitric acid.

*Charact.*—A colourless and strongly acid solution, giving a yellow precip. with solution of potash added in excess.

*Test.*—Sp. gr. 2·246. Does not give any precip. when a little of it is dropt into hydrochloric acid diluted with twice its volume of water.

*Prep.*—Mercury ℥iv.; nitric acid f℥v.; dist. water f℥iss. Mix the acid with the water in a flask, and dissolve the mercury in the mixture without the application of heat. Boil gently for 15 minutes; cool, and preserve in a stoppered bottle.

*Uses.*—An irritant and corrosive poison. Used occasionally as a caustic for cancer, lupus, sloughing ulcers, and small nævi. Should be applied with a glass rod.

*Unguentum Hydrargyri Nitratis.*—Mercury ℥iv.; nitric acid f℥xij.; prepared lard ℥xv.; olive oil f℥xxxij. Dissolve the mercury in the acid by a gentle heat; melt the lard in the oil, by a water-bath, in a porcelain vessel capable of holding six times the quantity; and while the mixture is hot, add the solution of mercury, also hot, mixing them thoroughly. If the mixture do not froth up, increase the heat till this occurs. Citrine ointment. Uses.—A stimulating application to indolent ulcers, to the eyelids in ophthalmia, and in a variety of skin diseases, such as herpes, ringworm, impetigo, lepra, psoriasis, rupia. In the milder skin diseases it may be diluted with lard, 1 to 3.

**Hydrargyri Oxidum Rubrum.** Red Oxide of Mercury.

HgO.

*Charact.*—An orange-red powder, readily dissolved by hydrochloric acid, and yielding a solution which, with caustic potash in excess, gives a yellow precip., and with solution of ammonia, a white.

*Tests.*—Entirely volatilized by a heat under redness, being at the same time decomposed into mercury and oxygen. Done in a test tube, no orange vapours are perceived. Dissolves without residue in hydrochloric acid.

*Actions and uses.*—Formerly employed to salivate, but not now used internally. May be employed as a caustic to exuberant granulations, indolent ulcers, and venereal warts, but it is not equal to other caustics treated of.

*Unguentum Hydrargyri Oxidi Rubri.*—Red oxide of mercury, reduced to very fine powder, gr. lxij.; yellow wax ʒss.; oil of almonds ʒss. Mix. Useful in chronic inflammation of the edges of the eyelids.

**Hydrargyrum.** Mercury.

*Charact.*—Brilliantly lustrous and easily divisible into sphericle globules. Fluid at common temperatures.

*Test.*—Volatilizes with heat without any residue.

*Actions and uses.*—In the metallic state, mercury, like other metals, is of little service, and but little employed in practice, being only, and that very rarely, had recourse to as a mechanical agent in obstruction of the bowels—a very questionable kind of treatment. When oxidated, however, and otherwise combined, it assumes an immense importance, few drugs possessing so great a variety of actions, or admitting of such a variety of applications. It then becomes physiologically an irritant, corrosive, cholagogue, cathartic, diuretic, stimulant, and an exciter of a singular condition or chain of symptoms, salivation being the most prominent. And as a result of these actions separately or combinedly, it is therapeutically an antiphlogistic, sedative, deobstruant, alterative, and antisyphilitic; or perhaps it is this latter specifically, or in virtue of some occult power. The irritant and corrosive actions of mercurials are seen in increased vascularity, inflammation, ulceration, and sloughing. Of all the physiological effects, however, the most wonderful is that termed mercurialism, or mercurial erethism. This singular state, which may be occasioned by repeated small quantities, or one large dose, is divisible into a few species. 1. A peculiar febrile excitement with increased pulse, fetor of the breath, and a metallic taste; then redness, tenderness, swelling, and sponginess of the gums, increase of saliva, ulceration of the gums, buccal membrane and fauces. 2. High fever, nervous symptoms, intense salivation, deep ulceration, sloughing and gangrene of the gums, cheeks, throat, tongue. This is a condition attended with great risk of life. 3. A train of nervous symptoms, a continued tremor and convulsive twitching of the muscles of the extremities, jaw, and tongue, with paralysis, leading to difficulty in walking or speaking; there is also delirium, loss of memory, sleeplessness, dry and brown skin. This has been called shaking palsy, or tremblement metallique, and occurs generally among gilders, and workers in quicksilver mines, exposed to the mercurial vapour. 4. Great depression, irregular action of the heart, sighing, trembling, a weak pulse, a sense of coldness, pale and contracted countenance, and proneness to death on sudden exertion. This variety of condition is probably in part owing to certain unknown constitutional peculiarities; for we find some individuals who are slowly acted upon, others violently affected by a single small dose, and some, again, in whom mercurialism shows itself after the mercurial has been stopped. Again, children under ten years of age, in general, bear as much as an adult. By watching the action of mercury in each particular case, we are, in general, enabled to keep its action within due bounds ; such as is shown by fetor, slight tenderness of the gums, and moderate salivation—action enough for specific curative purposes. Sudden changes of temperature while using it are apt to occasion eczema, and other cutaneous diseases (scaly), with fever, and internal inflammations, especially of the serous membranes. Scrofulous people offer an unfavourable soil for mercury, swelling and suppuration of glands, diseases of the skin and bones, being occasioned by its use. The results are still more grave when the syphilitic taint concurs. Various methods and remedies are recommended for combating the symptoms of mercurial action. At an early stage, brisk saline purgatives are useful, with a warm, uniform atmosphere, and the throat and neck kept cool. If there be much swelling and pain, leeches may be applied behind the jaws, and the warm bath at times. Nauseating doses of tartarated antimony and acetate of lead in 10-grain doses, 3 or 4 times a day, have been of service. The mouth may also be relieved by gargles of alum, tannin, catechu, borax, and honey, or a mild solution of chloride of lime. Cordials and opiates are also approved by some, and of course the mercury is discontinued immediately. But we must now come to the therapeutical powers of mercury. As an antiphlogistic it is employed in fevers ; it is most serviceable in severe remittents and yellow fever. It is more useful still in acute internal inflammations, and especially in those which give rise to the effusion of coagulable lymph, such as croup, laryngitis, pericarditis, peritonitis (particularly puerperal), meningitis, pneumonia, pleuritis, hepatitis, and emphatically so in iritis. In metritis and synovitis it is also of service, but is of more doubtful advantage in nephritis. Very large doses in the form of calomel often abort a tropical dysentery, and arrest malignant cholera. In acute inflammations, advantage is often derived from previous local blood-letting. As an antisyphilitic, mercury possesses an ancient reputation. It was formerly imagined to be the only remedy, and that large doses were indispensable; we now know that the virus may bé exterminated by other means, but perhaps most effectually by it; and well enough by more moderate doses. For this purpose, as well as the preceding, calomel, or the green iodide, combined with a little opium to prevent draining away by the bowels, are best adapted. The corrosive sublimate is preferred by others. They are given in small doses two or three times a-day until moderate salivation is induced. As a de-obstruant, it is employed in congestion and enlargement of the liver, in some cases of jaundice, and obstruction of the bowels, in glandular swellings, in morbid deposits, in inflammatory adhesions, in effusions into shut sacs, fibrinous effusions into the aqueous humour, in paralysis resulting from cerebral disorder, and partial palsy, depending on disorder of particular nerves. Many, now-a-days, go to the iodide of potassium instead, and probably in some constitutions with equally good results, and somewhat less risk of detriment. For most of the above purposes, slight mercurial action is necessary. As an alterative, given in small doses at intervals, and stopping short of mercurial action, the tongue becomes cleaner, the secretions more natural, the appetite improved, the skin more vigorous in action, and gradually various chronic morbid states, such as skin eruptions, torpidity of the bowels, and enlargement and induration of the mesenteric and other glands, disappear. Small doses of pil. hydrarg. or calomel, every other night answer well. As a sedative, its action is peculiar and limited, having this effect only in large doses (calomel) in enteric inflammation. As an anthelmintic, diaphoretic, and diuretic, it is most useful along with other drugs, whose action it seems to promote. It is not given in the metallic state; so the doses will be found under the different preparations.

*Emplastrum Hydrargyri.*—Applied as a stimulant over enlarged glands, and over the liver in chronic induration.

*Emplastrum Ammoniaci cum Hgdrargyro.*—As a resolvent in indolent buboes, nodes, and enlarged glands.

*Hydrargyrum cum Creta.*—Mercury, by weight, ℥j.; prep. chalk ℥ij. Rub in a porcelain mortar until metallic globules cease to be visible to the naked eye, and the mixture acquires an uniform grey colour.

*Uses.*—This is an admirable laxative for children, and acts by increasing the hepatic, pancreatic, and intestinal secretions. Along with a little rhubarb, it is of great service in the diarrhœa of the young, depending on irregular action of the liver with deficient biliary secretion. As an alterative, it is also serviceable in infantile cutaneous diseases. It is well adapted for adults, and it is not altogether correct to say that grown-up people require as much to produce catharsis as would induce salivation. Dose for children, gr. ij. to v. Adults a little more.

*Linimentum.*—Ointment of mercury ℥j.; solut. ammonia f℥j.; liniment of camphor f℥j. Melt the oint. and linim. with a gentle heat, then add the solut. gradually and agitate. A stimulating application to indolent swellings. Salivation may result from it.

*Pilula Hydrargyri.*—Mercurial or blue pill. Mercury ℥ij.; confection of roses ℥iij.; liquorice powder ℥j. Rub the mercury with the confection until metallic globules are no longer visible, then add the liquorice, and mix the whole well together. Divide in 5 gr. pills. Dose. cathartic, gr. v. to x. To produce the specific effect for which it is often employed, it is given in smaller doses, frequently repeated, and should be combined with a little opium. As a cathartic, taken at night, and followed in the morning by a purgative draught, it is useful in slight biliary disorders.

*Suppositoria Hydrargyri.*—Ointment of mercury gr. lx.; benzoated lard and white wax, of each, gr. xx.; oil of theobroma gr. lxxx. Divide into 12 equal parts.

*Unguentum Hydrargyri.*—Mercury lb.j.; prepared lard lb.j.; prepared suet ℥j. Rub them together until metallic globules disappear. This may be applied to produce salivation, from ℨss. to ℥ij. being rubbed into the inside of the thighs, or axilla. A quicker plan is to blister the surface previously. Used also in enlarged glands, and over the inflamed part in phlegmonous erysipelas.

*Unguentum Hydrargyri Compositum.*—Oint. of mercury ʒvi.; yellow wax; olive oil, of each, ʒiij.; camphor ʒiss. Mix. "Scott's Dressing." Useful for obstinate glandular swellings, and said to do good in carbuncle.

### Hydrargyrum Ammoniatum. Ammoniated Mercury.

$NH_2$, $Hg_2$, Cl., or $NH_2$ HgCl.

*Charact.*—An opaque white powder, on which cold water, alcohol, and ether have no action.

*Uses.*—Not used internally, but for making ointment.

*Unguentum Hydrargyri Ammoniate.*—Ammoniated mercury gr. lxij.; simple oint. ʒj. Mix. Useful in herpes, impetigo, sycosis menti, acne, &c.

### Hydrargyri Perchloridum. Perchloride of Mercury.

Synon. Corrosive Sublimate, Hydrarg. Bichlor., &c., HgCl., or $HgCl_2$.

*Charact.*—In heavy colourless masses of prismatic crystals, possessing a highly acrid metallic taste, more soluble in alcohol, and still more so in ether than water. Its aqueous solution gives a yellow precipitate with caustic potash, a white precipitate with ammonia, and a curdy white precip. with nitrate of silver.

*Tests.*—Entirely soluble in ether. When heated it sublimes without decomposing, or leaving any residue.

*Actions and uses.*—An intensely irritant poison, a few grains inflaming and corroding the alimentary tube, and occasioning death. In some cases there is a great depression of the nervous system and coma. In poisoning, give a moderate quantity of albumen, such as the white of egg (the yolk is also efficacious); in their absence, give flour, milk, or the proto-chloride of tin. Notwithstanding its poisonous properties, it is a great favourite with many for antivenereal purposes; and for chronic rheumatism, periostitis, and arthritis, depending on the syphilitic taint. I should be disposed to place it as an alterative for these purposes above calomel, or the blue pill, and on equal terms with the green iodide of mercury; corrosive sublimate, however, being given in much smaller doses. Dose, $\frac{1}{12}$ to $\frac{1}{8}$ of a grain, in pill, or in solution, as follows: ℞ Hydrargyri corrosivi sublimati gr. ij.; spiritus vini rectificati fℨss.; infusi columbæ fℨxviij.; liquoris morphiæ hydrochloratis fℨij. Misce. Sumat cochleare parvum bis terve die. Each teaspoonful contains $\frac{1}{12}$ of a gr. If there is much intestinal irritation excited, it should be stopped.

*Liquor Hydrargyri Perchloridi.*—Perchloride of mercury, chloride of ammonium, of each, gr. x.; dist. water Oj. Dissolve. Dose, fℨss. to fℨij. Each drachm contains $\frac{1}{16}$ gr.

*Lotio Hydrargyri Flava.*—Perchlor. mercury, gr. xviij.; solution of lime fℨx. Mix. Used much as Lotio. Nig. in syphilitic ulcers, &c.

*Incompatibles.*—Alkalies and their carb., lime, antim. tart., nitrate of silver, acetate of lead, iodide of potassium albumen, decoction of bark, soaps.

**Hydrargyri Subchloridum.** Subchloride of Mercury.

Synonym.—Calomelas.

$Hg_2$ Cl., or HgCl.

*Charact.*—A heavy and almost tasteless powder, of a dull-white hue; becoming yellowish by rubbing in a mortar. A solution of potash or lime renders it black. Entirely volatilized by a sufficient heat.

*Actions and uses.*—Irritant, alterative, antiphlogistic, or sedative, diuretic, cathartic, diaphoretic, cholagogue, sialogogue; and not more varied in its properties and applications than often useful in its results. When introduced into the system it is reduced to the metallic state. In very large doses it destroys not so much by its irritant power, as by the induction of intense salivation, and extreme nervous prostration. As a sedative or antiphlogistic it is given in doses of from gr. x. to xx., with benefit in the dysentery and cholera of warm climates; and in smaller doses, along with a little opium, it is of signal service in acute internal inflammations, such as peritonitis, pleuritis, pericarditis, hepatitis, metritis, &c. As a diuretic it acts best along with others, such as digitalis or squills, and seems to increase their activity. It is an excellent cathartic alone in small doses, and combined with other cathartics, such as jalap, or scammony, its action is all the more effectual and certain. It is thus an excellent vermifuge for children, killing and expelling the parasites from the intestines. As a diaphoretic it is most energetic, along with a little opium, and is thus given in febrile disorders. As an alterative it is given in small doses, frequently repeated (and with a little opium to prevent it draining away by the bowels), in syphilis, and other blood diseases manifested by cutaneous eruptions; and on the development of its physiological action, an improvement of the system oftentimes results. Children are not quite so susceptible to the action of this drug as adults. Of late doubts have been raised by certain experimenters on the lower animals, whether calomel (or mercury rather) increases the biliary secretion; whether, in fact, it does not rather arrest it. Now, whatever it may do among the lower animals, daily evidence is afforded among the higher, of its power of augmenting the secretion of bile; light-coloured fæces speedily assuming a normal hue. This is proof enough; and the last place to go to in order to test the physiological action of hydrargyrum (or any other drug) on Homo, is among the hounds. Opium will affect a dog differently from a duchess, a monkey from a man; and gentlemen will find that a breakfast of Nicotiana Tabacum will sit less easily on their stomachs, than on that of a goat. A truce, then, to induction from analogies of so unsatisfactory a nature as these; we mean, of course, in reference to the actions of drugs. Dose, gr. j. oft repeated as an alterative; gr. iij. to vj. cathartic; gr. iij. frequently antiphlogistic; gr. xx. sedative.

*Pilula Hydrargyri Subchloridi Composita.*—Subchlor. hydr., antimon. sulphurat., of each ʒj.; guaiacum resin ʒij.; castor oil sufficient to make a proper mass. Formerly called Plummer's Pill. Given in syphilis, &c. Dose, gr. v. to x.

*Lotio Hydrargyri Nigra.*—Subchlor. hydr. gr. xxx.; solution of lime f℥x. Mix. Commonly called Black Lotion, Black Wash. Used in syphilitic ulcers and sores, and in varicose ulcers.

*Unguentum Hydrargyri Subchloridi.*—Subchlor. hydr. gr. lxxx.; lard ℥j. Mix.

### Hydrargyri Sulphas. Sulphate of Mercury.

$HgOSO_3$, or $HgSO_4$.
Used only to prepare corrosive sublimate and calomel.

### Hyoscyami Folia. Hyoscyamus Leaves.

Hyoscyamus niger Linn. N. F. Solanaceæ. The leaves and branches of the indigenous biennial plant, dried; collected when about two-thirds of the flowers are expanded.

*Charact.*—Leaves sinuated and hairy. The fresh herb has a powerful unpleasant odour, and a slightly acrid taste, which nearly disappear on drying.

*Analysis.*—An alkaloid hyoscyamia, bitter extractive, fixed oil, gum, sugar, albumen, &c.

*Actions and uses.*—Narcotic and slightly irritant. In large doses it occasions delirium, with dilatation of the pupil, loss of vision, and profound stupor, the prelude of death. These effects are to be met by stimulating emetics, the stomach-pump, external and internal stimulants, and blood-letting. In smaller doses it is a useful anodyne and hypnotic, and is more suitable for some in the way of procuring sleep, allaying spasm, or soothing pain, than opium. As a general rule, however, it is much inferior to opiates for these purposes, but it possesses the advantage of not constipating the bowels. Many, however, who get on well with opiates, experience anxiety, headache, excitement, troublesome dreams, spectral illusions, and delirium, from its use; and these effects are the more likely to arise in the presence of cerebral affections. Hyoscyamus is given chiefly in irritable cough, in urinary diseases, in neuralgia, in spasmodic affections with nervous excitability; and, above all, it is in extensive use for correcting the tormina produced by different cathartics. Topically it is applied as an anodyne in painful glandular swelling, ulcerations, and piles. It has never made for itself a name as a deobstruant. Dose, of powdered leaves (seldom given), gr. v. to x.

*Extractum Hyoscyami.*—Dose, gr. ij. to x. in the form of pill.

*Tinctura Hyoscyami.*—Hyoscyamus leaves ℥ijss.; proof spt. Oj. Make as usual. Dose, m. xxx. to f℥j.

*Incompatibles.*—Potash and soda, nitrate of silver, the vegetable acids, and acetate of lead.

### Infusa. Infusions.

These are all placed under the drugs which give their name.

### Iodum. Iodine.

*Charact.*—Laminar crystals of a singular odour, dark colour, and metallic lustre, which, when heated, yield a violet coloured vapour; sparingly soluble in water, but freely dissolved by alcohol, by ether, and by a solution of ·iodide of potassium. The aqueous solution strikes a deep blue with starch.

*Adulterations.*—Charcoal, plumbago, black oxide of manganese, and water. The three first are not sublimed by heat, and the water is detected by pressing between folds of filtering paper, or by shaking in a dry bottle.

*Actions and uses.*—Irritant, corrosive, tonic, deobstruant, and an exciter of iodism; a peculiar condition to be afterwards described. In doses of a few grains, it occasions pain in the stomach, sickness, vomiting, headache, and giddiness; and in larger quantities, inflammation of the alimentary mucous membrane, &c., and death; orange-coloured erosions being found in the mucous coat of the stomach. From gr. lx. to gr. cxx. might occasion death. Iodism is produced by small doses continued for a lengthened period. The symptoms are headache, nausea, languor, giddiness, loss of appetite, debility; by and bye there is intense depression, muscular debility, entire want of appetite, tremors, emaciation, quick and feeble pulse, palpitation, a sinking feeling, clammy sweats, dinginess of the skin, catharsis, diuresis, priapism, and more rarely a wasting of the mammæ and testicles. Death may result unless the iodine be discontinued, but these symptoms gradually subside when it is disused. Idiosyncrasy comes in here again to give us variety; some take it largely without being iodized ; in others, the nasal and pulmonary mucous membranes are very much inflamed, and some again have their kidneys immensely stimulated. Now there is profuse diaphoresis, again pustular eruptions. The treatment is, suspension of the drug, emetics, and demulcent drinks. The applications of iodine in medicine are numerous; but most success will attend us, we think, if we confine it pretty much to the treatment of scrofula and its varied manifestations ; and these, without going the length of Lugol, are sufficiently numerous and grave. In bronchocele, where it was first used by Coindet of Geneva, its success is undoubted, but it fails if there be much induration of the gland. For this purpose it may be used internally, and in the way of inunction. In abscesses, tumours, enlarged glands, ulcers, osseous disease, and ophthalmia, springing from the scrofulous taint, it will be found extremely serviceable. It is recommended, too, by many in leucorrhœa, amenorrhœa, phthisis, gout, chorea, epilepsy, paralysis, and ascites, but often fails. Yet, in many of these diseases, where they are the offspring of scrofula, it will be found frequently of great benefit. The inhalation of the vapour of iodine in phthisis and bronchitis is worthy of continued trial—success having followed in some cases. It is highly probable that the successful results of this drug are due to a combined alterative and deobstruant action. The tincture is employed as an injection after tapping for the radical cure of hydrocele ; and in this form, as well as in that of ointment and liniment, it is topically applied as a stimulant, or resolvent, to enlarged glands, chronic swellings of joints, buboes, inflamed bursæ, and chronic abscesses. Iodine is seldom given in substance, but usually along with iodide of potassium in solution. Dose, gr. ½.

*Formula.*—℞ Iodi gr. iij.; potassii iodidi gr. xxx.; aquæ f℥v.; syrupi aurantii f℥j. Misce. Sumat cochleare magnum ter die.

*Linimentum Iodi.*—Iodine ℥jꝪ.; iodide of potassium ℥ss.; camphor ℥Ꝫ.; rect. spt. f℥x. Dissolve.

*Tinctura.*—Iodine ℥ss.; iodide of potass. ℥Ꝫ.; rect. spt. Oj. Dissolve. Dose, min. v. to xx.

*Unguentum Iodi.*—Iodine gr. xxxii.; iodide of potassium gr. xxxii.; proof spt. f℥j.; prepared lard ℥ij. Rub the iodine and the iod. pot. well together with the spt. in a porcelain mortar; add the lard gradually, and mix thoroughly.

*Vapor Iodi.*—Tinct. iodi f℥j.; aq. f℥j. Mix, and apply a gentle heat. A useful inhalation.

*Incompatibles.* — Ammonia, sulphur, phosphorus, sulphuric, nitric, prussic acid, metals and their salts, vegetable alkaloids.

**Ipecacuanha.** Ipecacuan.

Cephaelis Ipecacuanha D. C. N. F. Cinchonaceæ. The root dried; imported from Brazil.

*Charact.*—In pieces 3 or 4 inches long, about the size of a small quill, contorted and annulated. Colour, various shades of brown. Consists of two parts, the cortical or active portion, which is brittle, and a slender, white woody centre. Powder, pale brown, with a nauseous odour, and a somewhat acrid and bitter taste.

*Analysis.*—The cortical part contains an alkaloid named emetina, to which it owes its active properties; a fat, oily matter, a reddish-brown acid, named ipecacuanha acid, wax, gum, starch, &c.

*Adulterations.*—Spurious ipecacuan roots are occasionally, but not often, substituted; but attention to the above characters will conduce to their detection.

*Actions and uses*—Irritant, emetic, diaphoretic, expectorant, and if retained in the stomach (instead of in general being rejected), narcotico-acrid. We know this from the experiments of Magendie, who excited vomiting, coma, and death in a dog, by the introduction of emetina into the system through wounds, as well as by the stomach. As an emetic, it operates very much like tart. antim., some 20 minutes or so elapsing ere emesis results, and the act of vomiting being frequently repeated; but it does not depress quite so much, nor is it so apt to induce catharsis. It is well suited for old people, feeble women, and children, not, as before said, depressing so much as antimony. It is used in infantile fevers, where we wish to empty the stomach and abate the force of the circulation (for it is sedative in virtue of its emetic power), in hooping-cough, and in the fits of ague, asthma, and hysteria, which are sometimes checked by it. As a diaphoretic, it is of service in pulmonary catarrh, coryza, and acute rheumatism, and more so if combined with a little opium. As an expectorant, in small doses by diminishing the discharge, and in large doses by expelling it during vomiting, it is beneficial in chronic bronchitis. Some believe it to be tonic in doses of $\frac{1}{4}$ grain or so, but this is doubtful. It is employed with success in nauseating doses in the dysentery, acute and chronic, of warm climates, where it is supposed by some to act as a specific sedative, by others as an astringent; and by some again its good results are thought to be due to its action on the skin. Some people are extremely and peculiarly susceptible to its action, the invisible dust of the powder floating in the air of their apartment exciting an attack of spasmodic asthma. *Emetina* is but little used; $\frac{1}{16}$th gr. will excite vomiting. Dose of the powder, gr. xv. to xxx. as an emetic; gr. j. to gr. ij. as an expectorant.

*Formula.*—For chronic bronchitis. ℞ Vini ipecacuanhæ fʒiij.; syrupi scillæ fʒj.; tincturæ lobeliæ æthereæ fʒjss.; liquoris morphiæ hydrochloratis fʒjss.; infusi senegæ ad ʒvj. M. Sumat cochleare magnum ter die.

*Pulvis Ipecacuanhæ Compositus.*—Ipecacuan, powder, ʒss.; opium, in powder, ʒss.; sulphate of potash ʒiv. Mix well, and pass through a fine sieve. This, commonly called Dover's Powder, is an excellent diaphoretic; it should not be given where there is much irritability of the stomach, or in cerebral disorder. Dose, gr. v. to xv. The surface of the body should be kept warm; and that it may be retained on the stomach, little drink should be taken with or after it.

*Pilula Ipecacuanhæ cum Scilla.*—Compound powder of Ipecac. ℥iij.; squill in powder, ammoniac in powder, of each ℥i.; treacle, a sufficiency. Dose, gr. v. to x. A useful expectorant pill.

*Trochisci Ipecacuanhæ.*—Gr. ¼ in each lozenge.

*Vinum Ipecacuanhæ.*—Ipecacuan, bruised, ℥j.; sherry Oj. Macerate 7 days, with frequent agitation; filter. Dose, expectorant, min. v. to xl.; as an emetic, fℨiij. to fℨvj.

*Incompatibles.*—Salts of lead and mercury, vegetable acids, and astringent infusions.

### Jalapa. Jalap.

Exogonium Purga Bentham. N. F. Convolvulaceæ. The tubercles, dried; imported from Mexico.

*Charact.*—From the size of a nut to that of an orange, ovoid, the larger tubers often incised, covered with a brown wrinkled cuticle; when cut, of a yellowish-grey hue, with dark-brown concentric circles.

*Analysis.*—A hard and soft resin, the active principle, gum, sugar, starch, &c.

*Actions and uses.*—Cathartic. In large doses, irritant, occasioning violent hypercatharsis, which may even prove fatal. Its action in medicinal doses is energetic, griping occasionally, and producing frequent stools; and it affects chiefly the small bowel. It is given in constipation, and along with potass. bitart. in dropsies, where it occasions copious watery evacuations; and combined with a little calomel, it forms a useful vermifuge. It purges when applied to a wound. Dose, powder, gr. x. to gr. xxx. for adults; gr. ij. to viij. for children.

*Extractum Jalapæ.*—Dose, gr. v. to xv.

*Pulvis Jalapæ Compositus.*—Jalap ℥v.; acid. tart. potash, ℥jx.; ginger, powder, ℥j. Mix well, and pass through sieve. An excellent hydragogue cathartic. Dose, gr. **xx.** to lx.

*Tinctura.*—Jalap ℥ijss.; proof spt. Oj. M. By maceration and percolation, as usual. Dose, f℥ss. to f℥ij.

### Jalapæ Resin. Resin of Jalap.

A resin obtained from jalap by means of rect. spt.

*Charact.*—In dark-brown opaque brittle fragments, translucent at the edges, easily reduced to a pale-brown powder, acrid in the throat, soluble in rect. sp., partially so in ether.

*Actions and uses.*—An active cathartic. Dose, gr. ij. to v.

### Kamala. Kamala.

Rottlera Tinctoria. The powder which adheres to the capsules; imported from India. N. F. Euphorbiaceæ.

*Charact.*—Granular, orange-red, inflammable; not easily mixed with water, but the greater part dissolved in boiling alcohol, forming a red solution. Soluble in ether also, the residue consisting mostly of tufted hairs.

*Uses.*—This has been used in India as an anthelmintic in tape-worm. It is somewhat irritating to the bowels. Dose, gr. xxx. to ℥¼.

### Kino. Kino.

Pterocarpus Marsupium. The juice obtained from incisions in the trunk, inspissated; from Malabar. N. F. Leguminosæ.

*Charact.*—In small angular tears, reddish-black, ruby-red on the edges, very astringent.

*Analysis.*—Tannin in large quantity, catechuic acid, gum. Water takes up little, alcohol dissolves nearly two-thirds of it.

*Actions and uses.*—Astringent, and used in the same diseases as catechu. Dose, powder, gr. x. to xxx.

*Pulvis Kino Compositus.*—Take of kino ℥iij. and three quarters; opium ℥¼.; cinnamon ℥j. Mix and pass through sieve. Dose gr. v. to xx. Gr. j. of opium in xx.

*Tinctura.*—Take of kino ʒij.; rectified spt. Oj. Macerate seven days, filter, and add spt. to make a pint. Dose, fʒss. to fʒij.

### Krameriæ Radix. Rhatany Root.

Krameria triandria Ruiz and Pavon. The root, dried; from Peru. N. F. Polygalaceæ.

*Charact.*—About an inch diameter, numerous branches, long, brownish-red, and rough externally, reddish-yellow internally, powerfully astringent.

*Analysis.*—Tannin, a trace of gallic acid, krameric acid, gum, &c. Yields its active principles to cold water and alcohol.

*Actions and uses.*—A powerful astringent. Useful in hæmatemesis, menorrhagia (passive), chronic diarrhœa, atonic mucous discharges, colliquative sweating, and incontinence of urine. A topical styptic, and an ingredient of many dentrifices. Dose, powder, gr. x. to gr. xxx.

*Extractum.*—Prepared by maceration of the root in water, and evaporation. Dose, gr. v. to xx.

*Infusum.*—Rhatany ʒss.; boiling dist. water ʒx. Infuse an hour; strain. Dose, fʒj. to fʒij.

*Tinctura.*—Rhatany ʒijss.; proof spt. Oj. Macerate 48 hours, then percolate, and make up to a pint. Dose, fʒss. to fʒij.

### Lac. Milk.

The fresh milk of the cow, Bos Taurus. Used in mistura scammonii.

### Lactuca. Lettuce.

The flowering herb of Lactuca virosa. N. F. Compositæ.

*Actions.*—Narcotic, sedative, and diuretic, but not of much consequence.

*Extractum.*—This is not so useful a preparation as the inspissated juice. Dose, gr. v. to. x.

### Laurocerasi Folia. Cherry-Laurel Leaves.

Prunus Laurocerasus Linn. The common or cherry-laurel. The fresh leaves; a native of the shores of the Black Sea, but now cultivated in Britain. N. F. Rosaceæ.

*Charact.*—Ovate-lanceolate, distantly toothed, glands at base, smooth and shining, deep-green on strong short footstalks, emitting a ratafia odour when crushed.

*Analysis.*—A volatile oil, resembling the volatile oil of bitter almonds, and containing free prussic acid. The properties of the leaf depend on this.

*Actions and uses.*—Narcotic and sedative. Poisouous in large doses, owing to the prussic acid they contain. Used in spasmodic cough, and in phthisis; but it is better to employ the prussic acid itself.

*Aqua.*—Prepared by distilling the fresh leaves in water. Dose, min. v. to min. xxx.

**Limonis Cortex.** Lemon Peel.

Citrus Limonum D. C. The fresh outer part of the rind of the ripe fruit; imported from Southern Europe. N. F. Aurantiaceæ.

*Syrupus.*—Dose, f℈j. Tinctura, f℥ss. to f℥ij.

**Limonis Oleum.** See *Oleum Limonis.*

**Limonis Succus.** Lemon Juice.

Citrus Limonum D. C. The expressed juice of the ripe fruit.

*Charact.*—A slightly muddy yellowish liquor, with acid taste, and agreeable flavour.

*Actions and uses.*—A pleasant refrigerant in fevers, and useful occasionally in acute rheumatism, but it has been rated too high in this disease. At one time held in high repute for scorbutus, but now that we know the value of variety in diet, and especially of a liberal supply of vegetables, we depend less upon it. It is generally taken as a drink alone, or in the form of a lemonade, with any of the alkaline bi-carbonates.

**Lini Farina.** Linseed Meal.

Linum Usitatissimum Linn. The seeds ground and deprived of their oil by expression.   Useful in the form of poultice as an emollient.

*Cataplasma.*—Linseed meal ʒiv.; olive oil fʒss.; boiling water fʒx.   A poultice for inflamed parts.

### Lini Oleum.   See *Oleum Lini.*

### Lini Semina.   Linseed.

Linum Usitatissimum Linn.   The seeds; cultivated in Britain.

*Charact.*—Small, flat, oval, glistening, brownish seeds.

*Uses.*—A demulcent in dysentery and hæmorrhoids in the form of enema, and by the mouth in catarrh and urinary diseases.

*Infusum.*—Linseed 160 grains ; fresh liquorice root 60 grain; boiling dist. water 10 ounces.   Infuse one hour, and strain.   Dose, fʒj. to fʒiv.

### Linimenta.   Liniments.

These will be found under the different drugs.

### Liquores.   Solutions.

These also found under the drugs from which they derive their title.

### Lithiæ Carbonas.   Carbonate of Lithia, $LO\ CO_2$

*Charact.*—White powder, or small crystalline grains, alkaline in reaction, soluble in 100 parts of cold water.

*Uses.*—Diuretic, and very useful in gout, owing to its power of eliminating the urates.   In this respect it stands higher than the salts of potash.   Useful also in some skin diseases, such as urticaria. prurigo, and lichen.   Dose, gr. iij. to viij.

### Lithiæ Citras.   Citrate of Lithia, $3\ LO\ C_{12}\ H_5\ O_{11}$.

*Charact.*—An amorphous, white powder, deliquescent, and soluble in water.

*Uses.*—Same as the carbonate.   Dose, gr. v. to x.

*Liquor Lithiæ Effervescens.*—Carbonate of lithia gr. x. ; water Oj.   Along with $CO_2$.   Dose, fʒv. to fʒx.

### Lobelia. Lobelia.

Lobelia Inflata Linn. The herb in flower, dried; imported from North America. Indian tobacco. N. F. Lobeliaceæ.

*Charact.*—Stem angular; leaves alternate, ovate, toothed, hairy beneath; capsule ovoid inflated, ten-ribbed.

*Analysis.*—Lobelin—the active principle, a shining yellow hygroscopic substance, somewhat analogous to the active principle of tobacco; lobelic acid, gum, resin, fixed oil, &c.; more recently an oily, transparent, volatile fluid, lobelina (an alkaloid, possessing in minute doses the poisonous action of the plant) has been detected.

*Actions and uses.*—Emetic, expectorant, antispasmodic. It is a powerful narcotic poison. A teaspoonful of the powder, if not rejected by the stomach, may prove fatal. It is not much used in this country as an emetic, being thought somewhat dangerous. As an antispasmodic it has been used with success in the paroxysm of asthma and hooping-cough; in dyspnæa attending pulmonary emphysema, and organic diseases of the heart, and as an expectorant in bronchitis. In large doses, it causes violent vomiting —a burning sensation in the throat, followed by prostration, stupor, and convulsions. Coffin, an English quack, or his followers, can testify abundantly to these properties, many of their patients having been poisoned by its incautious use. Dose, powder, gr. xv. as an emetic. Gr. j. to gr. ij. as an antispasmodic and expectorant.

*Tinctura.*—Lobelia ℥ijss.; proof spt. Oj. Macerate 48 hours, and percolate. Dose, min. x. to fʒss.

*Tinctura Ætherea.*—Lobelia ℥ijss.; spirit of ether Oj. Dose, min. x. to min. xl. As an antispasmodic this is the best form.

In poisoning, give internal and external stimulants.

### Lupulus. Hop.

Humulus Lupulus Linn. The dried catkins of the female plant; cultivated in England. N. F. Urticaceæ.

*Charact.*—Greenish-yellow scales, with an adherent golden yellow powder at their base; taste bitter; odour aromatic.

*Analysis.*—Lupulin and a volatile oil (on which its efficacy depends); gum, lignin, colouring matter, &c. The lupulin is separated simply by rubbing and sifting.

*Actions and uses.*—A feeble narcotic and tonic. Used in medicine chiefly as a hypnotic in sleeplessness, connected with anxiety, nervous irritation, and delirium tremens, but not much to be relied on. A pillow filled with hops has long been a popular soporific. As a tonic, their power is not great; they are no more than a fair stomachic. Beer well impregnated with hops has been alleged to correct the lithic acid diathesis of profuse eaters of animal food.

*Extractum.*—Dose, gr. v. to gr. x.

*Infusum.*—Hops ℨss. Boiling dist. water fℨx. Infuse two hours, and strain. Dose, fℨj. to fℨij.

*Tinctura.*—Hops ℨijss.; proof spt. Oj. Macerate, and percolate. Dose, fℨss. to fℨij.

### Magnesia. Magnesia.

MgO.
*Charact.*—A white powder, insoluble in water, but readily dissolved by acids without effervescence.

### Magnesia Levis. Light Magnesia.

MgO.
*Charact.*—A bulky white powder differing from the foregoing only in its greater lightness.

### Magnesia Carbonas. Carbonate of Magnesia.

$$(MgO\ CO_2)_3 + MgO + 5\ HO,\ \text{or}\ (MgCO_3)_3.\ MgO.\ 5\ H_2\ O.$$

*Charact.*—A white granular powder; the magnesiæ carbonas penderosum of Dublin.

### Magnesiæ Carbonas Levis. Light Carbonate of Magnesia.

$$(MgO\ Co_2)_3 + MgO + 5\ HO,\ \text{or}\ (MgCO_3)_3.\ MgO.\ 5\ H_2\ O.$$

*Charact.*—A very light powder, found under the microscope to be partly amorphous, with many slender prisms intermixed.

*Actions and uses.*—Magnesia is laxative, antacid, and anti-lithic. As a laxative, it is very mild, and given chiefly to children, where it is also very useful in correcting the hyperacid condition of the alimentary canal which so often prevails. It is of great service in preventing heartburn and gastrodynia, given either alone or with a tonic or aromatic, a little before meals ; and it is beneficial in gout at times, owing to its antacid and antilithic action. As an antilithic, it acts by correcting acidity, and by forming the soluble lithate of magnesia, where free lithic acid or the lithate of ammonia prevails. Combined with rhubarb and ginger, it forms a good laxative and stomachic, long popularly known as Gregory's Powder. It has been used for solidifying copaiba, and as an antidote for arsenic. The carbonates of magnesia are the weakest. Dose, magnesia ; magnesia levis gr. x. to gr. xx. as an antacid and antilithic, thrice a-day ; as a laxative for adults, gr. lx.; for children, gr. iij. to gr. xij. Double the above of the carbonates.

*Pulvis Rhei Compositus.*—Rhubarb powder ℨij.; light magnesia ℨvi.; ginger powder ℨj. Mix well, and pass through a fine sieve. Dose, gr. xx. to gr. lx. as a laxative.

*Liquor Magnesiæ Carbonatis.*—Synonym. Fluid Magnesia. Prepared by impregnating water, in which freshly-precipitated carbonate of magnesia is suspended, with $CO_2$. One fluid ounce contains gr. xiij. of carb. magnesiæ. Dose, fℨi. to fℨij.

### Magnesiæ Sulphas. Sulphate of Magnesia.

MgO $SO^3$ + 7 HO, or $MgSO_4$. 7 $H_2$ O. Epsom Salts.

*Charact.*—In minute, colourless, transparent rhombic prisms, soluble in water.

*Actions and uses.*—A refrigerant cathartic, producing watery evacuations, without, in general, causing nausea or griping. It is well adapted for most forms of febrile and inflammatory affections. Dose, gr. lx. to ℨj. Its nauseous taste is well concealed by acid. sulph. dil.

*Enema.*—Sulphate of magnesia ℨj.; olive oil fℨj.; mucilage of starch ℨxv. M.

**Manganesii Oxidum Nigrum.  Black Oxide of Manganese.**

$MnO_2$.

A heavy black powder.  Used for yielding chlorine.

### Manna.  Manna.

Fraxinus Ornus Linn., and Fraxinus Rotundifolia D. C. A concrete exudation from the stem, obtained by incisions; imported from Sicily.  N. F. Oleaceæ.

*Charact.*—In yellowish-white stalactiform pieces, from one to six inches long, and one or two inches wide, porous, friable, and with a sweetish taste.

*Analysis.*—A saccharine principle—mannite—obtained by boiling in alcohol, uncryst. sugar, gum, and nitrogenous matter.

*Actions and uses.*—Mild laxative, and chiefly given to children, or along with other cathartics, as senna.  Dose, for children, ʒj. to ʒss.; adults, ʒss. to ʒj.  Mannite, children, ʒss. to ʒij.; adults, ʒss.

### Marmor Album.  White Marble.

$CaO\ CO_2$, or $CaCo_3$.

Used for the production of $CO_2$.

### Mastiche.  Mastich.

Pistacia Lentiscus.  A resinous exudation from the stem, obtained by incision.  From Turkey and the Levant. N. F. Anacardiaceæ.

*Charact.*—Small yellowish brittle tears; soft and ductile when chewed.

*Actions and uses.*—A drug of trifling value.  Once thought useful in leucorrhœa, and ulceration of the uterus; but now we know better.  An ingredient of " dinner pills," and useful for filling the cavities of carious teeth.

### Maticæ Folia.  Matico Leaves.

Artanthe Elongata Miguel, Comment.  The dried leaves; imported from Peru.  N. F. Piperaceæ.

*Charact.*—From two to eight inches long, veined on

upper surface; downy beneath, with a slightly astringent warm taste.

*Analysis.*—A volatile oil, tannin, and a resin.

*Actions and uses.*—Astringent; but for internal use it has proved almost a failure, hæmorrhages not being at all successfully arrested by it. It is a tolerable styptic in small bleedings, from leech-bites and incisions, but we have better ones.

*Infusum.*—Matico ʒss.; boiling dist. water f℥x. Infuse half-an-hour, and strain. Dose, f℥j. to f℥jv.

### Mel. Honey.

Apis Mellifica Linn. The Hive Bee. A saccharine secretion deposited by the insect in the honeycomb; British, and imported.

*Charact.*—A viscid brownish-yollow translucent liquid, with a sweet taste.

*Mel Depuratum.*—Clarified honey. Take of honey five pounds; melt the honey in a water-bath, and strain while hot through flannel previously moistened with warm water.

*Analysis.*—Grape-sugar, cane-sugar, acetic acid, mannite, wax, &c.

*Actions and uses.*—Demulcent, and slightly laxative. Used chiefly as an ingredient of gargles, for sore-throat, and aphthous ulcerations of the mouth. The mel. boracis is useful in aphthæ, and tenderness of the mouth and gums.

### Mezerei Cortex. Mezeron Bark.

Daphne Mezereum Linn. Mezereon, or Daphne Laureola Linn. Spurge Laurel. The bark, dried. N. F. Thymelaceæ.

*Charact.*—In tough pliable olive-brown strips, or quilled pieces, white within; taste hot and acrid.

*Analysis.*—A neutral crystalline principle contained in the inner bark—daphnin—an acrid resin combined with wax, sugar, &c.

*Actions and uses.*—A stimulating diaphoretic and alterative, once a good deal used as an antivenereal remedy, but now, probably owing to its acridity, as well as its frequent failure, seldom employed. It is very apt to disorder the primæ viæ. As a masticatory, Dr Withering found it serviceable in a case of difficult deglutition from paralysis. It is much employed on the Continent as an epispastic; here we believe in better ones.

*Extractum Mezerei Æthereum.*—Used in Lin. Sinap. Co.

### Mica Panis. Crumb of Bread.

The soft part of bread made with wheat flour. Used in Cataplasma Carbonis, and as an excipient in various pills.

### Mori Succus. Mulberry Juice.

Morus Nigra Linn. The juice of the ripe fruit; cultivated in Britain. N. F. Urticaceæ.

*Charact.*—Dark violet colour, faint odour, sweet acidulous taste.

*Actions and uses.*—Refrigerant and laxative. Proves a grateful drink in fevers, by cooling and allaying thirst. When too much is taken it is apt to produce diarrhœa.

*Syrupus.*—Mulberry juice Oj.; refined sugar lb.ij.; rect. spt. f℥ijss. Dissolve the sugar in the juice by a gentle heat. Add the spt. lastly. The product should weigh three pounds six ounces. Dose, f℥j. to f℥ij.

### Morphiæ Acetas. Acetate of Morphia.

$C_{34} H_{19} NO_6, C_4 H_3 O_3 + HO$, or $C_{17} H_{19} NO_3, C_2 H_4 O_3$. A white powder soluble in water and spirit.

*Uses.*—Same as the hydrochlorate, but not so trustworthy. Dose, gr. $\frac{1}{8}$ to $\frac{1}{4}$.

*Liquor Morphiæ Acetatis.*—Acetate of morphia gr. iv.; dilute acetic acid min. viij.; rect. spt. f℥ij.; dist. water f℥vj.

Dose, min. x. to lx.

### Morphiæ Hydrochloras. Hydrochlorate of Morphia.

Synonym.—Morphiæ Murias. The hydrochlorate of an alkaloid, $C_{34} H_{19} NO_6 HCl+6 HO$, or $C_{17} H_{19} NO_3 HCl. 3 H_2 O$. Prepared from opium.

*Charact.*—White flexible acicular prisms of a silky hue, with a bitter taste, and soluble in water and spirit.

*Tests.*—Entirely destructible by heat, leaving no residue. Gr. xx. of the salt, dissolved in ʒss. warm water, with ammonia added slightly in excess, give, on cooling, a crystalline precipitate, which, when washed with a little cold water, and dried by exposure to the air, weighs 15·18 grains.

*Prep.*—See Brit. Pharm.

*Actions and uses.*—Narcotic, sedative, anodyne, hypnotic. This preparation is a narcotic poison the same as opium, gr. x. having proved fatal. It is used for the same purposes, such as, subduing pain, allaying spasm, soothing irritability, and procuring sleep; and while, in general, in no way inferior, possesses certain advantages over that drug. For example, it does not, in general, constipate the bowels so much ; nor occasion so often giddiness, headache, sickness, impaired appetite, weight about the stomach, indigestion, and feeling of wretchedness ; nor is it so fruitful of excitement, apprehension, feverishness, and horrible dreams. Its taste also commends it, especially where we wish the patient not to know he is getting an opiate, being much less disagreeable. As a set off to these advantages, we have to note that the morphia is rather more liable to occasion an itchiness of the skin, with an eruption ; and irritability of the bladder, but only in rare cases. The injection of a few drops of a strong solution into the areolar tissue, is now a common, and, at times, successful way of palliating various neuralgic pains, such as sciatica and tic-douloureux. This salt, like opium and some other drugs, when continued for any length of time, requires to be increased in dose, the system, by getting habituated to it, tolerating more. Dose, gr. ¼ to gr. ss. When applied by the skin, the cuticle is removed by blistering, and a grain or so sprinkled over the raw surface.

*Liquor.*—Take of hydrochlorate of morphia gr. iv.; dilute hydrochloric acid min. viij.; rectified spirit fʒij.; distilled water fʒvj. Mix the acid, spirit, and water, and dissolve the hydrochlorate in the mixture.   Dose, min. x. to lx.

*Trochisci.*—Hydrochlor. morph.; tinct. tolu; sugar and gum.   Each lozenge contains gr. $\frac{1}{36}$ of hydrochlor. morph. Dose, No. 6 or 8 daily.

*Trochisci Morphiæ et Ipecacuanhæ.*—Same as preceding, with the addition of ipecac.   Each contains $\frac{1}{36}$ of hydrochlor. morph. and gr. $\frac{1}{12}$ of ipecac.   These lozenges are useful for allaying irritable cough.   6 or 8 daily.

*Suppositoria Morphiæ.*—Morph. hydrochlor gr. vj.; benz. lard gr. lxiv.; oil of theobroma gr. xc.; white wax gr. xx. Mix.   Divide into xij.

*Incompatibles.*—Astringent decoctions and infusions; alkalies and alkaline earths; earthy and metallic salts in general.

### Moschus.   Musk.

Moschus moschiferous Linn.   Native of Thibet and other parts of central Asia.   The inspissated secretions from the preputial glands, dried; imported from China.   Class, mammalia; order, ruminantia.

*Charact.*—Small reddish-black unctuous grains, with a strong, peculiar, and diffusible odour, and bitter taste; contained in an oval membranous sac, about 2 inches in diameter, covered on the outer side with stiff greyish hairs.

*Analysis.*—Ammonia, stearine, elaine, cholesterine, volatile oil, gelatine, albumen, an undetermined acid, and different salts.

*Actions and uses.*—Antispasmodic.   It is not much employed, being dear; but it does good in hysteria and in the hiccough and subsultus tendinum of fevers.   In chorea, its influence is variable or doubtful.   Dose, gr. x.

### Mucilagines.   Mucilages.

These will be found under the different drugs.

### Myristica.   Nutmeg.

Myristica officinalis Linn.   Suppl.   The kernel of the

seed; imported from Sumatra and the Molucca Islands. N. F. Myristicaceæ.

*Actions and uses.*—An aromatic stimulant, and carminative. Useful at times in vomiting. It is narcotic in virtue of its essential oil, in large quantity, and therefore contra-indicated in those who have an apoplectic habit of body, or a tendency to paralysis. Dose, gr. v. to gr. xx.

*Spiritus Myristicæ.*—Volatile oil of nutmeg f℥j.; rect. spt. f℥xlix. Dissolve. Dose, fℨss. to fℨj.

### Myrrha. Myrrh.

Balsamodendron Myrrha. Ehrenb. A gum-resinous exudation from the stem; collected in Arabia Felix and Abyssinia. N. F. Amyridaceæ.

*Charact.*—In reddish-yellow tears, somewhat translucent; odour aromatic, taste acrid and bitter.

*Analysis.*—Volatile oil, resin, gum, carbonate of magnesia and lime, and oxide of iron.

*Actions and uses.*—A warm stimulant and tonic. In small doses, it stimulates the stomach, promoting digestion. It has been used as an expectorant in chronic bronchitis, though not with anything like marked success; and it has occasionally done good in phthisis, probably by its combined tonic and expectorant action. It was at one time in vogue as an emmenagogue, and as a remedy in genito-urinary mucous discharges, but it has failed to maintain a reputation in these diseases. In consequence of its stimulant and heating nature, it should not be given where there is a tendency to inflammatory action. Employed also in the form of wash for tender mouth and gums. Dose, gr. x. to xxx.

*Tinctura.*—Myrrh, in coarse powder, ℥ijss.; rect. spt. Oj. Macerate 48 hours, then percolate; add enough spt. to make a pint. Dose, fℨss. to ℨj.

### Nectandræ Cortex. Bebeeru Bark.

Nectandra Rodiæi Schomburgk. The green-heart tree. The bark imported from British Guiana. N. F. Lauraceæ.

*Charact.*—In large flat heavy pieces, one to two feet long, two to six inches broad, about ¼ inch thick; greyish-brown externally, cinnamon-brown internally. Taste very bitter and astringent. Used for preparing the beberiæ sulphas.

### Nux Vomica. Nux Vomica.

Strychnos Nux Vomica Linn. The seeds; imported from the East Indies. N. F. Apocynaceæ.

*Charact.*—Nearly circular and flat, about an inch diameter, umbilicated on one side; ash-grey colour externally, thickly covered with short satiny hairs, internally translucent, tough, and horny; taste intensely bitter, without odour.

*Analysis.*—Strychnia and brucia, combined with igasuric acid, concrete oil, wax, &c.

*Actions and uses*—A special stimulant, acting on the medulla oblongata, and medulla spinalis; and a nerve-tonic. In poisonous doses it occasions violent tetanic spasms, without sensibly affecting the sensorium. Two drachms of the powder have killed in two hours, and even gr. xv. have caused death. Death may result from irritation in the alimentary canal, after recovery from the primary effects on the nervous system. Nux vomica is mostly employed for its stimulant and tonic action on the nervous system; and affects chiefly the motor nerves, as is seen by the twitchings of the voluntary muscles which it occasions when largely or protractedly used. Benefit is obtained by it in chronic paralysis, general and more limited; and it seems to have done most good in the former, and been more successful in paraplegia than hemiplegia. In paralysis of the muscles of the bladder, and in constipation (along with a purgative), arising from an atonic state of the muscular coat of the large bowel, it has been of signal service. A few rare cases of epilepsy have improved under it; and some have trusted it in prolapsus ani, nervous diarrhœa, and amenorrhœa. Dose, gr. j. to gr. iij. gradually increased.

*Formula.*—℞ Extracti nucis vomicæ gr. xii.; extracti rhei gr. xxiv.; extracti colocynthidis compositi gr. xxiv.

Misce. Divide iri pilulas xii. Capiat unam bis die. Useful for restoring tone in constipation from atony of the muscular coat.

*Extractum.*—See Brit. Pharm. Dose, gr. ss. gradually increased to iij.

*Tinctura.*—Nux vomica ℥ij.; rect spt. Oj. Apply steam to the nux vom. till it is softened, then dry rapidly, and reduce to powder. Macerate 48 hours, and percolate as usual, adding spt. to make a pint. Dose, m. x. to xx.

### Oleum Anygdalæ. Almond Oil.

The oil expressed in England from the almonds, bitter and sweet.

*Charact.*—Pale-yellow, almost odourless, with a bland oleaginous taste.

*Uses.*—Laxative, but chiefly employed externally, and for ointments.

*Ung. Cetacei.*—Spermaceti ℥v.; white wax ℥ij.; almond oil Oj. or a sufficiency. M. A simple dressing.

*Ung. Simplex.*—See *White Wax.*

### Oleum Anethi. Oil of Dill.

The oil distilled in Britain from dill fruit.

*Charact.*—Pale-yellow, taste acrid, sweetish, pungent smell.

*Uses.*—An aromatic carminative. Dose, min. i. to v. on sugar.

### Oleum Anisi. Oil of Anise.

Pimpinella Anisum. Anise. N. F. Umbelliferæ. The oil, distilled from the fruit in Europe. And Illicium Anisatum Linn. Star Anise. The oil, distilled from the fruit in China.

*Charact.*—Pale-yellow colour, and a warm sweetish taste. Concretes at 50°.

*Uses.*—An aromatic stimulant and carminative, and useful in flatulent colic and griping of children, along with a little magnesia. It is alleged to favour the secretion of

milk in nurses. An ingredient of the tinct. camph. co.
Dose, min. i. to v. on sugar.

*Essentia Anisi.*—Essence of anise. Oil of anise fℨj.;
rect. spt. fℨiv. Mix. Dose, min. x. to xx.

*Formula for Children.*—℞ Sacchari albi gr. cxx.; magnesiæ levis gr. lx.; olei anisi min. xii. M. A few grains
in milk.

### Oleum Anthemidis. English Oil of Chamomile.

The oil distilled in Britain from chamomile flowers.

*Charact.*—Greenish-blue, gradually becoming yellow,
with the odour and aromatic taste of the flowers.

*Uses.*—An excellent carminative in the flatulence of dyspepsia, and in pains of colic. Dose, min. ij. to v. on a bit
of sugar.

### Oleum Cajuputi. Oil of Cajuput.

Melaleuca Minor D. C. N. F. Myrtaceæ. The oil distilled from the leaves in the Molucca Islands.

*Charact.*—Mobile, transparent, of a pale bluish-green
colour; strong agreeable odour, and aromatic hot taste,
leaving a sensation of coldness in the mouth.

*Uses.*—Stimulant and rubefacient. A good deal used in
the East for chronic rheumatism, hysteria, gout, and nervous disorders. Was tried in Asiatic cholera, but did not
prove of service. Topically, it is employed in cases of rheumatism. Dose, min. j. to iv. on sugar.

*Spiritus.*—Oil of cajuput fℨj.; rect. spt. fℨxlix. Dissolve.
Dose, min. xxx. to fℨi.

### Oleum Carui. Oil of Caraway.

The oil distilled in Britain from caraway fruit.

*Charact.*—Colourless, or pale-yellow colour, aromatic
odour, and spicy taste.

*Uses.*—Carminative, and a corrective of other drugs, such
as aloes in the pil. aloes barb. Dose, min. j. to v.

*Aqua Carui.*—Dose, fℨj. to fℨij.

### Oleum Caryophylli. Oil of Cloves.

The oil distilled in Britain from cloves.

*Charact.*—Colourless at first, but gradually becoming red-brown, having the odour of cloves, and a spicy, hot taste. Sinks in water.

*Uses.*—Aromatic stimulant, chiefly used to flavour, and correct the griping qualities of other drugs. A drop or two into the cavity of a carious tooth often palliates toothache. Dose, min. j. to iij.

### Oleum Cinnamomi. Oil of Cinnamon.

The oil distilled from cinnamon; imported from Ceylon.

*Charact.*—Yellowish at first, gradually becoming red, having the odour and taste of cinnamon. Sinks in water.

*Uses.*—A warm stimulant, used principally for its pleasant flavour as an adjunct. Dose, min. j. to v.

*Aqua Cinnamomi.*—Cinnamon, bruised, ℥xx.; water cong. ij. Distil one gallon. A pleasant vehicle for other drugs, and an article of the mist. cretæ.

### Oleum Copaibæ. Oil of Copaiva.

The oil distilled from copaiva.

*Charact.*—Pale yellow colour, odour and taste of copaiva.

*Actions and uses.*—Same as copaiva, but not quite so effectual in most cases. It seems not to occasion so much nausea. Dose, min. x. to xxx.

### Oleum Coriandri. Oil of Coriander.

The oil distilled in Britain from coriander fruit.

*Charact.*—Yellowish, having the odour of coriander.

*Uses.*—Aromatic and carminative. Dose, min. j. to v.

### Oleum Crotonis. Croton Oil.

Croton Tiglium Linn. The oil expressed from the seeds in England. N. F. Euphorbiaceæ.

*Charact.*—Slightly viscid; brownish-yellow colour; taste acrid, odour somewhat nauseous.

*Tests.*—Agitated with its own volume of alcohol, and gently heated, it forms a clear solution, from which about ½ of the oil separate on cooling.

*Analysis.*—Crotonic acid, and a bland fixed oil.

*Adulterations.*—Castor oil; detected by its solubility in alcohol.

*Actions and uses.*—An intensely strong irritant and cathartic. In large doses it is poisonous, and even a few drops occasion severe hypercatharsis. It is a hydragogue cathartic, producing copious watery stools, and operating speedily. It is given for the most part in obstinate constipation, dropsy, comatose affections, neuralgia, convulsions, and apoplexy. In tic-douloureux, with constipation, common among some sedentary females, it is often of great service, so much so, indeed, as to have led some to call it a specific, in which view, however, we do not concur. It occasions an acrid sensation in the throat, unless given in the form of pill, well covered with powder. When given in apoplexy, or coma, a drop or two on sugar may be placed on the back of the tongue. It is contra-indicated in cases of debility, and where there is a tendency to inflammation of the digestive organs. Applied to the skin, croton oil excites inflammation, followed by a pustular eruption, and is therefore an active counterirritant. If applied to the face or scalp, however, it is apt, in some cases, to induce erysipelatous inflammation. Dose, $\frac{1}{4}$ to ij. min.

*Formula.*—℞ Olei crotonis gtt. ij.; extracti colocynthidis compositi gr. viij. Misce. Divide in pilulas ij. Dust well with powder of liquorice, or magnesia.

*Linimentum Crotonis.*—Croton oil f℥j.; oil of cajuput and rect. spt., of each f℥iiiiss. Mix. A strong counterirritant.

**Oleum Cubebæ.** Oil of Cubebs.

The oil distilled in Britain from Cubebs.

*Charact.*—Pale greenish-yellow, with the peculiar odour and taste of cubebs.

*Uses.*—Same as the powder, but hardly so effectual. Dose, min. v. to xx.

**Oleum Juniperi.** Oil of Juniper.

Juniperis communis Linn. N. F. Coniferæ. The oil distilled in Britain from the unripe fruit.

*Charact.*—Pale greenish-yellow, of a sweetish odour, and aromatic, hot taste.

*Actions and uses.*—A stimulating diuretic, of considerable power; used chiefly along with others. In renal disease, or in presence of imflammatory symptoms, it should be withheld. It quickly imparts its odour to the urine. "Hollands" owes its flavour and diuretic properties to this oil. Dose, min. iij. to v.

*Spiritus Juniperi.*—English oil of Juniper f℥j.; rect. spt. f℥xlix. Dissolve. Dose, min. xxx. to lx.

### Oleum Lavandulæ. Oil of Lavender.

Lavandula vera D.C. N. F. Labiatæ. The oil distilled in Britain from the flowers.

*Charact.*—Pale yellow, odour pleasant, like lavender, and a hot, bitter, aromatic taste.

*Uses.*—Stimulant and carminative, but inferior to others, such as peppermint. Principally used for giving an agreeable flavour to mixtures, and in perfumes. Dose, min. j. to v.

*Spiritus.*—Eng. oil of lavender f℥j.; rect. spt. f℥xlix. Dissolve. Dose, min. xxx. to lx.

*Tinctura Lavandulæ Composita.*—Eng. oil lavender f℥jss.; oil of rosemary m. x.; cinnamon, bruised, gr. cl.; nutmeg, bruised, gr. cl.; red sandal-wood gr. ccc.; rect. spt. Oij. Macerate the cinnam., nutmeg, and red s.-wood in the spt. for 7 days; then press out and strain; dissolve the oils in the strained tincture, and add sufficient rect. spt. to make two pints. Commonly known as red lavender, and given as an aromatic stimulant in sickness, flatulence, and dull spirits. It is useful combined with the aromatic spt. of ammonia. Dose, f℥ss. to f℥ij.

### Oleum Limonis. Oil of Lemon.

The oil expressed or distilled from fresh lemon peel; imported chiefly from Sicily.

*Charact.*—Pale-yellow, odour agreeable, taste bitter and warm.

*Uses.*—An aromatic stimulant, and used chiefly for imparting an agreeable flavour to other drugs. German oculists drop it into the eye in strumous ophthalmia, where it is said to be a useful stimulant. An ingredient of the spt. ammon. arom. Dose, min. ij. to v.

### Oleum Lini. Linseed Oil.

The oil expressed without heat from linseed.

*Charact.*—Yellow, with a faint odour, and oleaginous taste, and viscid.

*Uses.*—Emollient. Some prefer it to olive oil for mixing with lime water as an application to recent burns.

### Oleum Menthæ Piperitæ. Oil of Peppermint.

Mentha Piperita Linn. The oil distilled in Britain from the fresh herb when in flower.

*Charact.*—Pale-yellow, with the odour of peppermint; taste warm aromatic, followed by a sensation of coldness in the mouth.

*Actions and uses.*—A strong aromatic and diffusible stimulant, carminative, and antispasmodic. It is of great service often in this way, in gastrodynia, flatulence, and griping pains in the bowels. It is widely used for covering the taste, and correcting the disagreeable properties of other drugs. Dose, min. ij. to v. on sugar.

*Aqua Menthæ Piperitæ.*—Eng. oil peppermint f℥jss.; water, cong. jss. Distil one gallon. Dose, f℥j. to f℥ij.

*Spiritus Menthæ Piperitæ.*—Eng. oil peppermint f℥j.; rec. spt. f℥ix. Dissolve. Dose, min. x. to xxx.

### Oleum Menthæ Viridis. Oil of Spearmint.

Mentha Viridis Linn. The oil distilled in Britain from the fresh herb when in flower.

*Charact.*—Pale-yellow, with the odour and taste of spearmint.

*Uses.*—Same as peppermint, but not so strong. Dose, min. j. to v.

*Aqua Menthæ Viridis.*—Eng. oil of spearmint f℥jss.; water, cong. Ojss. Distil one gallon. Dose, f℥j. to f℥ij.

### Oleum Morrhuæ.   Cod Liver Oil.

Gadus Morrhua Linn.   The oil extracted from the fresh liver by a steam heat not exceeding 180⁰.

*Charact.*—Pale-yellow, with a slight fishy odour, and fishy taste.

*Analysis.*—Gaudine, oleic, and margaric acids, glycerine, traces of butyric, acetic, fellic, and choleic acids, iodine, chlorine, bromine, phosphorus, phosphoric acids, soda, lime, &c.   The therapeutical powers of the oil are due to the presence of iodine, bromine, &c.

*Actions and uses.*—Alterative.   Cod liver oil was long popularly employed as a kind of restorative in phthisis, and other emaciating diseases, but fell somewhat into disuse until about 20 years ago, when it was lauded in a book written by Professor Bennett.   There can be no doubt but that cod liver oil is of great service in scrofula and the diseases connected with it, such as glandular swellings, abscesses, disease of joints and bones, ophthalmia, tabes mesenterica, &c.   Some cases of phthisis have been benefited by it too, and chronic rheumatism.   It does not, however, deserve the very high encomiums that some physicians have passed upon it, to the effect that it would ultimately banish consumption from the land !   The fact is, that only a few adults are able to assimilate it, many more having to abandon it owing to the nausea which it occasions, and on account of its disturbance of the digestive functions.   Children, as a rule, tolerate it best, and derive most benefit from it.   It has been employed in the form of inunction as well as internally, but with doubtful benefit.   Dose for children, fℨj. three or four times a-day; adults, fℨss. to fℨij. thrice a-day.   The quantity may be increased considerably when the stomach becomes habituated to it.

### Oleum Myristicæ Expressum.   Expressed Oil of Nutmeg.

A concrete oil of an orange colour got by means of expression and heat from nutmegs.

Used in emp. calefac. and emp. picis.

**Oleum Myristicæ.**   Volatile Oil of Nutmeg.

The oil distilled in Britain from nutmeg.

*Charact.*—Straw-yellow, having the odour and taste of nutmegs.

*Uses.*—An aromatic stimulant, and used chiefly as a corrective to other drugs.  Topically it has been applied as a stimulant in palsy and rheumatism.  Dose, min. j. to v.

*Spiritus Myristicæ.*—Volatile oil of nutmeg f℥j.; rect. spt. f℥ix.  Dissolve.  Dose, min. x. to xxx.

**Oleum Olivæ.**   Olive Oil.

Olea Europæa Linn.   N. F. Oleaceæ.   The oil expressed from the fruit in the south of Europe.

*Charact.*—Pale-yellow, with little odour, and a bland oleaginous taste; congeals partially at about 36°.

*Adulterations.*—Poppy oil, cocoa-nut oil, rape seed oil. " Mixed with a twelfth of its volume of sol. nit. hydr., prepared by dissolving with a gentle heat, ℥iv. hydr. in ℥jxss. nitric acid ; if pure, it becomes in three or four hours like a firm fat, without any separation of liquid oil."

*Uses.*—Emollient and laxative.  Used for the most part as an emollient in the form of liniment and ointment, and as an addition to clysters in enteric inflammation and spasm. Used largely in the prep. of ointments and liniments. Dose, f℥ss. to f℥j., by the mouth, but seldom given ; in clyster, f℥ij.

**Oleum Pimentæ.**   Oil of Pimento.

The oil distilled in Britain from pimento.

*Charact.*—Colourless, but becoming brown when long kept ; odour and taste of pimento.  Sinks in water.

*Uses.*—An aromatic stimulant, but little employed in medicine.  Communicates warmth and flavour to other drugs.  Dose, min. ij. to v.

**Oleum Ricini.** Castor Oil.

Ricinus Communis Linn.   N. F. Euphorbiaceæ.   The

oil expressed from the seeds in England, or imported from the East Indies and America.

*Charact.*—Viscid, colourless, having a slightly nauseous odour, and a somewhat acrid taste.

*Tests.*—Entirely soluble in one volume of alcohol, and in two volumes of rectified spt.

*Analysis.*—Three fatty acids, ricinic, elaiodic, and margaritic. The active part or principle has not yet been detected, but is worthy of investigation.

*Adulterations.*—Seldom any now ; if so, easily detected by the above tests.

*Actions and uses.*—One of our mildest and most effectual cathartics, its operation being seldom attended by abdominal pain or irritation, though sometimes with nausea and vomiting. It acts on the whole bowel, occasioning three or four thin, but not watery, evacuations. It is an admirable laxative in hæmorrhoidal affections, in spasmodic and inflammatory diseases of the bowel, or urethra, in stricture of the rectum, prostatic disease ; during pregnancy and after delivery, in infantile disorders, and after surgical operations about the pelvis and abdomen. Dose, f3j. to f3j.

### Oleum Rosmarini. English Oil of Rosemary.

Rosmarinus Officinalis Linn. The oil distilled from the flowering tops.

*Charact.*—Colourless, with the odour of rosemary, and an aromatic taste.

*Actions and uses.*—An aromatic stimulant, used in hysteria, and for discutient fomentations. Dose, min. ij. to v.

*Spiritus.*—Eng. oil of rosm. f3j.; rect. spt. f3xlix. Dissolve. Dose, min. x. to xxx., but chiefly used in lotions.

### Oleum Rutæ. English Oil of Rue.

Ruta Graveolens Linn. N. F. Rutaceæ. The oil distilled from the fresh herb.

*Charact.*—Pale-yellow, odour disagreeable, taste acrid and bitter.

*Actions and uses.*—Stimulant and antispasmodic. Given in amenorrhœa, hysteria, colic, and infantile convulsions.

Externally it may be used as a rubefacient. Dose, min. j. to v.

**Oleum Sabinæ.** Oil of Savin.

The oil distilled in Britain from fresh savin. Juniperus Sabina.

*Charact.*—Pale-yellow.

*Actions and uses.*—Irritant, stimulant, emmenagogue. In large doses a poison ; in smaller doses, stimulates the uterus, and is employed in chlorosis, and amenorrhœa. It should not be given where there is a tendency to irritation or inflammation of the uterus or intestines. Dose, min. ij. to v.

**Oleum Terebinthinæ.** Oil of Turpentine.

Pinus Palustris, Pinus Tæda, Pinus Pinaster. N. F. Coniferæ. The oil distilled from the oleo-resin, turpentine ; imported from America and France.

*Charact.*—Colourless, with a strong peculiar odour, and bitter and pungent taste.

*Actions and uses.*—Anthelmintic, cathartic, diuretic, stimulant, epispastic. As an anthelmintic it often proves successful in tapeworm, operating by killing the parasite ; it is also useful in the lumbrici and ascarides. As a cathartic it succeeds best along with castor oil, and may be given in constipation resulting from cerebral disease, in spasmodic diseases, such as chorea, hysteria, epilepsy, tetanus ; in sciatica, lumbago, and other neuralgic affections; in purpura hemorrhagica, tympanitis, and passive hæmorrhages. As a diuretic it is not much employed ; but it is of service in gleet and chronic crystirrhœa, and, from increasing the quantity of lithic acid in the urine, it does good sometimes in gravel. It is contra-indicated if there be any inflammatory tendency. As a stimulant, it has been given in the adynamic stage of continued fever, in chronic rheumatism, in iritis, mucous hæmorrhages from defective vascular tone, and in neuralgia. Externally it is one of our most useful and effectual counterirritants. It is applied to the soles of the feet in the stupor of continued fever, in coma, apoplexy, and narcotic poisoning; over the chest in cardiac and pulmonary disease, and over the abdomen in peritonitis, painters' colic, and renal disease. It is also thrown up the rectum as an anthelmintic, and as a counterirritant in coma. Dose, cathartic, f3ij. to f3j.; diuretic and stimulant, min. x. to xxx.; anthelmintic f3ss. to f3j.; children, f3ss. to f3j.

*Confectio.*—Oil turpentine f3j.; liquorice powder 3j.; clarified honey 3ij. M. Anthelmintic. Dose, gr. lx. to cxx.

*Enema.*—Oil turpentine f3j.; mucilage of starch f3xv. Mix.

*Linimentum.*—Soft soap 3ij.; camphor 3j.; oil of turpentine f3xvj. Mix. Stimulant. Useful as a dressing for extensive burns when the vital powers are sinking; also in rheumatic pains and neuralgia.

*Linimentum Terebinthinæ Aceticum.*—Oil turp. f3j.; acetic acid f3j.; liniment of camphor f3j. M. A strong counter-irritant (called St John Long's Liniment).

*Unguentum.*—Oil turp. f3j.; resin gr. lx.; yellow wax 3ss.; prepared lard 3ss. M.

### Oleum Theobromæ. Oil of Theobroma.

Synonym.—Cacao butter.

A concrete oil obtained by expression and heat from the ground seeds of Theobroma Cacao.

*Charact.*—In cakes of a yellowish colour; about the consistency of tallow, of a bland and agreeable taste. Used for making suppositories.

### Opium. Opium.

Papaver Somniferum Linn. N. F. Papaveraceæ. The inspissated juice; obtained by incision from the unripe capsules of the poppy, grown in Asia Minor.

*Charact.*—Irregular lumps, from 3iv. to lb.ij., enveloped in a poppy leaf, and generally covered with rumex seeds; when fresh, plastic, tearing with an irregular slightly moist chestnut-brown surface, shining when rubbed smooth with the finger, having a most peculiar odour and nauseous bitter taste.

*Adulterations.*—Moisture, sand, stones, leaves, woody fibre, seeds, &c.  The best test of opium is the quantity of morphia yielded by it.  Christison says, a pound of good opium, treated according to the Edinb. process, should yield at least 10 p. ct. of salt.

*Analysis:*—

### 1.—Alkaloids.

| Substances. | Action. |
| --- | --- |
| Morphia ($C_{34}$ $H_{19}$ $NO_6$) . . . | Narcotic. |
| Codeia ($C^{36}$ $H^{21}$ $O^6$ N) . . . | Narcotic. |
| Narcotina ($C^{46}$ $H^{25}$ $O^{14}$ N) . . | Bitter tonic. |
| Thebaina ($C^{36}$ $H^2$ $O^6$ N) . | Stimulant, resembling Strychnia. |

### 2.—Neutrals.

| | |
| --- | --- |
| Narcein ($C^{46}$ $H^{29}$ $O^{18}$ N) . . | Inert. |
| Meconin ($C^{10}$ $H^5$ $O^4$) . . . | Inert. |
| Porphyroxin ($C^{66}$ $H^{36}$ $O^{23}$ N) . . | Inert. |

### 3.—Acid.

| | |
| --- | --- |
| Meconic acid ($C^{14}$ H $O^{11}$) . . | Inert. |

### Unimportant.

Bitter extractive, albumen, gluten, caoutchouc, lignin, salts, &c.

*Actions and uses.*—Narcotic, sedative, antispasmodic, hypnotic.  In large doses it is a narcotic poison, occasioning giddiness, stupor, depression of the circulation and respiration, relaxation of the muscles, contraction of the pupils, then deep stupor, and death.  These are to be met by the stomach-pump, stimulating emetics, cold affusion, ammonia to the nostrils, making the patient move about supported, internal stimulants, as brandy and coffee, galvanic shocks, and artificial respiration, maintained, if need be, for hours. In smaller doses, opium produces, first, excitement of the system, increased pulse and heat, with various very pleasurable sensations; then, in about an hour or so, fulness in the head, a benumbing of the limbs, disinclination to exertion, and apathy are experienced, and ultimately the flight of pain, and the advent of sleep. This sleep may continue from 6 to 12 hours, after which there is generally sickness, want of appetite, headache, languor, with depression and indisposition for any effort. Constipation and a checking of the mucous secretions also result. If approaching sleep be battled with and resisted, we may have a state of high excitement of the brain and nervous system prolonged for hours, during which there is an intensifying of the various faculties of the mind; excogitation, and speech becoming more original, profound, or brilliant; or, if the individual cannot be troubled with the application of his mental powers to any walk of study, he may indulge in the strangest fancies, and perform the oddest freaks. Other symptoms are observed, and probably due to idiosyncrasy. For example, some, instead of obtaining sleep, are rendered feverish and extremely miserable—with anxiety, restlessness, frequent pulse, headache, and horrible visions. Again, there is dry tongue, intense thirst, vomiting, discomfort of body, and wretchedness of mind. In some there is unusual susceptibility to the action of the drug, a small dose proving a powerful soporific; and this is almost always the case with children. Individuals, again, are to be met with who tolerate considerable quantities without experiencing the usual effects. Further, and this is of considerable importance, habit diminishes susceptibility more or less in all. The man who is merged into a deep sleep by a grain of opium, or 30 minims of the tincture to-day, may, if he continues to use it, require ten times that quantity in fewer months; and from an ounce to ten ounces of the tincture, is a common feat daily to the regular opium eater. This large quantity, however, is not partaken of with impunity. Each successive dose is followed by depression and misery, though productive for the time of perhaps pleasant feelings and mental activity; and the body also suffers: there is want of appetite, indigestion, and emaciation, sallow complexion, and often early decrepitude, and shortening of life. Certain states of the system, too, countervail or modify its action; larger doses are borne in most cases of extreme pain or spasm; in diarrhœa and dysentery, in the advanced stages of peritonitis and pneumonia, in uterine hæmorrhage, in delirium tremens (apparently at least), in tetanus and hydrophobia, and in some kinds of mania. Combination with other drugs also alters its action; it has fewer disagreeable concomitants when given with camphor; and along with ipecacuan, we may often safely extend the dose. The physiological action of opium is developed by whatever channel it may find its way into the circulation, whether by the rectum or mouth, vein, wound, or skin-denuded surface. But we must now come to the therapeutics of the drug. It is given, speaking generally, to procure sleep, to subdue spasm, and assuage pain. It is a valuable remedy in the advanced stages of pleurisy, pneumonia, peritonitis ; in gastritis, enteritis, dysentery, diarrhœa, and cholera. It is also useful in acute rheumatism, in gout (for allaying the pain), in spasm of the ureter or gall duct from the passage of calculi, in colic, neuralgia, tetanus, and hydrophobia. In continued fever, it is given to induce sleep, where there is watchfulness and delirium, without much vascular excitement, but here it should be given with care, and well watched. It is invaluable in the cerebral disturbance which sometimes occurs from the eighth to the tenth day of the eruption of small-pox; and in intermittent fever, a large dose at the beginning of the cold stage sometimes arrests the fit. Along with ether, it is of service in asthma; ordinary catarrh is often cut short by an early dose, and it is as yet the best remedy we possess in diabetes, that is, along with attention to diet. In rupture of the uterus, given speedily in full doses, it has at times saved the patient's life. Externally, in the form of lotion, liniment, plaster, &c., it is used to subdue pain and check inflammation, as in neuralgia, erysipelas, gout, rheumatism, &c., and up the rectum in piles, spasm, and tenesmus. It is also injected into the urethra, to allay pain, in ischuria, nephritis, spasmodic stricture, and urethral inflammation. Dose of the solid opium, or powder, gr. j. to gr. iij.

*Confectio Opii.*—Comp. powd. of op. gr. cxcij.; syrup f℥j. M. Dose, gr. v. to xx.

*Morph. Hydrochlor.*—See *Hydrochlorate of Morphia.*

*Emplastrum Opii.*—Opium, in powder, ℥j. resin plaster ℥jx. Mix. An anodyne in neuralgic and rheumatic pains.

*Enema Opii.*—Tincture of opium f℈ss.; mucilage of starch, f℥ij. Mix. Useful in dysentery, irritation of the rectum, &c. Opium acts in this way nearly as energetically as by the mouth.

*Extractum Opii.*—Dose, gr. ¼ to ij.

*Extractum Opii Liquidum.*—Dose, min. x. to xl.

*Linimentum Opii.*—Tincture of opium f℥ij.; liniment of soap f℥ij. Mix. An anodyne liniment for rheumatic and other pains.

*Pilula Saponis Co.*—Opium in fine powder ℥ss.; hard soap ℥ij.; dist. water, a sufficiency. Reduce the soap to a fine powder, add the opium with the water, and beat into an uniform mass. Dose, gr. iij. to v.

*Pilula Plumbi cum Opio.*—See *Acetate of Lead.*

*Pulvis Opii Compositus.*—Opium powder ℥iss.; black pepper, powder, ℥ij.; ginger powder ℥v.; carraway fruit, powder, ℥vj.; tragacanth ℥ss. Mix thoroughly; pass through fine sieve. Dose, gr. ij. to v.

*Tinctura Opii.*—Opium ℥jss.; proof spt. Oj. Macerate 7 days, strain, express, and filter; then add p. spt. to make Oj. Dose, min. v. to xl.

*Tinctura Opii Ammoniata.*—Opium gr. c.; saffron, benzoic acid, of each gr. clxxx.; oil of anise f℈j.; strong solution of ammon. f℥iv.; rect. spt. f℥xvj. Macerate for 7 days, filter. Commonly called Scotch paregoric. Anodyne and antispasmodic. Dose, f℈ss. to f℈j.

*Trochisci Opii.*—Contain ext. op. (¹⁄₁₆th gr. in each lozenge), tolu, sugar, acacia, liquorice water. Dose, 1 to 6 lozenges.

*Vin Opii.*—Ext. op. ℥j.; cinnamon and cloves, of each gr. lxxv.; sherry Oj. Macerate 7 days. Dose, min. x. to xl.

*Incompatibles.*—Plumb. acet., zinc. sulph., copper and iron, corros. sub., and astringent vegetable preparations.

**Os Ustum.** Bone Ash.

The residue of bones which have been burned to a white ash in contact with air.

Used in the prep. of calc. phosph. and sodæ phosph.

**Ovi Vitellus.** Yolk of Egg.

The yolk of the egg of Gallus Banckiva.

Used in mist. spt. vini gallici.

**Oxymel.**

Clarified honey ʒxl.; acetic acid fʒv.; dist. water fʒv. Liquefy the honey by heat.

**Papaveris Capsulæ.** Poppy Capsules.

The nearly ripe dried capsules of the white poppy, papaver somniferum Linn. Cultivated in Britain.

*Charact.*—About 2¼ in. diam., globular, crowned by a sessile stellate stigma.

*Uses.*—Chiefly for fomenting inflamed and pained parts, in the form of decoction.

*Syrupus Papaveris.*—Dose, fʒss. to fʒj.

*Decoctum Papaveris.*—Poppy capsules, bruised, and freed from the seeds, ʒjv.; dist. water Oiij. Boil 10 minutes, and strain. The product should be Oij. For fomenting inflamed parts, and painful swellings.

**Pareiræ Radix.** Pareira Root.

Cissampelos Pareira Linn. F. F. Menispermaceæ. The dried root, from Brazil.

*Charact.*—Cylindrical, oval pieces, entire, or split longitudinally, ¼ in. to 4 in. diam., and 4 in. to 4 ft. in length. Bark greyish-brown, longitudinally wrinkled, crossed transversely by annular elevations ; interior woody, yellowish-grey, with well marked, often incomplete, concentric rings. Taste at first sweetish and aromatic, afterwards very bitter.

*Analysis.*—Cissampelina, on which its activity depends, and which is an alkaline white powder; a soft resin, various salts, &c.

*Actions and uses.*—Diuretic. It seems to act specifically on the urinary organs, giving tone to the mucous membrane, and ultimately diminishing secretion. It is thus useful in chronic inflammation of the bladder. Dose, powder (but not a good form), gr. xxx. to lx.

*Decoctum Pareiræ.*—Pareira ʒjss.; dist. water Oj. Boil 15 minutes and strain. The product should be Oj. Dose, fʒj. to fʒij.

*Extractum Pareiræ.*—Dose, gr. x. to xx.

*Extractum Pareiræ Liquidum.*—Dose, fʒss. to fʒij.

### Phosphorus.

A non-metallic element obtained from bones.

*Charact.*—A colourless, wax-like solid, which emits white vapours when exposed to the air. Sp. g. 1·77.

Used for preparing acid. phosph. dilut. Phosphorus has been recommended strongly of late, with cod liver oil, in atony of the nervous system. It has been given in pills with suet, gr $\frac{1}{50}$th in each; also in the form of phosphorated oil.

### Physostigmatis Faba. Calabar Bean.

The seed of physostigma venenosum, from W. Africa.

*Charact.*—About the size of a large horse-bean, with a hard, brittle, shining, integument of a brownish-red colour.

*Actions.*—Narcotic and sedative. Used chiefly to cause contraction of the pupil after the use of Belladonna. Has been tried in tetanus with good results. Dose, powder, gr. i. to iv.

Extractum Physostigmatis. Dose, gr. $\frac{1}{16}$th to $\frac{1}{4}$.

### Pimenta. Pimento.

Eugenia Pimenta. N. F. Myrtaceæ. The dried unripe berries of the allspice tree, from the West Indies.

*Uses.*—Aromatic stimulant, little used in medicine.

*Aqua.*—Pimento ʒxvj.; water cong. ij. Distil one gallon. Carminative for children, but inferior to dill and anise. Dose, fʒj. to fʒij.

### Piper Nigrum. Black Pepper.

Piper Nigrum Linn. N. F. Piperaceæ. The dried unripe berries, chiefly from the East Indies.

*Analysis.*—Piperin, a neutral crystalline principle ; an acrid soft resin, gum, bassorin, &c.

*Actions and uses.*—A hot aromatic stimulant, but not much used in medicine.   Piperin in doses of gr. ij. to vj., every hour or two, has been lauded by some as a remedy in ague, and it appears to have succeeded frequently.   It is given in the form of pill with conserve.

*Confectio Piperis.*—Black pepper, powder, ℥ij.; caraway, powder, ℥iij.; clarified honey ℥xv.   Mix well.   Given in hæmorrhoids with debility.   Dose, gr. lx. to ℥iij.

### Pix Burgundica.  Burgundy Pitch.

Abies Excelsa.   Spruce Fir.   A resinous exudation from the stem, melted and strained ; imported from Switzerland.

*Charact.*—Hard and brittle, gradually taking the form of the vessel in which it is kept ; pale yellow colour.

*Adulterations.*—It is sometimes a mere mixture of turpentine resin and palm oil.   It should be without bitterness, free from vesicles, and give off no water when heated.

*Uses.*—An external stimulant, and useful for affording support to a weak part.

*Emplastrum Picis.*—Burgundy pitch ℥xxvi.; common frankincense ℥xiij.; resin ℥jvss.; yellow wax ℥jvss.; expressed oil of nutmeg ℥j.; olive oil f℥ij.; water f℥ij.   Add the oils and water to the frankincense, burg. pitch, resin, and wax, previously melted together ; then, constantly stirring, evaporate to a proper consistence.   As a stimulant to the chest in chronic bronchitis, and over the seat of rheumatic pains.

### Pix Liquida.  Tar.

A bituminous liquid obtained from the wood of Pinus Sylvestris Linn., and other pines, by destructive distillation.

*Charact.*—Thick, viscid, brownish-black, of a peculiar aromatic odour.

*Actions and uses.*—Formerly employed as a stimulant, diaphoretic, and expectorant, in chronic catarrh, and in the form of inhalation in phthisis and other chest complaints,

but now seldom used internally. It is one of the best remedies for external use in lepra, psoriasis, and tinea capitis.

*Unguentum Picis Liquidæ.*—Tar ℥v.; yellow wax ℥ij. An
excellent form for various scaly and pustular skin diseases.

### Plumbi Acetas.  Acetate of Lead.

$PbO\ C^4\ H^3\ O^3 + 3\ HO$, or $Pb\ (C_2\ H_3\ O_2)_2.\ 3\ H_2\ O.$

*Charact.*—In white masses of interlaced acicular crystals,
slightly efflorescent, having an acetous odour, and a sweet
astringent taste.  Its solution in water slightly reddens
litmus, gives a yellow precip. with iodid. potass. and is precipitated white by sulphuric acid, acetic acid being set free.

*Test.*—Its solution in dist. water is clear, or has only a
slight muddiness, which vanishes on the addition of acetic
acid.

*Actions and uses.*—Irritant, and a sedative astringent.  In
large doses, it occasions inflammation of the alimentary
canal, and the antidotes are sulphate of magnesia, phosphate
and sulphate of soda, emetics, and doses of castor oil and
opium.  When lead is conveyed into the body in small, but
protracted quantities, it induces a variety of effects, the
aggregate of which has been termed lead-poisoning, or
plumbism.  The symptoms are constipation, dyspepsia,
dejection of spirits, and fits of colic.  Ultimately apoplectic
symptoms may ensue, or paralysis of the extensor muscles
of the arms and fingers.  A blue line upon the gums is also
observed.  Painters, plumbers, and workers in lead are most
liable to this, and it is supposed that the carbonate of lead
is the preparation most likely to induce it.  The treatment is
abandonment of the occupation for a time, baths, tonics, iodide
of potassium, and the antidotes named above.  The diseases
for which acetate of lead is given are diarrhœa, dysentery,
and passive hæmorrhages, in which, by its combined sedative and astringent action, it is of great service.  In hæmoptysis, hæmatemesis, hæmaturia, and menorrhagia, it proves of
great use ; and it is often successful in the way of arresting
the profuse expectorations of some cases of bronchitis and
phthisis, together with the diarrhœa and colliquative sweat-

ing of the latter. It should not be too long administered where there is a tendency to dyspepsia or irritable stomach. Externally, in the form of lotion (often with a little opium), it is widely used in erythema, erysipelas, and superficial inflammations generally ; in ophthalmia, leucorrhœa, gonorrhœa, and in skin eruptions attended with inflammation. In ulceration of the cornea, it should not be used, as it is apt to produce an indelible white stain. Dose, gr. j. to v.

*Pilula Plumbi cum Opio.*—Acetate of lead, fine powder, gr. xxxvj.; opium, in fine powder, gr. vj.; confection of roses, gr. vj. Beat into a mass. Excellent for sedative and astringent purposes. Dose, gr. iij. to vj.

*Unguentum.*—Acetate of lead gr. xij.; benzoated lard ℨi. Mix.

*Incompatibles.*—Hard water, mineral acids and their salts, the alkalies, lime water, opium, iod. potass., tinct. galls, albuminous fluids, and many other vegetable infusions.

**Plumbi Carbonas. Carbonate of Lead.**

$2 (PbO, CO_2) + HO, PbO.$

*Charact.*—A soft heavy white powder, darkened by sulph. hydrog., insoluble in water, soluble with effervescence in dilute nitric acid, which solution is precipitated yellow by iod. potass., and white by sulph. acid.

*Uses.*—External astringent, and aids the cicatrization of excoriations and ulcerations. It sometimes does good in chronic eczema, and other skin diseases attended with itching and discharge.

*Unguentum Plumbi Carbonatis.*—Carbonate of lead, in fine powder, gr. lxij.; simple ointment ℨj. Mix.

**Plumbi Subacetatis Liquor. Subacetate of Lead.**

$2 PbO, C_4 H_3 O_3,$ dissolved in water.

*Charact.*—A dense clear colourless liquid, of alkaline reaction, and sweet astringent taste, becoming turbid by exposure to the air, and forming with mucilage of gum-arabic an opaque white jelly. Sp. gr. 1·26.

*Uses.*—External astringent, and applied in the same cases as the acetate. Should be diluted with 20 to 40 parts of water. Not used internally.

*Liquor Plumbi Subacetatis Dilutus.*—Solut. Subacet. lead fℨij.; rect. spt. fℨij.; dist. water f℥xixss. Mix. A useful lotion for superficial inflammations, and for the inflammatory stages of many skin diseases.

*Unguentum.*—Sol. subacet. of lead f℥vj.; camphor gr. lx.; white wax ℥viij.; olive oil Oj. M. Soothing and astringent application to superficial inflammations.

### Plumbi Iodidum.   Iodide of Lead.

PbI, or PbI₂.

*Charact.*—A fine powder of a golden yellow colour, tasteless and odourless.

*Uses.*—Seldom given internally. Employed chiefly in the shape of ointment to indolent ulcers, enlarged glands, and in skin diseases occurring in scrofulous persons. In porrigo capitis it seems to work much good. Dose gr. j. to iij.

*Emplastrum.*—Iod. Plumb. ℥j.; soap plaster and resin plaster, of each ℥iv.

*Unguentum.*—Iod. Plumb. gr. lxij.; ung. simp. ℥j. M. This has been used occasionally with temporary benefit in cancerous tumours.

### Plumbi Nitras.   Nitrate of Lead.

PbO, NO₅, or Pb (NO₃)₂.

Used for the preparation of plumb. iodid.

### Plumbi Oxidum.   Oxide of Lead.

PbO.

Synonym.—Lythargyrum.

*Charact.*—In brick-red heavy scales.

*Uses.*—Seldom employed by itself. Occasionally as an external astringent in excoriations and superficial ulcerations.

*Emplastrum Plumbi.*—Oxide of lead ℔iv.; olive oil cong. j.; water Oiijss. Diachylon plaster. A useful strapping for wounds, &c., and the basis of a number of plasters.

### Podophylli Resina.

A resin obtained from podophyllum, by means of rectified spirit.

*Charact.*—A greenish-brown amorphous powder, soluble
in rect. spt. and in ammonia ; precipitated from the former
solution by water, from the latter by acids.

*Test.*—Almost entirely soluble in pure ether.

*Actions and uses.*—Cathartic, cholagogue, alterative. This
drug, which has been extensively employed in America for
a considerable period, has of late had many patrons in this
country. We have bestowed some little attention upon it,
and do not think it so highly worthy of the encomiums bestowed upon it by a few distinguished physicians. As an
alterative, it possesses no great power ; for skin diseases,
secondary syphilis, and its varied concomitants, do not seem
to improve very rapidly under it. It seems, however, to be
useful, in the way of stimulating and improving the biliary
secretions, thus doing good in hepatic derangements of minor
importance ; the stools, tongue, and appetite, also sharing
in the amelioration. This benefit—these results—we think,
may be obtained equally well by means of aloes, or rhubarb
and taraxacum, not to speak of moderate doses of blue pill,
and without the tormina—the painful griping—often occasioned by this drug. It is somewhat uncertain in its action,
or else some are much more susceptible than others ; for
what will painfully operate on one, may not affect another.
Dose, gr. ¼ to j. in pill.

*Formula.*—℞ Podophylli resinæ gr. iij.; pulveris rhei
gr. xxiv.; extracti hyoscyami gr. xx. Misce. Divide in
pilulas duodecim. Dose, one or two. It is better to give
small doses, until it is seen how the patient bears it.

### Podophylli Radix. Podophyllum Root.

Podophyllum Peltatum Linn. The dried rhizome, imported from North America.

*Charact.*—In pieces of different lengths, about two lines
thick, wrinkled longitudinally, reddish-brown externally,

whitish within, breaking with a short fracture; accompanied with pale-brown rootlets. Powder yellowish-grey, sweetish in odour, bitterish subacrid, and nauseous in taste.

*Uses.*—Employed for preparing the resina.

### Potassa Caustica. Caustic Potash.

Hydrate of Potash, KO, HO, or KHO, with some impurities.

*Charact.*—In hard white pencils, deliquescent, and strongly alkaline and corrosive.

*Actions and uses.*—Caustic, and a powerful corrosive and irritant poison; antidotes,—vinegar, fixed oils, lemon juice. It is not used internally, but as a caustic for making issues. This is done by covering the part with several layers of adhesive plaster, and rubbing the potass on through an aperture in the centre. A poultice is afterwards applied, and when the slough separates, a pea is inserted. Owing to its deliquescent character, it is not so convenient a caustic for general purposes; it may, however, be employed for the destruction of tumours, and the useless and unhealthy parts of ulcers. Mixed with gutta percha, it is less apt to attract moisture; and equal parts of the caustic and lime, with a little glycerine, form an excellent dry caustic for the destruction of growths. *Vienna paste* is a mixture of caustic potash and lime, thus:—Caustic potash ʒv.; slaked lime ʒvj.; rect. spt. enough to make a mass.

*Liquor Potassæ.*

*Charact.*—A colourless transparent fluid, feeling somewhat soapy; odourless, of an extremely alkaline and caustic taste. Should be kept in well-stoppered bottles, as it absorbs carbonic acid from the air. Prepared by mixing ʒxij. slaked lime in lb. j. of carb. potash, dissolved in a gallon of water, brought to the boiling point in a clean iron vessel; and the boiling continued for ten minutes with constant stirring.

*Actions and uses.*—In large doses, a corrosive and irritant poison, destroying animal textures. In small doses it is antacid and antilithic, and is given in dyspepsia, attended with acidity and gastrodynia, where it is of considerable service. In the lithic acid diathesis, from its solvent power over the urinary deposits, and in the acidity of the stomach of gouty patients, it is often beneficial. It is given with doubtful benefit in chronic skin diseases, such as lepra and psoriasis; but probably with more success in some of the manifestations of scrofula. In gonorrhœa it diminishes the acridity of the urine, lessening the pain of micturition. Taken for some time, it diminishes nutrition, and is thus useful in some fatty diseases, and for promoting the absorption of redundant fat in those who happen to labour under excess of adipose tissue. Dose, min. xv. to lx. largely diluted in some aromatic water.

### Potassa Sulphurata. Sulphurated Potash.

Tersulphuret of potassium, K S$_3$ with sulphate of potash. Synon. "Liver of sulphur." Potassii sulphuretum.

*Charact.*—In solid greenish masses, liver-brown when recently broken; acrid to the taste.

*Actions and uses.*—Narcotic and irritant, occasioning inflammation of the alimentary canal, and tetanic spasms. In small doses, it was formerly employed as a stimulant and alterative in obstinate skin diseases, and in chronic rheumatism, but owing to its irritant properties, and want of success, it has been abandoned. It was at one time thought to be an antidote in metallic poisoning, but this has been disproved. It is now chiefly used in the form of bath in cutaneous eruptions, chronic rheumatism, and lead colic. The proportion is ℥iv. to cong. xxx. or so of water. Dose, gr. ij. to viij. in cinnamon water.

*Unguentum.*—Sulphurated potash gr. xxx.; prep. lard ℥j. Used in scabies with much benefit.

### Potassæ Acetas. Acetate of Potash.

KO, C$_4$ H$_3$ O$_3$, or KC$_2$ H$_3$ O$_2$.

*Charact.*—White foliaceous satiny masses, deliquescent, with a watery solution, of which tartaric acid causes a crystalline precip.; sulphuric acid, the discharge of acetic acid, and a dilute solution of perchloride of iron strikes a blood-red colour.

*Tests.*—Neutral to test paper, entirely soluble in rect. spt. solution, unaffected by sulphide of ammonium.

*Actions and uses.*—Cathartic and diuretic. It is rarely employed as a cathartic, but it is an excellent and widely used diuretic. In dropsies, especially ascites and hydrothorax, it is often beneficial; and it is generally useful combined with decoctum scoparii. Its influence in jaundice and some chronic skin diseases is doubtful. Dose, gr. x. to xxx., and as a laxative, gr. cxx.

*Incompatibles.*—Tartaric acid, the mineral acids, and their soluble salts.

### Potassæ Bicarbonas. Bicarbonate of Potash.

$KO\ HO\ 2\ CO_2$, or $KH\ CO_3$.

*Charact.*—Colourless right rhombic prisms, not deliquescent, of a saline alkaline taste.

*Actions and uses.*—Antacid, antilithic, and diuretic. Used for the same purposes as the liquor potassæ, but acts more powerfully on the kidneys. Dose, gr. x. to xx. as an antacid and antilithic; and gr. lx. as a diuretic.

### Liquor Potassæ Effervescens. Potash Water.

A solution of potass. bicarb. in water, with $CO_2$ pressed into it. A useful drink in rheumatic and other fevers, and in the lithic acid diathesis. Dose, f℥v. to ℥x.

*Incompatibles.*—Lime water, acetate of ammonia, chloride of ammonium, most of the metallic salts.

### Potassæ Bichromas. Bichromate of Potash.

$KO\ 2\ CrO_3$, or $K_2\ C_2\ O_7$.

Large, red, translucent, four-sided tables. Not used in medicine. Employed for preparing the soda valerianas.

### Potassæ Carbonas. Carbonate of Potash.

$KO\ CO_2$, or $K_2\ CO_3$, with about 16 per cent of water of crystallization.

*Charact.*—A white crystalline powder, alkaline and caustic to the taste, readily soluble in water.

*Actions and uses.*—Corrosive and irritant; antilithic,

antacid, and diuretic. Corrodes the mucous membrane of the alimentary canal, giving rise to vomiting (sometimes bloody), burning pain, and, provided death is averted, irritability of the stomach, indigestion, and emaciation. The antidotes are vinegar and fixed oils. Owing to its irritant nature and strong taste, it is not so much used as the bicarbonate, but it is an excellent remedy in deposits of lithic acid and the lithates. It is sometimes, in solution, injected into the bladder. Dose, gr. v. to xv. in a good deal of fluid, two or three times a-day.

*Incompatibles.*—Same as the bicarbonate, but sulphate of magnesia in addition.

### Potassæ Chloras. Chlorate of Potash.

$KO\ Cl\ O_5$, or $KClO_3$.

*Charact.*—In colourless rhomboidal crystalline plates, with a saline taste, sparingly soluble in cold water. Explodes when triturated with sulphur.

*Actions and uses.*—It were hard to give a short name to this drug; it is refrigerant, but it is much more. Phagedenic ulcers, such as cancrum oris, seem to improve under it, and in some cases of scarlatina, continued fever, and even malignant cholera, temporary advantages, at least, have been gained. The tongue will sometimes get clean under it, too, in infantile remittents, and other disorders of children, but it is not easy to say how. It is held by some to supply oxygen to the blood, and thus proves useful in malignant fevers with defective arterialization. Dose, gr. x. to xxx. in water, with a little syrup. For children, gr. ij. to v.; and in cancrum oris, this should be given every hour or two.

*Trochisci.*—1 to 6 lozenges.

### Potassæ Citras. Citrate of Potash.

$3\ KO\ C^{12}\ H^5\ O^{11}$, or $K_3\ C_6\ H_5\ O_7$.

*Charact.*—A white powder of feebly acid taste, deliquescent, and soluble in water.

*Uses.*—Refrigerant. Useful in gout, rheumatism, and scorbutus. Dose, gr. xx. to lx.

### Potassæ Nitras. Nitrate of Potash.

$KO\ NO_5$, or $KN\ O_3$. Synon.—Nitre.

*Charact.*—In white masses or fragments of striated six-sided prisms, colourless, of a cool saline taste. Deflagrates when thrown into the fire.

*Actions and uses.*—In large doses it is an irritant, producing inflammation of the alimentary lining membrane, sinking of the pulse, attended with sickness, vomiting, purging, and sometimes proving fatal. In smaller doses it is diuretic, and useful in anasarca and ascites, but not equal to the acetate or acid tartrate. It is also a sedative and refrigerant, and is in consequence of service occasionally in hæmoptysis. It is a good deal employed by some physicians in acute rheumatism, but for this it is not anything like a reliable remedy. When its use is continued for some time, it causes irritability of the stomach and nausea. It should not be given where there is an inflammatory affection of the kidneys, bladder, stomach, or bowels. Dose, gr. x. to xxx. In acute rheumatism, large doses, such as from 4 to 6 drachms, are given in the 24 hours.

*Nitre Whey.*—This is prepared by boiling gr. cxx. in Oj. of fresh milk, and straining. It forms a refrigerant drink in fevers.

*Incompatibles.*—Alum, sulphuric acid, metallic sulphates, sulphate of magnesia.

### Potassæ Permanganas. Permanganate of Potash.

$KO\ Mn_2\ O_7$, or $KMn\ O_4$.

*Charact.*—Dark purple, slender prismatic crystals, odourless, with a sweet astringent taste, soluble in water. A single small crystal suffices to form, with an ounce of water, a rich purple solution.

*Uses.*—Stimulant and antiseptic. Used for making the liquor, and for gargles and disinfecting solutions. Dose, gr. j. to ij.

*Liquor Potassæ Permanganatis.*—Permangranate of potash gr. jv.; dist. water f℥j. Dissolve. This fluid, diluted with water, is now pretty extensively employed (often under the name "Condy's"), topically, to foul or gangrenous ulcers and fœtid sores, and as a gargle in ulceration of the mouth and fauces; and these often improve speedily under it. It may be also employed as an injection to correct the fetor of dysenteric evacuations, and offensive discharges from the vagina and uterus in cases of malignant ulceration. The usual strength is f$\mathrm{3}$j. of the liquor, or gr. ss. of the solid, to $\mathrm{3}$ij. water.

**Potassæ Prussias Flava.** Yellow Prussiate of Potash.

Synonym.—Ferrocyanide of Potassium.
$K_2 FeC_6 N_3 + 3 HO$, or $K_4 FeC_6 N_6. 3 H_2 O$.
*Uses.*—Not employed in practice in this country. In America it was tried as a sedative, but did little good. Used chiefly for preparing acid. hydrocyan. diluti.

**Potassæ Sulphas.** Sulphate of Potash.

$KO SO_3$, or $K_2 SO_4$.
*Charact.*—Colourless six-sided prisms, terminated by six-sided pyramids, which decrepitate strongly when heated; sparingly soluble in water.
*Actions and uses.*—A mild cathartic, but not much used, being rather insoluble. It is a good purgative for women after delivery, if we wish to check the secretion of milk. Dose, gr. xv. to lx.

**Potassæ Tartras.** Tartrate of Potash.

$2 KO, C_8 H_4, O_{10}$, or $K_2 C_4 H_4 O_6$.
*Charact.*—Small colourless six-sided prisms. Heated with sulphuric acid it forms a black tarry-looking fluid, evolving inflammable gas, and the odour of burned sugar.
*Actions and uses.*—A mild cathartic, but not much employed. It accelerates the action of other cathartics, such as scammony and jalap. Also slightly diuretic. Dose, diuretic, gr. xx. to xl., purgative, gr. c. to cc.

**Potassæ Tartras Acida.** Acid Tartrate of Potash.

$KO, HO, C_8, H_4, O_{10}$, or $KH C_4 H_4 O_6$.
Synonym.—Potassæ Bítartras. Cream of Tartar. Ob-

tained from argol, which is deposited on the inside of wine-casks.

*Charact.*—A finely gritty white powder; crystallized on one surface; of an agreeable acid taste, sparingly soluble in water, insoluble in spirit. Heated in a crucible it evolves inflammable gas and the smell of burned sugar, and leaves a black residue.

*Adulterations.*—Alum, wheaten flour, starch, and bisulphate of potash.

*Actions and uses.*—An excellent mild cathartic, producing frequent watery discharges. Along with sulphur, it is a common and very suitable purgative in piles; and with jalap it forms an admirable hydragogue cathartic in dropsies. In small doses, largely diluted, it is also a useful diuretic. Dose, ℥ss. to ℥j., and as a diuretic, gr. xx. to xl. often repeated.

*Imperial,* a refrigerant and diuretic drink in fevers, is made by dissolving gr. clx. or so in Oj. boiling water, and adding a little sugar and lemon peel.

*Cream of Tartar Whey* is made of the same strength with boiling milk, the curd being removed. It is used for the same purpose, aud both may be taken at pleasure.

*Incompatibles.*—The mineral acids, alkalies, lime water, acetate of lead, carbonates of potash and soda.

### Potassii Bromidum. Bromide of Potassium.

K Br.

*Charact.*—In white transparent cubical crystals, with no odour, but a pungent saline taste, readily soluble in water, less soluble in spirit.

*Actions and uses.* — Calmative, sedative, alterative, deobstruant. This drug has had a somewhat variable career. At one time it had sunk so low in professional estimation that it was omitted from the London Pharmacopœia. During the past few years (so much for the changes produced by the whirligig of time), it has attained a reputation hardly equalled by any other medicine, not excepting its neighbour the iodide itself. Is there sound cause for this? does it possess virtues entitling it to the laudation it receives? We think that it does. Some medicines attain very great, but generally short-lived, renown, by a flaming puff from one or two individuals at most; but the bromide has reached its high and secure anchorage gradually, and by the sound support of many of our most acute, observant, and experienced physicians. These have found virtues in it which they look in vain for elsewhere. As an alterative and deobstruant, it cannot be placed so high as the iodide in strumous disorders, syphilis, rheumatism, neuralgia, and cutaneous affections; but in enlargement of the spleen and liver, in fibrous tumours of the uterus and ovarian disease, it operates with greater power. In the last-named malady, I think we may fairly believe it has enabled us to stay the knife of the ovariotomist, suspicious enlargements gradually softening down, and finally passing away. But this deobstruant action of the bromide is by no means its most important; it is as a remedy in nervous disorders that it so very much excels. It is a great nerve-calmative, possessing none of the evil after-effects attachable to those narcotics to which we were wont to resort instead. The following are the disorders in which its valuable properties are best seen :—In sleeplessness, whether constitutional or arising from pain or disease, as during acute ailments and fever. In nervousness produced by severe mental application, or agitation, and unrest of mind, or dissipation of diverse kinds. In functional or hysterical epilepsy (where it wards off the attacks); in delirium tremens, acute mania, nympho-mania, and melancholia. In dynamic or functional diseases of the larynx and lungs, such as hooping-cough, asthma, croup, and laryngismus stridulus. Of late, I have used it with the most cheering success in the spasmodic cough of children, whether due to centric causes, or reflex, as from the irritation of teething; and I think I have seen it alleviate the dyspnœa produced by a thoracic aneurism. In infantile convulsions, I have in one or two instances found it of much service in subduing and probably averting the fits.

In hydrocephalus, too, by its influence, sleep is obtained, and head pain somewhat relieved. On the ground that its beneficial action in respiratory disorders is due to its action on the pneumogastric, it has been recommended in disease of other organs supplied by that nerve; such as in irritable stomach. In dynamic stricture of the æsophagus, it occurred to me to try it in one case which came under my care, and benefit was conferred. In diabetes—a disease connected in some obscure or occult way with nervous irritation—it has proved of some little service, the urine becoming more normal both in quality and quantity. In Asiatic cholera, it has done some good in the way of arresting the vomiting and allaying the cramp in the earlier stage of collapse. On the footing also that exophthalmic goitre may have a neu-, rotic instead of a humoral (blood) origin, it has been tried in that disease with the favourable results of allaying the nervous symptoms, and subduing the palpitation. It is said to impair the strength of the generative system. Dose gr. v. to xxx. For children, I give 2 grain doses every four hours—that is, in oft-recurring spasmodic cough.

*Incompatibles.*—Acids, and acidulous and metallic salts.

### Potassii Iodidum. Iodide of Potassium.

KI.

*Charact.*—In colourless cubic crystals, readily soluble in water, less so in spirit.

*Adulterations.*—Occasionally with carbonate of potash; detected by nitrate of baryta, with which it gives a white precip. If iodate of potash be present, a blue colour is developed by the addition of mucilage of starch, or tartaric acid.

*Actions and uses.*—Alterative, deobstruant, diuretic, and an exciter of iodism, but possesses less of this power than iodine. Few medicines have been, or are still being, run upon so extensively as this one, it being the common resort of practitioners in disorders mild and grave, doubtful and obscure, after other drugs have failed; and yet it is some- what difficult to state precisely what it can do, and what it cannot perform, while admitting that it can achieve no ordinary amount of good. It may be employed for all the diseases for which iodine is given, and it is more agreeable to the patients, better tolerated by the system, and less apt to produce the peculiar and disagreeable physiological effects of that drug. It is serviceable in bronchocele, in scrofula, and its long train of disorders, enlarged glands, abscesses, osseous disease; and highly beneficial in articular and chronic rheumatism, dropsy, periostitis, chronic enlargement of different viscera, and neuralgia. In some forms of this latter malady, probably of syphilitic origin, we will obtain the most decided benefit when ammon., chlor., iron, quinia, beberia, and arsenic, have been tried in vain. But it is probably in secondary syphilis that we find the best results, and few at the present day would think of omitting it from their list of remedies for this disorder, if they did not, as is highly probable, resort to it at once. Ulcers improve and heal under it, swellings soften and vanish, sore-throat gradually ameliorates, scales and pustules drop from the skin, and caries more or less quickly gives place to healthy bone. Of late it has been very extensively employed in this city in cases of aneurism, and with undoubted benefit. I have witnessed several cases of well-marked thoracic aneurism almost cured by it; and one instance of abdominal which has been much under my own observation, has also improved considerably under its influence. It relieves better than an opiate can do the distressing pain of the malady; and it also undoubtedly favours coagulation and consolidation. How it does so is not easy to say; my own theory is that it acts as a sedative to the nerves regulating the bloodvessels, diminishing the tone of the muscular coat, and thus slowing the circulation. The force of the heart's action may also be impaired, and thus contribute to the small and feeble pulse which the drug induces. When the iodide is pushed too far, disturbed digestion may result; and there is often also headache, simple catarrh, articular pains, emaciation, nervous irritability, tremors, sometimes ptyalism, and there have been one or two instances of absorption of healthy parts, such as the mammæ and testes. Large doses, however, are often taken continuously and protractedly, without any other result than a little gastric irritation, and often not even that. In large doses it has been given with the view of removing the discoloration of the skin produced by nitrate of silver, but there is little to show in the way of success. More lately a strong solution has been applied topically and with benefit in lead palsy. I think the iodide is rendered more efficacious in some instances by a combination with iodine. Dose, gr. ij. to x. In aneurism and severe neuralgia, 20 to 30 grain doses may be given three or four times a-day. Give in water, or a bitter infusion, such as Calumba. The latter especially in those cases where disturbed or irritable stomach is likely to be occasioned.

*Unguentum Potassii Iodidi.*—Iod. potass. gr. lxiv.; dist. water f℥j.; prepared lard ℥j. Dissolve the iod. potass. in the water, then mix well with the lard. A few drops of caustic potash preserves this ointment, and restores its whiteness when it has become yellow. Useful for rubbing over enlarged glands and tumours, and to aid the internal action of the iodide.

*Ung. Iodi Co.*—See *Iodum.*

*Formula for Secondary Syphilis.*—℞ Potassii iodidi, gr. lx.; iodi gr. v.; infusi dulcamaræ ℥vj. Misce. Sumat cochleare magnum ter die.

*Incompatibles.*—Acids, and acidulous and metallic salts.

### Prunum. Prune.

Prunus Domestica Linn. The plum. The dried drupe; from plants cultivated in southern Europe.

*Uses.*—A mild laxative, and occasionally added to infusions of senna, into the confection of which they enter.

### Pterocarpi Lignum. Red Sandal-Wood.

Pterocarpus Santalinus Linn. The wood, from Coromandel and Ceylon.

*Uses.*—Used only as a colouring ingredient in the compound tincture of lavender. The essential oil in min. xxx. doses is pretty effectual in gonorrhœa.

### Pulveres. Powders.

These will be found under the names of the respective drugs from which they derive their name.

### Pyrethri Radix. Pellitory Root.

The root of anacyclus pyrethrum; imported from the Levant. N. F. Compositæ.

*Charact.*—Short tapering pieces, 3 to 4 inches long, about the diameter of the little finger. Externally dark-brown, internally dirty-yellow. Odourless, but when chewed causes a pricking sensation in the mouth.

*Analysis.*—Pyrethrin (on which its acrimony depends), gum, tannin, &c.

*Actions and uses.*—A powerful special stimulant, acting on the glands about the mouth, and producing a copious flow of saliva. Used for toothache with much benefit; in facial neuralgia with less success; in paralysis of the tongue with good results. In relaxed uvula it has also done good. For these purposes a bit is placed in the mouth and gently chewed.

*Tinctura.*—Pellitory root ℥iv.; spt. rect. Oj. M. Used alone, or with spt. camph. and chloroform, for toothache.

### Pyroxylin. Gun Cotton.

Used for making collodion and collodium flexile.

### Quassiæ Lignum. Quassia Wood.

Picræna excelsa. The wood from Jamaica. N. F. Simarubaceæ.

*Charact.*—In yellowish-white chips; intensely bitter.

*Analysis.*—A neutral bitter principle, quassin; lignin, gum, a trace of volatile oil, salts of lime, &c.

*Adulterations.*—Other woods resembling it are at times substituted. They are not so bitter, and their infusions are rendered black by the persalts of iron, while that of quassia is unaffected.

*Actions.*—A powerful and pure bitter tonic.  It is chiefly. employed in dyspepsia from want of tone of the digestive organs.  In the form of infusion it is a suitable vehicle for alkaline remedies in heartburn, and for saline cathartics in the constipation of indigestion from defective tone.  It possesses somewhat feeble narcotic properties.  An infusion in the way of clyster is a useful anthelmintic in thread-worm. It is not given in powder.

*Infusum Quassiæ.*—Quassia chips gr. lx.; cold dist. water f℥x.  Infuse for half-an-hour, and strain.  Dose, f℥j. to f℥ij.  As it is not altered in colour by iron, it forms a suitable vehicle for the chalybeates.

*Extractum.*—Dose, gr. iij. to v. in pill.

*Tinctura.*—Quass. ℥¾; proof spt. Oj.  Dose, f℥ss. to f℥ij.

*Incompatibles.*—With the infusion, nitrate of silver, and acetate of lead.


### Quercus Cortex.  Oak Bark.

Quercus Pedunculata.  N. F. Cupuliferæ.  The dried bark of the small branches and young stems ; collected in spring from trees growing in Britain.

*Charact.*—Covered with a greyish epidermis, cinnamoncoloured on the inner surface, brittle, and powerfully astringent.

*Analysis.*—About 20 per cent. of tannin, some gallic acid, sugar, pectin, and salts.

*Actions and uses.*—Astringent.  In the form of decoction, it may be used in chronic diarrhœa and dysentery, and in intestinal hæmorrhage.  Topically it is much employed as an injection in leucorrhœa, in prolapse of the uterus and rectum, and as a gargle in relaxed uvula and sore-throat.  It may also be applied to the flabby granulations of unhealthy ulcers.  It is, on the whole, an astringent entitled to more support than it has met with of late.

*Decoctum Quercus.* —Oak bark, bruised, ℥j¼.; dist. water,

Oj. Boil ten minutes, and strain. Dose, f℈j. to f℥iv. This is also the proper strength for injection, &c.

*Incompatibles.*—Same as tannin.

### Quiniæ Sulphas. Sulphate of Quinia.

The sulphate of an alkaloid, $C_{40}$ $H_{24}$ $N_2$ $O_4$ HO $SO_3$+ 7 HO, or $(C_{20}$ $H_{24}$ $N_2$ $O_2)$ 2 $H_2$ $SO_4$ 7 $H_2$ O. 7 HO, prepared from yellow cinchona bark, and from the bark of cinchona lancifolia.

*Charact.*—Filiform silky wool-white crystals, of an intensely bitter taste, sparingly soluble in water, yet imparting to it a peculiar bluish tint. A few drops of a dilute acid added renders it freely soluble in water. The solution gives, with chloride of barium, a white precipitate, insoluble in nitric acid; and when treated first with solution of chlorine, and afterwards with ammonia, a fine emerald-green colour is developed.

*Adulterations.*—Sulphate of lime, gum, mannite, starch, fatty matters, and sulphate of cinchonia. A solution of gr. x. in f℈j. dist. water, and two or three drops sulphuric acid, if decomposed by a solut. of ℥ss. carb. soda in two waters, and heated till the precip. shrinks and fuses, yields, on cooling, a solid mass, which, when dry, weighs 7·4 grains, and in powder dissolves entirely in solution of oxalic acid. If salicin be present, it becomes bright red on the addition of a few drops of sulphuric acid.

*Actions and uses.*—Tonic and antiperiodic. In small doses it strengthens the pulse, and invigorates the nervous and muscular system. Its most conspicuous and singular property is that whereby it arrests periodic diseases, especially intermittent fevers—a power not possessed in an equal degree by any other drug. How it operates in these cases is not known; it may be in virtue of its tonic property (yet other more bitter tonics do not succeed so well), or by breaking in some occult way more or fewer of the links of that chain of elements which may constitute the fevers in question. Not being able to account for or explain its
·eration, it is said to be a specific. In these diseases,

large doses are necessary, and it is given during the stage of intermission. In some cases, large doses, and even smaller ones, occasion headache, giddiness, nausea, pain in the stomach, flushed countenance, ringing in the ears ; and more rarely, numbness of the feet, blindness, deafness, and delirium. (Cinchonism.) It is contra-indicated in acute local inflammations, and where there is much tendency to vomiting or dysentery. Quinia, in small doses, is also an excellent tonic, not in cases of dyspepsia so much as in general debility, induced by protracted diseases and long confinement. It has, moreover, been employed for almost every malady under the sun ; tetanus, acute rheumatism, erysipelas, cholera, diphtheria, continued fever, delirium tremens, &c., but its success in these cases being extremely small and variable, it may be permitted to doubt whether, when good accrued, other causes had not a better title to credit. In the minor periodic diseases, such as neuralgia, headache, and other regularly-recurring pains, it is of great service ; and in some strumous diseases, such as ophthalmia, it is also highly beneficial. In debility connected with anemia, it is not equal to iron. Dose, tonic, gr. ss. to ij.; anti-periodic, gr. v. to xx.; and for smaller periodic diseases, gr. j. to v. It is best given in water with a few drops of dilute sulphuric acid. It should not be prescribed in the infusum rosæ acidum, as it is precipitated by the tannin in that preparation.

*Pilula Quiniæ.*—Sulphate of quinia gr. lx. ; confection of hips gr. xx. Mix. Dose, gr. ij. to x.

*Tinctura Quiniæ.*—Sulphate of quinia gr. clx. ; tinct. orange peel Oj. Dose, fʒss. to ʒij.

*Vinum Quiniæ.*—Wine of quinia. Sulphate of quinia gr. xx.; citric acid gr. xxx. ; orange wine Oj. Dose, fʒss. to fʒj.

*Incompatibles.*—The alkalies and their carb., lime water, tartaric acid, and infusions and tinctures containing tannin.

### Resina. Resin.

The residue of the distillation of the turpentines from various species of Pinus Linn. and Abies Lam.

*Charact.* — Semi - opaque, yellowish, brittle ; fracture shining ; odour and taste slightly terebinthinate. It is readily fusible ; burns with a dense yellow flame and much smoke.

*Uses.*—External stimulant ; used chiefly for giving consistency to plasters and ointments.

*Emplastrum Resinæ.*—Resin ℥jv. ; lead plaster lb. ij. ; hard soap, in powder, ℥ij. M. Stimulant, and for affording support to weak parts.

*Unguentum Resinæ.*—Resin ℥viij. ; yellow wax ℥jv. ; simple oint. ℥xvj. M. A stimulant to indolent and foul ulcers.

### Rhamni Succus. Buckthorn Juice.

Rhamnus Catharticus, Common Buckthorn. The recently expressed juice of the ripe berries. N. F. Rhamnaceæ. Black, shining, four-sided berries, with an acrid taste.

*Uses.* — Powerful cathartic ; producing copious watery stools, and occasioning a good deal of nausea and severe tormina. Formerly given in dropsy, but, owing to the severity of the drug, now little used.

*Syrupus.*—Dose f℈j.

### Rhei Radix. Rhubarb Root.

One or more undetermined species of Rheum Linn. N. F. Polygonaceæ. The root, deprived of the bark, and dried ; from Chinese Thibet, and Tartary.

*Charact.*—Roundish cylindrical or flattish pieces, frequently bored with one hole, yellow externally, internally marbled with waving greyish and reddish lines ; taste bitter, faintly astringent and aromatic.

*Analysis.*—Rhabarberic acid (rhabarberin, or chrysophanic acid of others), gallic acid, tannin, uncrystallizable sugar, starch, gum, colouring matter, pectic acid, oxalate of lime, iron, silica, &c.

*Actions and uses.*—Tonic, cathartic, and a feeble astringent, the latter property being overborne by the cathartic, and only coming into play afterwards. In small doses, it improves digestion and appetite, and renders the intestinal secretions more healthy. In larger doses, it is an excellent cathartic, acting on the whole bowel, and especially the duodenum, and increasing the peristaltic action. It is well suited for the early stages of diarrhœa, as a laxative in constipation from debility of the digestive organs, and in the disorders of children, such as flatulence and irritation of the alimentary canal. It is extensively employed in combination with bicarbonate of soda as an aperient and stomachic. It renders the serum of the blood yellow, and, while using it, the urine is almost of a blood-red colour. Dose of the powder, tonic, gr. iij. to v. ; cathartic, gr. xv. to xxx.

*Extractum Rhei.*—Dose, gr. v. to xx.

*Infusum Rhei.*—Rhubarb ℈¼ ; boiling dist. water f℥x. Infuse one hour. Dose, f℥ss. to f℥ij.

*Pilula Rhei Composita.*—Rhubarb powder ℨiij.; socotrine aloes, in fine powder, ℨij¼ ; myrrh powder ℨjss.; hard soap ℨjss.; Eng. oil of peppermint f℈jss.; treacle by weight ℨjv. Dose, gr. v. to x. They are purgative and mildly tonic.

*Pulvis Rhei Compositus.*—(Gregory's Powder). Rhubarb ℨij. ; light magnesia ℥vj. ; ginger ℨj. Mix well, and pass through a fine sieve. A stomachic powder, antacid, laxative, and mildly tonic. Dose gr. xxx. to lx., and for children gr. v. to x.

*Tinctura Rhei.*—Rhubarb ℥ij.; cardamoms, bruised, ℈¼.; coriander, bruised, ℈¼. ; saffron ℈¼. ; proof spt. Oj. By maceration and percolation as before. Dose, f℈j. to f℈ij., as a stomachic ; as a purgative, f℥ss. to f℥j.

*Vinum.*—Rhub. ℥jss. ; canella alba bark gr. lx. ; sherry Oj. Dose, f℈j. to f℈ij.

*Syrupus.*—Dose, f℈i. to f℥ss.

### Rhœados Petala.  Red-Poppy Petals.

Papaver Rhœas. N. F. Papaveraceæ. The petals dried ; from indigenous plants.

*Charact.*—When fresh, scarlet, and of a heavy poppy odour; when dry, scentless and more dingy red.

*Uses.*—Feebly narcotic, but only used for making the syrup.

*Syrupus Rhœados.*—Used only for colouring mixtures.

**Rosæ Caninæ Fructus.**  Fruit of the Dog-Rose.  Hips.

Rosa Canina Linn.  The Dog Rose; and other allied species.  N. F. Rosaceæ.  The ripe fruit of indigenous plants, deprived of the hairy seeds (achenes).

*Charact.*—1 in. or more long, ovate, scarlet, shining; taste sweet, subacid, agreeable.

*Uses.*—Refrigerant, but only used for the confection of hips.

*Confectio Rosæ Caninæ.*—Hips lb.j.; refined sugar lb.ij. Beat well together.  Used as a basis for pills and electuaries, and compatible with the persalts of iron.

**Rosæ Centifoliæ Petala.**  Cabbage Rose Petals.

Rosa Centifolia Linn.  The fresh petals, fully expanded; from plants cultivated in Britain.

*Charact.*—Taste sweetish, bitter, and mildly astringent; roseate odour.

*Uses.*—An agreeable perfume, and for making the water.

*Aqua.*—Fresh petals of the 100-leaved roses lb.x.; water cong. ij.  Distil one gallon.  A pleasant perfume, and useful for lotions.

**Rosæ Gallicæ Petala.**  Sed-Rose Petals.

Rosa Gallica Linn.  The unexpanded petals, and dried; from plants cultivated in Britain.

*Charact.*—Colour purplish-red, retained after drying; taste bitterish, acid, and astringent; odour roseate, developed by drying.

*Actions and uses.*—Mildly astringent, but chiefly used for their colour and odour, and as adjuncts to more active remedies.

*Confectio Rosæ Gallicæ.*—Fresh petals lb.j.; refined sugar lb.iij.  Beat and rub well together.  Feebly astringent. Dose, gr. lx. to cxx.  Used for the most part as a basis for pills, but should not be employed with the persalts of iron.

owing to the tannin it contains.  Also as a linctus in sore-mouth.

*Infusum Rosæ Acidum.*—Red-rose petals ʒss.; dilute sulphuric acid fʒj.; boiling dist. water fʒx.  Infuse half-an-hour, and strain.  A pleasant refrigerant, and feebly astringent.  Dose, fʒss. to fʒij.  A good vehicle also for the neutral laxative salts.

*Syrupus Rosæ Gallicæ.*—Dried petals ʒij.; refined sugar ʒxxx.; boiling dist. water Oj.; filter, then dissolve the sugar by means of heat.  Used for flavouring and colouring purposes.  Dose, fʒj.

*Incompatibles.*—Same as under tannin.

### Sabadilla.  Cevadilla.

Asagræa Officinalis.  N. F.  The dried fruit; imported from Vera Cruz and Mexico.

*Charact.*—Fruit about ½ in. long, consisting of 3 light-brown papyraceous follicles, each containing from 1 to 3 seeds, which are about ¼ in. long, blackish-brown, shining, with an acrid bitter taste.

*Analysis.*—Cevadic acid, fatty matter, wax, veratria in union with gallic acid, gum, colouring matter, and sab-adilline.

*Actions and uses.*—Anthelmintic, stimulant, cathartic, but also highly poisonous.  It is employed on the Continent in tape-worm and ascarides; and as an external stimulant in chronic rheumatism and paralysis, and for destroying pediculi.  It is used for preparing veratria.  Its internal use requires the utmost caution.  Dose, powder of the seeds, gr. j. to ij. for children, followed by a little castor oil; adults, gr. vj. or so.

*Prep. Veratria.*—See *Veratria.*

### Sabinæ Cacumina.  Savin Tops.

Juniperus Sabina Linn.  The fresh and dried tops; collected in spring, from plants cultivated in Britain.

*Charact.*—Twigs densely covered with minute imbricated

appressed leaves in four rows ; odour strong ; taste acrid, bitter, resinous, and disagreeable.

*Analysis.*—Resin, volatile oil, on which its properties depend ; gallic acid, extractive, &c.

*Actions and uses.*—Emmenagogue, and irritant. It has a stimulating effect on the uterus, and is occasionally employed in amenorrhœa with chlorosis. Being poisonous, however, its use demands caution, and it should not be employed where there is a tendency to inflammation of the uterus or pelvic viscera. Savin is occasionally surreptitiously used in order to produce abortion, but serious risk to life may be occasioned without the accomplishment of the cherished object. In cases of poisoning, use emetics, afterwards demulcents, opiates, and general antiphlogistic treatment. Externally, the ointment is employed as an irritant to keep up discharges from a blistered surface, making a kind of chronic blister. Dose, powder, gr. iv. to x.

*Tinctura Sabinæ.*—Savin ℥ijss.; proof spt. Oj. Proceed in the usual way. Dose, xx. to lx.

*Unguentum Sabinæ.*—Fresh savin, bruised, ℥viij.; white wax ℥iij.; prepared lard ℥xvj. Melt the lard and wax together, add the savin, and digest 20 minutes. Then remove the mixture, and impress through calico. Useful for keeping issues and blisters open.

*Sabinæ Oleum.*—See *Oleum Sabinæ.*

### Saccharum Purificatum. Refined Sugar.

$C_{24} H_{22} O_{22}$, or $C_{12} H_{22} O_{11}$.

Saccharum Officinarum Linn. The crystallized refined juice of the stem; from plants cultivated in the West Indies, &c.

*Uses.*—Nutritive, emollient, and demulcent. Used in coughs, in irritant poisoning, and for making syrups, lozenges, confections, &c.

*Syrupus.*—Refined sugar lb. v.; dist. water Oij. Dissolve with the aid of heat. Used for suspending insoluble substances, and as an agreeable adjunct to mixtures.

### Saccharum Lactis.  Sugar of Milk.

$C_{24} H_{24} O_{24}$, or $C_{12} H_{24} O_{12}$.

Crystallized sugar, obtained from the whey of cow's milk by evaporation.

*Uses.*—Employed in medicine as an excipient for active drugs, such as calomel.  Also as an article of diet.

### Sambuci Flores.  Elder Flowers.

Sambucus Nigra Linn.  N. F. Caprifoliaceæ.  The fresh flowers, from indigenous plants.

*Charact.*—Flowers small, white, odorous, crowded in large cymes.

*Uses.*—Mildly emollient, used for preparing the aqua.

*Aqua Sambuci.*—Fresh elder flowers, separated from the stalks, lb. x.; water cong. ij.  Distil one gallon.  Used generally as a vehicle for alkalies in cutaneous diseases, in collyria, and as a perfume.

### Santonica.  Santonica.

The unexpanded flower-heads of an undetermined species of Artemisia Linn.  Imported from Russia.

*Charact.*—Flower-heads rather over a line long, and nearly ¼ line broad, fusiform, blunt at each end, greenish-brown, smooth, resembling seeds in appearance, but consisting of imbricated involucral scales with a green midrib, enclosing 4 or 5 tubular flowers; odour strong, taste camphoraceous.

*Actions and uses.*—Anthelmintic, and adapted for ascarides and lumbrici; but it has not been much used for a long time, and has now been displaced by its active principle santonin.  Dose of the powder, gr. x. to xxx., in milk or honey.  A purgative should be given the following day.

### Santoninum.  Santonin.

$C_{30} H_{18} O_{6}$, or $C_{15} H_{18} O_{3}$.

A crystalline neutral principle, obtained from santonica.

*Charact.*—White flat rhombic prisms, almost tasteless, fusible and sublimable by a moderate heat; scarcely soluble in cold water, sparingly in boiling water, but freely in chloroform and in boiling rect. spt. Becomes yellow by exposure.

*Prep.*—See Brit. Pharm.

*Actions and uses.*—An excellent anthelmintic in ascarides and lumbrici. Formerly, I was in the habit of combining the santonine with scammony, calomel, and a little ginger; and though a powder of this kind was successful in expelling the worms, I am now of opinion that it should be given alone, or simply along with a little sugar. The powder of scammony, &c., should follow after the last dose. Dose, gr. j. to iij. every night for three nights.

### Sapo Durus. Hard Soap.

Soap made with olive oil and soda. Used in various pills and plasters. Slightly laxative.

### Sapo Mollis. Soft Soap.

Soap made with olive oil and potash.

*Uses.*—For liniment, terebinth.

*Emplastrum Saponis.*—Hard soap ℥vj.; litharge plaster, lb. ij¼., resin ℥j. M. For affording protection and support to tender parts.

*Linimentum Saponis.*—Hard soap ℥ijss.; camphor ℥j¼.; Eng. oil. rosemary f℥iij.; rect. spt. f℥xviij.; dist. water f℥ij. M. Soap liniment. (Opodeldoc.) An external stimulant in chronic swellings, rheumatism, and sprains.

### Sarsæ Radix. Jamaica Sarsaparilla.

Smilax Officinalis Humb. and Bonpl. N. F. Similaceæ. The dried root; native of Central America, imported from Jamaica.

*Charact.*—Roots, size of a goose-quill, generally many feet in length, reddish-brown, covered with rootlets, and folded in bundles about 18 inches long; scentless; taste mucilaginous, feebly bitterish, faintly acrid.

*Analysis.*—A white crystallizable neutral principle, smilacin, volatile oil (lost in drying), acrid bitter resin, lignin, starch, &c.

*Actions and uses.*—Diaphoretic, tonic, and alterative. Much discrepancy of opinion exists in regard to the therapeutic actions of this drug, but it seems to possess, when fresh, no insignificant power. It is given in scrofula and secondary syphilis, and the concomitants of these diseases, such as ulcers, cutaneous eruptions, nodes, indurated glands, caries, necrosis, articular swellings, and rheumatism, often improve under a protracted course of it. We are well aware that it has often been employed for months in strumous and syphilitic cases, without apparent benefit; but this may have been owing to inert specimens of the drug, the active part being easily expelled. This want of success has led many eminent men to doubt its virtues, and if they employ it at all, it is only as a vehicle for more active alteratives, such as the iodide of potassium. There are others who, sceptical in regard to its alterative or anti-syphilitic powers, still think it a kind of restorative after an exhausting course of mercury (a line of practice not now common), or in cases of debility from grave strumous disease; and some believe it capable of strengthening the generative powers. Dose, powder, but a bad form, gr. lx. to cxx.

*Decoctum Sarsæ.*—Jamaica sarsaparilla, not split, ℥ijss.; boiling dist. water Ojss. Digest for an hour, boil for ten minutes in a covered vessel, strain. The product should be Oj. Dose, f℥iij. three or four times a-day.

*Decoctum Sarsæ Compositum.*—Jam. sarsap. ℥ijss.; sassafras chips ℥¼.; guaiac wood turnings ℥¼.; fresh liquorice root ℥¼.; mezereon gr. lx.; boiling dist. water Ojss. Digest. Prepare as the last. The product should be Oj. Dose, f℥jv. three or four times a-day.

*Extractum Sarsæ Liquidum.*—Dose, f℥ij. to f℥ss.

*Incompatibles.*—Acetate of lead, and lime water.

### Sassafras Radix. Sassafras Root.

Sassafras Officinale Nees. N. F. Lauraceæ. The dried root; from North America.

*Charact.*—In branched pieces, sometimes 8 in. in diam.

at the crown; bark externally greyish-brown, internally rusty-brown; of a warm aromatic taste, and pleasant odour. Also in chips.

*Analysis.*—A volatile oil, tannin, &c.

*Actions and uses.*—Diaphoretic, but not much employed. A constituent of decoct. sarsæ co. An infusion may be made, ʒj. to Oj. water, the dose of which is fʒij. to fʒiv.

### Scammoniæ Radix. Scammony Root.

Convulvus Scammonia Linn. N. F. Convolvulaceæ. The dried root ; from Syria.

*Charact.*—Tap-shaped roots, sometimes 3 in. diam. at the top ; brown without, white within, tasteless. Ether agitated with the powder, and evaporated, leaves a residue having the properties of scammony resin.

*Uses.*—For making the resin of scammony.

### Scammoniæ Resina. Resin of Scammony.

A resin obtained by means of rect. spt. from scammony root or scammony.

*Charact.*—In brownish translucent pieces, brittle, resinous in fracture, of a fragrant odour, if prepared from the root.

*Tests.*—It cannot form singly an emulsion with water. Its tincture does not render the fresh cut surface of a potato blue. Dissolved entirely by ether.

*Actions and uses.*—This preparation, which must be distinguished from the gum-resin scammony (from which it may also be prepared), is a drastic cathartic, and much prized for its purity, scammony having been much adulterated. It produces copious watery discharges, and is useful in dropsies, and along with other cathartics, in habitual constipation. Being easily disguised in milk, &c., it is well adapted for children. Dose, gr. iij. to viij.; and for children, gr. ss. to ij.

*Mistura Scammonii.*—Resin of scammony gr. iv.; milk fʒij. Triturate, and mix gradually and well. An excellent cathartic, the milk covering the taste of the resin. Dose, fʒij. to fʒiv.; and for children, fʒss. to fʒij.

### Scammonium. Scammony.

Convolvulvus Scammonia Linn.   N. F. Convolvulaceæ.
A gum-resin, obtained by incision from the living root, in
Syria.

*Charact.*—Ash-grey, and rough exernally ; fresh fracture
resinous, shining, black when dry, odour and flavour
cheesy; causes, when chewed, a prickly sensation in the
back of the throat; easily triturated into a dirty-grey
powder, and converted with water into a smooth emulsion.

*Analysis.*—About 76 per cent of resin, 10 per cent gum,
starch, moisture, woody fibre, &c.   The resin is the active
part.

*Adulterations.*—This drug has been very much adulterated.   The substances are chalk, gum tragacanth, flour,
guaiacum resin.

*Tests.*—Does not effervesce with hydrochloric acid.   Boiling water agitated with the powder, cooled and filtered,
does not strike a blue colour with tincture of iodine.   Ether
removes from 80 to 90 per cent of resin ; and what remains
is chiefly soluble gum, with a little moisture.

*Actions and uses.*—A drastic cathartic, producing copious
watery evacuations, and griping a good deal.   It is generally
combined with other purgatives, as in the compound colocynth pill, and thus forms an excellent cathartic in torpidity of the intestines, head affections, and dropsies.
Along with a little calomel, it is often given to children,
in worms and other disorders.   Dose, if pure, gr. viij. to x.;
and for children, gr. j. to iij.

*Confectio.*—Scammony powder ℥iij.; ginger ℥iss.; oil of
carraway f℈j.; oil of cloves f℈ss.; syrup f℥iij.; clarified
honey ℥iss.   Dose, gr. x. to xxx.

*Pulvis Scammonii Compositus.*—Scammony ℥jv.; jalap
℥iij.; ginger ℥j.   Mix well, and pass through a fine sieve.
A hydragogue cathartic.   Dose, gr. x. to xx.; for children,
gr. iij. to v.

*Incompatibles.*—Acids.

### Scilla. Squill.

Urginea Scilla Steinheil. N. F. Liliaceæ. The bulb; from the Mediterranean coasts; sliced and dried.

*Charact.*—Pear-shaped, from ¼ to 4 pounds in weight; outer scales membraneous, brownish-red, or white; inner scales thick, whitish, fleshy, juicy; taste mucilaginous, strongly and disagreeably bitter, somewhat acrid.

*Analysis.*—An intensely bitter, uncrystallizable, semi-transparent substance, named scillitine; an acrid poisonous resinoid substance, a fatty matter, sugar, mucus, citrate of lime.

*Actions and uses.*—Diuretic, expectorant, emetic, cathartic, and a narcotico-acrid poison. In large doses, it produces inflammation of the alimentary and urinary canals, and gr. xxjv. have proved fatal. As an emetic or cathartic, it is seldom given, being less certain and suitable than many others we possess. It is a good deal employed, along with others, such as digitalis, juniper, and spt. of nitrous ether, as a diuretic in dropsies; and it succeeds better in general than in local effusions, and in asthenic cases, indeed, it is not admissible where inflammatory symptoms are present. A little calomel, or a saline purgative, also favours its operation. It is one of our most common and efficient expectorants, and is useful in chronic bronchitis, and pneumonia, and in the viscid sputa of other chest affections. In some few cases it exerts its irritant action unusually (it may be owing to idiosyncrasy), not only on the alimentary canal, but also on the bronchial mucous membrane; here the addition of a little opium or hydrochlorate of morphia answers admirably, both in the way of prevention and cure. Some physicians believe it admissible even in acute chest diseases, but if given alone in these cases, it is rather apt to aggravate matters; combined, however, with opium and ipecacuan, it answers very well. Dose, as a diuretic and expectorant, powder, gr. j. to iij.

*Acetum Scillæ.*—Squill, bruised, ℥iiss.; diluted acetic acid Oj.; proof spt. f℥iss.; macerate the squill in the acid seven days, strain and add the spt. Dose, min. xv. to xl.

*Pilula Scillæ Composita.*—Squill, in fine powder, ℨj¼.; ginger ℨj.; ammoniac ℨj.; hard soap ℨj.; treacle ℨij.; or a sufficiency. Mix. An expectorant pill. Dose, gr. v. to x.

*Syrupus Scillæ.*—Vinegar of squill Oj.; refined sugar lbs. ijss. Dissolve with the aid of heat. Dose, fℨss. to fℨj.

*Tinctura Scillæ.*—Squill, ℥ijss.; proof spt., Oj. M. Proceed in the usual way. This is commonly prescribed in diuretic mixtures, such as in decoctum scoparii. Dose, min. x. to xxx.

*Incompatibles.*—Persalts of iron, and the alkalies.

### Scoparii Cacumina. Broom Tops.

Sarothamnus Scoparius Wimmer. (Spartium Scoparium.) N. F. Leguminosæ. The fresh tops, dried; from native plants.

*Charact.*—Long, straight, angular, green twigs of a bitter taste.

*Analysis.*—A yellow crystalline substance scoparin, volatile oil, a concrete oil, mucilage, albumen, &c.

*Actions and uses.*—An excellent diuretic in dropsies, inducing, sooner or later, a profuse flow of urine. There is reason to believe that heat impairs its active properties. A cold infusion in water and a little spt. is a good form. It is not given in substance.

*Scoparin,* though not officinal, is an active diuretic. Dose, gr. v.

*Decoctum Scoparii.*—Broom tops ℥ss.; dist. water Oss. Boil 10 minutes in a covered vessel, and strain. Dose, fℨj. to fℨiij., three or four times a-day.

*Succus Scoparii.*—Broom tops lb.vij.; spt. a sufficiency. Bruise the tops in a mortar; press out the juice, and to every 3 measures of juice add 1 of spt.; set aside 7 days, and filter. This is an excellent preparation, and has been much wanted. Dose, fℨj. to fℨij.

*Formula for diuretic purposes.* — ℞ Spiritus ætheris nitrosi fℨss.; spiritus juniperi fℨiij.; succi scoparii fℨvj.; tincturæ digitalis fℨij.; aquæ ad f℥vi. Misce. Sumat cochleare magnum ter die. A powerful diuretic mixture.

### **Senegæ Radix.**  Senega Root.

Polygala Senega Linn.  N. F. Polygaleæ.  The root, dried ; from North America.

*Charact.*—A contorted knotty root-stock, with a branched tap-root, from the thickness of a quill to that of the little finger ; cortical part yellowish, sweetish, then acrid, causing salivation ; woody part whitish, inert.

*Analysis.*—A volatile acid, polygalic, the active principle tannin, pectic acid, fixed oil, albumen, gum, &c.

*Actions and uses.*—An excellent stimulating expectorant, well adapted for chronic bronchitis in old people, and for the advanced stages of pneumonia.  It is of service, too, in hooping-cough when it has run on for several weeks, and some have found it useful in the latter stages of croup. Dose, powder, gr. x. to xxx.

*Infusum Senegæ.*—Senega ʒss. ; boiling dist. water fʒx. Infuse for an hour.  Dose, fʒj. to fʒij.

*Tinctura Senegæ.*—Senega ʒiiss. ; proof spt. Oj.  Proceed as usual.  Dose, fʒss. to fʒij.

### **Senna Alexandrina.**  Alexandrian Senna.

Cassia Lanceolata Lamarck ; and Cassia Obovata Colladon.  N. F. Leguminosæ.  The leaflets (from Alexandria) freed from the flowers, leaf-stalks, and pods ; and from the leaves, fruit, and flowers of Solenostemma Arghel.

*Charact.*—Lanceolate leaflets, about one inch long, base unequally oblique, of a greyish green colour.

*Adulterations.*—Arghel leaves, and a few of the leaves of tephrosia apollinea, and coriaria myrtifolia, a poisonous article.  The spurious are known by being equal at the base, and the arghel leaves are paler, thicker, and more wrinkled.  The tephrosia leaves have their veins proceeding parallel, and without bifurcation, to the very edge. Those of the coriaria myrtifolia have three prominent longitudinal nerves, and their infusion gives a black precip. with a solution of sulphate of iron.

### Senna Indica.  Tinnivelly Senna.

Cassia Elongata Lemaire.  The leaflets from plants grown in southern India.

*Charact.*—Green, thin, flexible, lanceolate, acute ; leaves about 1¼ in. long., and unequal at the base.

*Analysis.*—A deliquescent uncrystallizable bitter substance, named cathartin, mucus albumen, malic acid, &c.

*Actions and uses.*—An admirable cathartic, stimulating the peristaltic action, and affecting chiefly the small intestines.  Its action is frequently attended with nausea and griping, but less so if combined with a saline purgative. It seems to enter the circulation before catharsis is induced, hence breast milk acquires from it a laxative property, and its cathartic effect is developed when an infusion is introduced by the veins.  A little ginger, coriander, or anise, corrects its griping property.  It is seldom given in the form of powder, but if so the dose is gr. cxx. to ℥ss.

*Confectio Sennæ.*—This contains a host of substances, such as tamarinds, figs, prunes, coriander, cassia, pulp, &c. Dose, gr. lx. to ℨxx.  It is commonly called lenitive electuary.

*Infusum Sennæ.*—Senna ℨj.; ginger gr. xxx.; boiling dist. water f℥x.  Infuse an hour.  Dose, f℥j. to f℥ij.

*Syrupus Sennæ.*—A pleasant cathartic for children.  Dose, fℨj. to fℨjv.

*Tinctura Sennæ.*—Senna ℥ijss.; raisins, freed of seeds, ℥ij., carraway ℥ss.; coriander ℥ss.; proof spt. Oj.  Make, as usual, by maceration and percolation.  Dose, fℨj. to fℨjv. Seldom given alone, but as an addition to the infusion, and other cathartics.

*Mistura Sennæ Co.*—Magnes. sulph. ℥iv.; ext. glycyrrh. ℥ss.; tinct. sennæ f℥ijss.; tinct. cardam. co. fℨx.; inf. senna ad Oj.  Dose, f℥j. to f℥iss.


### Serpentariæ Radix.  Serpentary Root.

Aristolochia Serpentaria.  The dried rhizome, from the south of North America.  N. F. Aristolochiaceæ.

*Charact.*—A yellowish-brown tufted head, with numerous attached radicles, about 3 in. long, with a subdued valerianic odour, and a warm camphoraceous taste.

*Analysis.*—A volatile oil, soft resin, gum albumen, starch, &c.

*Actions and uses.*—Tonic, stimulant, and diaphoretic, but not much relied on in this country. It has been used in continued fever, intermittents, amenorrhœa, and gangrenous affections, but has not been very successful. In the adynamic stages of continued fever, some little temporary benefit is obtained. Dose, powder (not a good form), gr. **x.** to **xxx.**

*Infusum Serpentariæ.*—Serpentary ℈ss.; boiling dist. water f℥x. Infuse two hours. Dose, f℥j. to f℥ij.

*Tinctura Serpentariæ.*—Serpentary ℥ijss.; proof spt. Oj. Proceed as usual. Dose, f℥ss. to f℥ij.

### Sevum Præparatum. Prepared Suet.

Ovis Aries Linn. The Sheep. The internal fat of the abdomen, purified by melting and straining.

*Uses.*—It is employed for the same purposes as lard. It has more consistence, and a higher melting point. A constituent of the emp. cantharid.

### Sinapis. Mustard.

Sinapis Nigra, and Sinapis Alba. Black mustard, and white mustard. N. F. Cruciferæ. The seeds, reduced to powder, mixed; native.

*Charact.*—Greenish-yellow, of an oily appearance, and an acrid burning taste; exhales when moist a powerful penetrating odour, irritating the nostrils and eyes.

*Analysis.*—The black mustard seeds contain a bitter uncrystallizable acid, named myronic, a peculiar principle resembling vegetable albumen, named myrosyne, and another principle, crystallizable and somewhat volatile, termed sinapisin. It is by the joint action of these principles, when water is added, that the pungent oil, on which the activity of mustard depends, is developed.

*Adulterations.*—Wheaten flour, detected by iodine; other impurities may be detected by the colour of the specimen, or under the microscope.

*Actions and uses.*—Emetic, epispastic, stimulant. It is a powerful stimulating topical emetic, operating speedily, and is suitable in cases of depression of the vital powers, such as narcotic poisoning, and in the suffocative catarrh of the old and feeble. As an epispastic or external irritant, it is in daily use, in the form of poultice (sinapism), to produce derivation, as for instance, on the chest in pulmonary disease, on the abdomen in colic and abdominal diseases. It is also applied over the seat of neuralgic and rheumatic pains, and to the thighs and soles of the feet in the adynamic stage of continued fever; in coma, apoplexy, and narcotic poisoning. Nothing need be said of mustard as a condiment. Dose, as an emetic, ʒj. or so, in fʒiv. to fʒviij. tepid water.

*Cataplasma.*—Mustard ʒijss.; linseed meal ʒijss.; boiling water fʒx. Mix gradually the meal with the water, and add the mustard, constantly stirring. A good form, producing redness in from twenty minutes to half-an-hour. If sinapisms are applied too long, vesication and ulceration may result.

*Linimentum Sinapis Compositum.*—Oil of mustard fʒj.; ether. ext. mezereon gr. xl.; camph. gr. cxx.; castor oil fʒv.; rect. spt. fʒiv. M. External stimulant, and a useful counterirritant.

*Oleum Sinapis.*—Oil distilled with water from the seeds of sinapis nigra. Used for preparing the linimentum.

*Incompatibles.*—Vinegar.

### Soda Caustica. Caustic Soda.

Hydrate of Soda. NaO HO, or Na HO.

*Charact.*—In hard whitish fragments of cakes, intensely alkaline and very corrosive.

*Actions.*—Corrosive and irritant; antidotes, fixed oils, and vinegar.

*Liquor Sodæ.*—Irritant. Used for preparing valerianate of soda, and sulphurated antimony.

### Soda Tartarata. Tartarated Soda.

$NaO, KO, C_8 H_4 O_{10} + 8 HO$, or $Na KC_4 H_4 O_6 4 H_2 O$.

Synon.—Sodæ et potassæ tartras. Rochelle salts. Prepared by the combination of carb. sodæ, and potass. acid tart.

*Charact.*—In colourless, right rhombic prisms, 8 and 12-sided, of a saline taste.

*Actions and uses.*—A mild laxative, with a not unpleasant taste, and suitable for persons with a delicate stomach. It is contained in the well known Seidlitz powders, the formula for which is as follows:—In the blue paper gr. cxx. rochelle salts, and gr. xl. bicarb sodæ; with some sugar and the least flavour of ess. limon. In the white paper gr. xxxvij. acid tartaric. Dose of the rochelle salts, gr. cxx. to ʒss.

### Sodæ Acetas. Acetate of Soda.

$NaO, C_4 H_3 O_3 + 6 HO$, or $Na C_2 H_3 O_2 3 H_2 O$.

*Charact.*—Colourless crystals, soluble in water; solution when dilute not precipitated by chlor. barium. or nit. argent.

Used in the preparation of ferri arsenias, ferri phosph., &c.

### Sodæ Arsenias. Arseniate of Soda.

$2 NaO, HO AsO_5 + 14 HO$ or $Na_2 H AsO_4 7 H_2 O$.

*Charact.*—In colourless hexahedral prisms, with an acrid taste; soluble in water.

*Actions and uses.*—Similar to those of the liq. arsenic; such as syphilitic, periodic, and cutaneous disorders. Also epilepsy, neuralgia, and rheumatism. Said to produce less irritation along the alimentary tract. It is best given in solution, and should be employed as usual with watching and caution. Dose, gr. $\frac{1}{16}$th, gradually increased to $\frac{1}{8}$th, after food.

*Liquor Sodæ Arseniatis.*—Arseniate of soda gr. jv.; dist. ·ater fʒj. Dissolve. Dose, min. v. gradually increased to x.

**Sodæ Bicarbonas.**   Bicarbonate of Soda.

NaO, HO, 2 $CO_2$, or NaHC $O_3$.

*Charact.*—In powder, or in indistinct rectangular prisms, white, odourless, with a mild alkaline taste.

*Actions and uses.*—An excellent antacid, antilithic, and diuretic, but it is not so energetic a diuretic as the bicarbonate of potash. It is much employed in the heartburn and vomiting of dyspepsia, along with tonics; and for making effervescing drinks. Used also as a lotion in skin diseases, papular and vesicular. Dose, gr. x. to lx.; for lotion, gr. x. to xx. to f℥j. water.

*Liquor Sodæ Effervescens.* Syn.—Soda water. Bicarb. sodæ, water, and $Co_2$; f℥x. contain gr. xv.

*Trochisci.*—Each lozenge contains gr. v. sodæ bicarb., with gum and sugar.

*Incompatibles.*—Acids, metallic salts, except those of magnesia, lime water.

**Sodæ Carbonas.**   Carbonate of Soda.

NaO, $CO_2$+10 HO, or $Na_2$ $CO_3$, 10 $H_2$ O.

Prepared on the large scale from sea-salt.

*Charact.*—In large transparent crystals, of the oblique rhombic form, with a disagreeable, alkaline, and caustic taste, odourless. Heat fuses it, depriving it of its water of crystallization.

*Actions and uses.*—Irritant, diuretic, antacid, antilithic. As a diuretic it is not equal to the carbonate of potash. It is a good antacid, but is harsher to the taste than the bicarbonate. It operates as an antilithic, by correcting stomachic acidity, and rendering the urine alkaline, but phosphatic deposits may result from this alkalinity. The bicarbonate is not open to this objection, because the excess of carbonic acid keeps the earthy phosphates in a state of solution. Alkalies in solution, well charged with carbonic acid, are thus useful in averting gravel, and probably tend to break down calculi of the bladder. Dose, gr. v. to xxx.

*Sodæ Carbonas Exsiccata.*—Prepared by exposing the

carbonate in a porcelain capsule to a strong sand heat. It is about three times stronger than the other, and being of a strong caustic taste, it should be given either in the form of a pill, or in some sweet substance, such as the sugar of milk. Dose, gr. v. to x.

*Incompatibles.*—Acids and their salts, magnesia, and lime water.

### Sodæ Chloratæ Liquor. Solution of Chlorinated Soda.

A mixed solution of hypochlorite of soda, NaO, ClO, chloride of sodium, and bicarbonate of soda.

*Charact.*—A colourless liquid, with a sharp astringent taste, and feeble odour of chlorine. Decolorizes sulphate of indigo.

*Actions and uses.*—Stimulant and antiseptic, and used for the same purposes as the liquor calcis chloratæ, such as in fevers, dysentery, gangrenous sores, burns, chronic cutaneous diseases, and to correct fetid discharges in general. It is perhaps preferable to the liq. calcis chlor. as a disinfectant, as chloride of sodium which remains is not deliquescent. Dose, min. x. to xx. in syrup.

### Sodæ Citro-Tartras Effervescens. Effervescent Citro-Tartrate of Soda.

Bicarb. of soda ℥xvij.; tartaric acid ℥viij.; citric acid ℥vj. Mix thoroughly; place in a pan heated to 220° or so, stir, and separate the granules when they form by means of a sieve.

Common name, granular effervescent citrate of magnesia. A refrigerant and antacid drink in continued and rheumatic fevers. Dose, gr. lx. to ℥¼.

### Sodæ Nitras. Nitrate of Soda.

NaO, $NO_5$, or Na $NO_3$.

A native salt, colourless, purified by crystallization from water.

Employed only to prepare sodæ arsenias.

### Sodæ Phosphas. Phosphate of Soda.

2 NaO, HO, $PO_5$+24 HO, or $Na_2$ $HPO_4$ 12 $H_2$ O.

*Charact.*—Translucent, colourless, oblique rhombic prisms, inodorous, and with a cooling saline taste.

*Actions and uses.*—A gentle saline cathartic, and, in consequence, as well as owing to its not unpleasant taste, it is well adapted for children and delicate people. It possesses a solvent action on uric acid, and may be given as a laxative, where there is a tendency to this deposit. Dose, $\mathfrak{Z}$ss. to $\mathfrak{Z}$j. For children it may be given in soup or other diet without their knowledge.

*Incompatibles.*—Lime water, magnesia, the mineral acids, nitrate of silver, and acetate of lead.

### Sodæ Sulphas. Sulphate of Soda.

NaO, $SO_3$+10 HO, or $Na_2$ $SO_4$. 10 $H_2$ O. Synon.—Glauber salts.

*Uses.*—A saline cathartic, increasing the intestinal secretions considerably. It is more nauseous than the sulphate of magnesia, and grips rather more; hence it is less employed. Dose, $\mathfrak{Z}$¼. to $\mathfrak{Z}$j. in f$\mathfrak{Z}$iv. to $\mathfrak{Z}$vj. water.

### Sodæ Valerianas. Valerianate of Soda.

NaO, $C_{10}$ $H_9$ $O_3$, or $NaC_5$ $H_9$ $O_2$.

*Charact.*—White fragments, soluble in water and spt., with a feeble odour of valerian.

*Uses.*—Antispasmodic, but used chiefly for preparing valerianate of zinc. Dose, gr j. to v.

### Sodii Chloridum. Salt.

NaCl.

*Charact.*—In small white cubes, odourless, and with a pleasant saline taste.

*Actions and uses.*—Stimulant, cathartic, and emetic. It is used by mankind over the world as an adjunct to diet, and it stimulates gently the digestive organs. It also prevents so far the growth of worms in the intestines, these parasites being more profuse where little salt is used, or where it is necessarily absent for a time. As a cathartic, it is useful in the way of aiding others, and it is the chief constituent of many mineral waters. In pretty full doses, such as ʒj. or ʒij., it may be employed as an emetic, if sulphate of zinc or mustard be not at hand. Warmed, it is applied to the surface of the body as a stimulant, or irritant, in severe pains of various kinds; and a solution is sometimes thrown up the rectum as an anthelmintic. Dose, stimulant, gr. x. to xl. Emetic ʒj. to ʒij. in Oj. water.

### Spiritus Ætheris Nitrosi. Spirit of Nitrous Ether.

A spirituous solution containing nitrous ether, $C_4 H_5 O$, $NO_3$. Specific gravity, 0·845. A slightly yellow fluid, mobile, inflammable, of an apple-like odour; sweetish, cool, sharp taste.

*Actions and uses.*—A stimulating diuretic, diaphoretic, and antispasmodic. It is useful along with squill and potash in cardiac dropsy, and (but less so) in that arising from renal disease. It is given to increase the flow of urine, and thus to help the solution of deposits in gravel, and to diminish the acrimony of the urine in gonorrhœa. Along with liquor ammoniæ acetatis (Mindererus spirit), it is an excellent diaphoretic in catarrh, and the early stages of fevers. In large doses it is a narcotic poison; in smaller doses it sometimes produces griping and pain in the stomach. This is corrected by mixing it with juniper and potash. Dose, fʒss. to fʒij.

### Spiritus Rectificatus. Rectified Spirit.

Alcohol, $C_4 H_6 O_2$, with 16 per ct. of water. Sp. gr. 0·838, obtained by the distillation of fermented saccharine fluids, and by rectification, if necessary.

*Charact.*—Colourless, transparent, mobile, and inflammable, with a peculiar and agreeable odour and a hot taste.

*Actions and uses.*—Stimulant, irritant, sedative, diuretic, but seldom used alone in medicine. It is most extensively used, however, in pharmacy as a solvent, and for preparing alcohol (absolute), and the spiritus tenuior. A few observations on alcoholic fluids are made under Wine.

*Spiritus Tenuior, Proof Spt.*—Rect. spt. Ov.; dist. water

Oiij. Mix. Sp. gr. 0·920. The great majority of tinctures are made with this ; the remainder with rectified spirit.

### Spiritus Vini Gallici. Spirit of French Wine.

Synon.—Brandy.

*Mistura Spiritus Vini Gallici.*—Spirit of French wine, cinnamon water, of each f℥iv.; the yolk of two eggs ; refined sugar ℥ss. M. A useful and pleasant stimulant in the adynamic stage of fever, and in other states of prostration. Dose, f℥i. to f℥ij.

### Stramonii Folia. Stramonium Leaves.

Datura Stramonium Linn. Thorn apple. N. F. Solanaceæ. The leaves dried ; collected from native plants when in flower.

*Charact.*—Large, ovate, angulato-sinuate, glabrous, with a heavy odour, and slightly bitter mawkish taste.

### Stramonii Semina. Stramonium Seeds.

Datura-Stramonium Linn. The ripe seeds.

*Charact.*—Small, brownish-black, kidney-shaped, rough, of a nauseous and bitter taste.

*Analysis.*—In the seeds and leaves are found an alkaloid named daturia, in colourless prismatic crystals, somewhat volatile, and on which the properties of the drug depend. The seeds also contain fixed oil, resin, wax, &c.

*Actions and uses.*—The seeds and leaves are strongly narcotic, occasioning dryness and burning sensation of the throat and tongue, nausea, delirium, coma, interrupted by convulsions and death. 100 seeds have killed a child of two years of age in 24 ho. It is used chiefly, but not extensively (and perhaps not so widely as it ought), for anodyne and antispasmodic purposes, such as in sciatica, tic, lumbago, in chronic rheumatism, and other painful diseases. It is very commonly applied in the form of smoke, by means of a tobacco-pipe, in asthma, and in the attacks of dyspnœa, which result from pulmonary emphysema and cardiac disease, and in this way the paroxysms of shortness of breathing are often relieved. It should not be pushed too far, as danger may be incurred; and it is inadmissible in the old and feeble, or those with a tendency to palsy or apoplexy. Dose, powder of the leaves, gr. j. to jv.; of the seeds, gr. ¼ to j., gradually increased.

*Extractum Stramonii.*—Prepared from the seeds with proof spt. Dose, gr. ¼ to ½.

*Tinctura Stramonii.*—Stramonium seeds ℥ijss.; proof spt. Oj. Proceed as usual; the product should be Oj. Dose, min. x. to xxx.

### Strychnia. Strychnia.

An alkaloid, $C_{42} H_{22} N_2 O_4$, or $C_{21} H_{22} N_2 O_2$. Obtained from nux vomica.

*Charact.*—In colourless, minute octahedrons, inodorous, sparingly soluble in water, yet imparting to it its own intensely bitter taste; soluble in ether, chloroform, and boiling rect. spt. Gives a deep violet hue with sulphuric acid, and bichromate of potash. Not coloured by nitric acid.

*Adulterations.*—Brucia and colouring matter; nitric acid develops a red colour if brucia be present.

*Actions and uses.*—A special stimulant and nerve tonic, acting on the medulla oblongata, and medulla spinalis, but not affecting the sensorium. It is also an active poison, occasioning violent tetanic spasms and death; and so little as ⅔ gr. by the mouth has excited violent spasms and locked-jaw. One grain, if introduced into a wound, would probably prove fatal; and ⅙ gr. has killed dogs and other animals in less than a minute. Of late, chloroform, belladonna, and aconite, have been recommended as antidotes, but we fear that neither of these are greatly to be relied on. It is not a cumulative poison, nor does its power diminish after using it for a while, although a slight increase of the dose may be borne. It has been used chiefly in chronic paralysis, such as hemiplegia, paraplegia, partial palsy, amaurosis, and in paralysis of the muscles of the bladder. It is of more service in paraplegia than hemiplegia; and, as a general rule, not very successful in local palsies, such as of the optic nerve, or the bladder. While using it, the paralysed muscles are first affected, and thrown into spasms; there is starting of the limbs; and if improvement is to follow, it is not in general very long delayed. It should not be given where there is a determination of blood to the head, or congestion of the nervous centres, as it is likely to prove injurious. It is applied endermically, either in the form of the liquor, or gr. ss. of the alkaloid may be sprinkled over the raw surface. This method is adopted in amaurosis, and different limited palsies. Dose, gr. $\frac{1}{30}$ to $\frac{1}{12}$, carefully watched, and slowly increased.

*Liquor Strychniæ.*—Strychnia in crystals gr. jv.; dilute hydrochloric acid min. vj.; rectified spt. f$\mathfrak{Z}$ij.; dist. water f$\mathfrak{Z}$vj. Mix the hydrochloric acid with four drachms of the water, and dissolve the strychnia in the mixture by the aid of heat. Then add the spt. and the remainder of the water. As will be seen, there is gr. j. in f$\mathfrak{Z}$ij. The dose will then be min. v. (or gr. $\frac{1}{24}$) to min. x. (or gr. $\frac{1}{12}$), observing well its effects.

### Styrax Præparatus. Prepared Storax.

Liquidambar Orientale. N. F. Ebenaceæ. A balsam got from the bark, in Asia Minor; purified by rect. spt. and straining.

*Charact.*—A dirty-brown, or yellowish half-fluid resin, with a pleasant aromatic odour.

*Actions and uses.*—Expectorant, but thoroughly unimportant. It is an ingredient of the tinct. benzoin co., but seldom given alone. Dose, gr. x. to xx.

### Sulphur Præcipitatum. Precipitated Sulphur.

*Prep.*—Precipitated from sulphuret of calcium by means of hydrochloric acid. (Lac sulphuris. Milk of sulphur.)

*Charact.*—A yellowish-white soft powder, not gritty.

*Actions and uses.*—A mild cathartic, and preferred by some to the sublimed sulphur, as having, if anything, less taste and smell. Useful in hæmorrhoidal affections, stricture of the rectum, &c. Dose, gr. lx. to cxx.

**Sulphur Sublimatum.**   Sublimed Sulphur.

Prepared from sulphur by sublimation.

*Charact.*—A bright greenish-yellow powder, somewhat gritty, with little taste, but a peculiar odour when rubbed.

*Actions and uses.*—A gentle cathartic, and cutaneous stimulant, painlessly stimulating the peristaltic action, and effectual in its operation.   In spasm and stricture of the rectum, in piles, and where a mild intestinal action is wanted, it is very useful.   The eructations and evacuations after using it, as well as the insensible perspiration, being tainted by sulphuretted hydrogen, it is not so much prescribed as it might otherwise have been.   It is held in high repute by many as a laxative in skin diseases ; but while it is one of the best drugs locally applied in these, especially scabies, it is doubtful whether internally it possesses advantages superior to others.   It is one of the most popular diaphoretics of the day, few old women failing to use it where any eruption is supposed to be struggling through the skin. Dose, ʒj. to ʒij., in treacle or honey, as it does not mix freely in water.

*Confectio Sulphuris.*—Sublimed sulph. ʒjv.; acid tartrate of potash ʒj.; syrup, orange peel, fʒjv.   Mix.   Very useful in piles.   Dose, gr. lx. to cxx.

*Unguentum Sulphuris.*—Sublimed sulph. ʒj.; benzoated lard ʒjv.   Mix well.   Used in scabies, where it is supposed to act as a poison to the insect existing in the pustules.   The skin should be well cleaned previously, and the oint. rubbed well in to the involved parts.   It is also used in lepra and psoriasis.

**Sulphuris Iodidum.**   Iodide of Sulphur.

Iodine ʒiv.; sulphur ʒi.   Rub in a mortar, then place in a flask, and liquefy by a gentle heat.   Then allow it to cool and solidify.

*Charact.*—Brownish plates, with a strong odour of iodine.

*Uses.*—Much the same as iodine, but it is seldom given internally.   Dose, gr. j. to ij. in pill.

*Unguentum.*—Iodide of sulphur gr. xxx.; prepared lard

℥j. Mix. A very useful ointment in obstinate skin diseases, such as porrigo, herpes, acne, lepra, and psoriasis.

### Sumbul Radix. Sumbul Root.

Transverse sections of the dried root of a plant, the botanical history of which is not known.

*Charact.*—Circular pieces, light, from 1 to 2 in. diam., and from 2 to 3 in. in depth. Internally dirty greyish-yellow, externally light brown. Odour musk-like, taste aromatic and bitter.

*Actions and uses.*—Not a very important drug. Said to be useful in nervous diseases, such as epilepsy, hysteria, and delirium tremens. Employed also in cholera as a stimulant.

*Tinctura.*—Sumbul root ℥ijss.; rect. spt. Oj. Dose, min. x. to xxx.

### Suppositoriæ. Suppositories. These will be found under the drugs from which they are named.

### Syrupi. Syrups. These also found under the different drugs.

### Tabaci Folia. Leaf Tobacco.

Nicotiana Tabacum Linn. Virginian tobacco. The dried leaves; grown in America. N. F. Solanaceæ.

*Charact.*—Dark-brown, with yellowish spots, lanceolate acuminate, with an unctuous feel, a heavy odour, and a bitter nauseous taste.

*Analysis.*—A liquid, colourless, volatile alkaloid, named nicotina, and which is the active part, a concrete volatile oil, nicotianin, gum, albumen, starch, malic acid, &c.

*Actions and uses.*—A potent narcotico-acrid poison, the symptoms being sickness, exhaustion, relaxation of muscles, voluntary and involuntary, intense depression of the circulation, as indicated by the pulse, which is weak and fluttering; pallid countenance, coldness of the surface of the body, convulsions, and death. In small doses, tobacco is a laxative and diuretic, but very rarely employed as such, its use being attended with danger. It was formerly used as a relaxant of the muscular system in strangulated hernia and dislocations, but chloroform has entirely superseded it. Some few employ it yet to subdue spasm, as in tetanus, or to overcome obstruction, as in ileus, but it is better to seek these influences or results from drugs of less hurtful tendency. As an anthelmintic, in the form of enema, it has also fallen into disuse. Mode of administration, in the form of enema.

*Enema Tabaci.*—Leaf tobacco gr. **xx.**; boiling dist. water fℨviij. Infuse half an hour, and strain. This is the usual strength for injection.

In poisoning, if it has been taken by the mouth, give stimulating emetics. Tannin, and strong external and internal stimulants should also be administered.

### Tamarindus. Tamarind.

Tamarindus Indica Linn. N. F. Leguminosæ. The preserved pulp of the fruit, imported from the West Indies.

*Charact.*—A reddish-yellow pulp, preserved in sugar, with seeds and vegetable fibres, and of a pleasant acid taste.

*Adulterations.*—Copper, detected by plunging a clean iron knife into the pulp, when the metal will adhere.

*Actions and uses.*—Laxative and refrigerant, and given occasionally in fevers. It is an ingredient of the confect. senna. A pleasant cooling whey is made by boiling them with milk. Dose, ℨss. to ℥jss.

### Taraxaci Radix. Dandelion Root.

Taraxacum Dens Leonis D. C. N. F. Compositæ. The fresh roots; gathered between September and February, in Britain.

*Charact.*—Dark-brown tap-shaped roots, white within, brittle, and yielding a bitter milky juice, which on exposure turns pale-brown.

*Analysis.*—A bitter extractive named taraxacine, mannite, resin, sugar, gum, &c.

*Adulterations.*—To prevent the substitution of other roots, the genuine should be ordered with some of the leaves attached : these are runcinate and smooth, and easily known.

*Actions and uses.*—Tonic, and a weak aperient. It is a good deal used by some in functional disorders of the liver, and after using it for some time, the biliary secretion is promoted, the intestinal motions become more natural, and the appetite improves. Large doses are required, and in a good many cases very little influence seems to be exerted by it. It is not given in substance.

*Decoctum Taraxaci.*—Dandelion root, sliced, ℥j.; dist. water Oj. Boil 10 minutes, and strain. Dose, f℈ij. to f℥jv.

*Extractum.*—Dose, gr. x. to xxx.

*Succus Taraxaci.*—Dose, f℈j. to f℥ij.

### Terebinthina Canadensis. Canada Balsam.

Abies Balsamea. Balm of Gilead Fir. N. F. Coniferæ. The turpentine, obtained from the stem by incision, in Canada.

*Charact.*—Of a honey colour and consistence when fresh, but gradually thickens into a resinous looking mass ; with a terebinthinate odour, and an acrid taste.

*Actions and uses.*—A stimulant and tonic to the mucous membranes, especially of the bladder and urethra. It proves useful in gleet, leucorrhœa, and cystirrhœa. Dose, gr. xx. to xxx. three or four times a-day, mixed in magnesia.

### Theriaca. Treacle.

The uncrystallized residue of the refining of sugar.

*Actions and uses.*—Emollient and demulcent. Used chiefly for pills, electuaries, &c.

### Thus Americanum. Common Frankincense.

Pinus Tæda Linn., the Frankincense Pine, and Pinus Palustris, the Swamp Pine. The concrete turpentine from the south of North America.

*Uses.*—For plasters, chiefly to give odour and consistency. A constituent of the emp. picis.

### Tincturæ.  Tinctures.

These are all placed under the medicines whence they derive their title.

### Tragacantha.  Tragacanth.

Astragalus Verus Olivier, and other species.  N. F. Leguminosæ.  A gummy exudation from the stem; gathered in Asia Minor.

*Charact.*—In yellowish-white, broad, thin, somewhat curved plates, tough and elastic, inodorous and tasteless.

*Analysis.*—Soluble gum, 51 per cent, the remainder bassorin.

*Actions and uses.*—Demulcent, and used for same purposes as gum arabic, but not so widely employed.  Dose, gr. xxx. to cxx.

*Pulvis Tragacanthæ Compositus.*—Tragacanth ʒj.; gum arabic ʒj.; starch ʒj.; refined sugar ʒiij.  Mix well.  Used as a vehicle for powders containing calomel, &c.  Dose, gr. xx. to lx. as a demulcent.

*Mucilago.*—Tragacanth gr. lx.; boiling dist. water fʒx.  Macerate 24 ho., and express through calico.

### Trochisci.  Lozenges.

See the different drugs after which they are named.

### Ulmi Cortex.  Elm Bark.

Ulmus Campestris.  Broad-leaved Elm.  N. F. Cupuliferæ.  The dried inner bark, deprived of its outer layers, from indigenous trees.

*Charact*—A brownish-yellow bark, about half a line thick, inodorous, taste bitter and astringent.

*Analysis.*—Tannin, resin, gum, &c.

*Actions and uses.*—Tonic, but not very active or important.  Some prescribe it in skin diseases, as it is said to act a little on the cutaneous capillaries.  It is not given in substance.

*Decoctum Ulmi.*—Elm bark ʒijss.; dist. water Oij.  Boil down to Oj.  Dose, fʒij. to fʒiv.

**Unguenta.** Ointments.

See the drugs whence they derive their name.

**Uvæ Ursi Folia.** Bearberry leaves.

Arctostaphylos Uva Ursi. N. F. Ericaceæ. The dried leaves; from indigenous plants.

*Charact.*—Dark-green entire, obovate, shining, coriaceous leaves, convex above, 'concave and reticulated on the under surface, with an astringent bitter taste, and odour of hay.

*Analysis.*—A bitter principle, in long thin colourless prisms, named arbutin, tannin, gallic acid, resin, gum, &c.

*Adulterations.*—Leaves of the red whortle-berry (vaccinium vitisidæa), and of the common box (buxus sempervirens), are often mixed with the true. The former have their under surface dotted, not reticulated; and the latter are not astringent.

*Actions and uses.*—An astringent to the genito-urinary mucous membrane. Employed in chronic mucous discharges, such as gleet, leucorrhœa, and catarrh of the bladder. In chronic nephritis, and diabetes, it sometimes does a little good, and may be tried at least as a change from other remedies. Dose of the powder, gr. x. to xl.

*Infusum Uvæ Ursi.*—Bearberry leaves ʒss.; boiling dist. water fʒx. Infuse 2 hours. Dose, fʒj. to fʒij.

*Incompatibles.*—Same as tannin.

**Uvæ.** Raisins.

Vitis Vinifera Linn. The Grape Vine. The ripe fruit, dried in the sun, or with artificial heat; from Spain.

*Uses.*—Nutritive and demulcent. Used as agreeable adjuncts in tinctures, such as that of senna, and cardamoms.

**Valerianæ Radix.** Valerian Root.

Valeriana Officinalis Linn. N. F. Valerianaceæ. The root of indigenous plants, collected in autumn, and dried; that from wild plants on dry soil is best.

*Charact.*—A short tuberous yellowish-brown rhizome, with numerous root-fibres, from 2 to 4 in. long, of a penetrating odour, and a bitter, acrid, somewhat aromatic taste.

*Analysis.*—Valerianic acid, volatile oil crystallizable, resin, gum, &c. The active properties are due to the acid.

*Actions and uses.*—A powerful stimulant and antispasmodic. When given in large doses it affects the cerebral organs, occasioning headache and vertigo. It is now chiefly employed in hysteria, where it is of undoubted service, few remedies being equal to it in the way of subduing the paroxysm of that disease. Some cases of epilepsy in young people have been benefited by it, and in the nervousness of the adynamic stage of continued fever, good has resulted, but it is not very much to be relied on here. Dose, powder, gr. xx. to xl.

*Infusum Valerianæ.*—Valerian gr. cxx.; boiling dist. water f℥x. Infuse one hour. Dose, f℥j. to f℥ij.

*Tinctura Valerianæ.*—Valerian ℥ijss.; proof spt. Oj. Proceed as usual. Dose, f℥j. to f℥ij.

*Tinctura Valerianæ Ammoniata.*—Valerian ℥ijss.; aromatic spt. of ammonia Oj. Macerate 7 days. This is the best preparation of this drug. Dose, f℥ss. to f℥j.

*Formula.*—℞ Tinct. valerian. ammon. f℥vj.; tinct. assafœtidæ f℥iij.; infusi cuspariæ ad f℥vj. Misce. Sumat f℥ss. pro re nata. Useful in hysteria.

*Incompatibles.*—Salts of iron, alkalies; the earthy and metallic oxides.

**Vapores.** Inhalations. These found under the respective drugs from which they are named.

### Veratri Viridis Radix. Green Hellebore Root.

The rhizome of Veratrum Viride, dried. Collected in autumn in North America.

*Actions.*—Emetic and sedative. Diminishes the pulse very much, producing syncope if given freely. Dilates the pupils also. Given sometimes in rheumatism, neuralgia, and where we wish to abate the force of the circulation. Dose, powder, gr. iij. to v.

*Tinctura Veratri Viridis.*—Green Hellebore root ℥iv., spt. Oj. Dose, min. v. to xx.

### Veratria. Veratria.

An alkaloid ($C_{64} H_{52} N_2 O_{15}$) obtained from Cevadilla; not quite pure.

*Charact.*—A greyish white powder, uncrystallizable, of an intensely acrid and bitter taste, powerfully irritating to the nostrils, the smallest portion exciting violent sneezing. It is insoluble in water, sparingly in ether, more so in spirit. Acids dissolve it readily, traces of an insoluble brown resinoid matter being left.

Prepared from sabadilla by maceration in water and spirit, and precipitation by solution of ammonia, &c.

*Adulteration.*—Lime occasionally; heated in a platinum spoon, the pure leaves no residue.

*Actions and uses.*—A general stimulant, but a strong irritant poison, occasioning inflammation of the alimentary canal, vomiting, and diarrhœa; the least particle also inflaming the lining membrane of the nostrils, and producing coryza. In very small doses, it stimulates generally the secretions of the skin, kidney, and intestines. It was at one time highly praised as a remedy in neuralgia, for which purpose it was used internally and externally; but we do not now trust it much in this many-formed disease. On the Continent it has been used in pneumonia, and has acquired also a kind of name in acute rheumatism, but it is not believed in here for these diseases. In the form of ointment, it is recommended in strumous diseases of joints. Dose, gr. $\frac{1}{12}$th, in the form of pill. If heat in the throat, pain in the stomach, vomiting, or diarrhœa result, it should be discontinued.

*Unguentum Veratriæ.*—Veratria gr. viij.; olive oil fℨss.; prepared lard ℨj. Rub the oil and veratria well together, then add the lard.

In poisoning, give emetics, demulcent drinks, tannin, and stimulants, such as coffee, brandy, and ammonia.

**Vina.** Wines. See the different drugs which give them their name.

**Vinum Xericum.** Sherry.

A Spanish wine.

*Charact.*—A transparent liquid of a pale yellow colour, containing about 18 per cent of alcohol.

*Actions and uses.*—Stimulant. Used in the preparation of all the wines in the pharmacopœia. About the use and utility of alcoholic liquids in medicine there is considerable contrariety of opinion, the temperance question coming in often, even among professional men, to bias the mind, and prevent a calm estimate of their therapeutical effects and position. We think there is little doubt but that, whether in the form of wines, whisky, brandy, &c., they are often useful stimulants, helping to tide patients, for a little while at least, over periods of weakness and exhaustion. In fevers, in convalescence from acute diseases, and in debility from protracted discharges, they are often of service ; and in cases of shock from injury, or faintness and exhaustion from other causes, benefit is derived. In general, they should not be used where there is acute local inflammation.

**Zinci Acetas.** Acetate of Zinc.

$ZnO, C_4 H_3 O_3 + 2 HO$, or $Zn (C_2 H_3 O_2)_2 2 H_2 O$.

*Charact.*—Thin white translucent crystalline plates, of a pearly lustre, inodorous, and with a sharp styptic taste.

*Actions and uses.*—An excellent astringent for external use. Employed in chronic mucous discharges, as gleet and leucorrhœa ; and in skin diseases, such as lupus, eczema, and impetigo, when they are attended with much discharge. It is also used with benefit in ophthalmia. Internally, it is not much employed. Dose, gr. j. to iij. in pill with ext. rhei. For a lotion, gr. ij. to x. in ℥j. water.

*Incompatibles.*—Lime water ; the alkalies and their carbonates.

**Zinci Carbonas.** Carbonate of Zinc.

$ZnO, CO_2 + 2 ZnO + 3 HO$ or $ZnCO_3 (ZnO)_2, 3 H_2 O$.

*Charact.*—A whitish, heavy, tasteless, inodorous powder,

insoluble in water. Entirely soluble with effervescence in dilute sulphuric acid.

*Actions and uses.*—Astringent. Used externally for drying the skin in excoriations, and in the profuse discharges of chronic cutaneous diseases. An ointment, called " Turner's Cerate," is made with this, with wax, lard, &c. It is popularly used for all kinds of sores of limited extent.

### Zinci Chloridum. Chloride of Zinc.

$ZnCl$, or $ZnCl_2$.

*Charact.*—In snow-white opaque rods, inodorous, very deliquescent and caustic, with a powerfully styptic taste; soluble in water, alcohol, and ether.

*Actions and uses.*—A powerful caustic, involving the vitality of the organized textures, and occasioning severe burning pain, which lasts for several hours. It is used to destroy fungous tumours, nævi materni, fibrous growths, and as an application to malignant ulcer, fungus hæmatodes, &c. Of some benefit in open cancer, by promoting a new action in the neighbourhood. It is used also for making issues.

*Liquor Zinci Chloridi. Prep.*—See Brit. Pharm. In poisoning with this powerful caustic give emetics. and warm demulcent drinks.

*Chloride of Zinc Paste*, for the gradual destruction of growths, &c., is made by mixing one part of the caustic with two of flour. The paste is applied in a layer, one to two lines thick, and left on from six to ten hours, the contiguous parts being well protected.

### Zinci Oxidum. Oxide of Zinc.

$ZnO$.

*Charact.*—A soft white powder, inodorous and tasteless, becoming yellowish-white when heated. Insoluble in water, soluble in most acids.

*Actions and uses.*—Tonic and astringent. As a tonic it is employed in convulsive and spasmodic diseases, such as chorea and epilepsy, and in the latter disease it is often of service when given for a lengthened period. In spasmodic cough it is not much to be depended on, but in chronic catarrh it helps to diminish excessive expectoration. Some give it in scaly skin diseases, but it is inferior to arsenic in these. Externally it is pretty widely used for healing chaps, excoriations, superficial ulcers, and in herpetic eruptions, intertrigo, &c. Dose, gr. ij. to viij. in pill, with ext. tarax. and ext. gent., three times a-day, after food.

*Unguentum Zinci Oxidi.*—Oxide of zinc gr. lxxx.; benzoated lard ℥j. Mix. An excellent healing oint. for simple sores.

### Zinci Sulphas. Sulphate of Zinc.

ZnO, SO$_3$+7 HO, or ZnSO$_4$. 7 H$_2$ O.

*Charact.*—Transparent colourless crystals of the right rhombic form, inodorous, with a strong styptic metallic taste ; freely soluble in water.

*Actions and uses.*—Irritant, emetic, astringent, tonic. In large doses it is an irritant poison, but it is usually discharged by vomiting; or, if not, warm demulcent drinks should be given, and inflammatory symptoms met in the usual way, if they arise. As an emetic it is one of our best, operating immediately and effectually, and thus, as well as from its not depressing the circulation, being useful in narcotic poisoning. As a tonic some use it in those disorders for which the oxide is given, but it has not proved so successful. As an astringent internally it is used in chronic diarrhœa and dysentery, in bronchitis with excessive secretion, in leucorrhœa and gleet, and in all these with occasional benefit. Externally it is much employed in the form of injection in gonorrhœa, gleet, and leucorrhœa, as a lotion in old and weak ulcers, and as a collyrium in ophthalmia. Dose, as an astringent and tonic, gr. j. to v. in pill, with ext. gentian.; as an emetic, gr. xv. to xxx. in f℥jv. of water.

*Red Lotion* is a solution of this salt, of the strength of gr. ij. to jv. to f℥j. of water, and coloured with tinct. lavand. co.

It is useful as a stimulant to weak, an astringent to flabby, and a corrective to foul ulcers.

*A Caustic Paste* for reducing growths, is made by drying the sulphate of zinc, and mixing it with $\frac{1}{4}$th part, or so, of glycerine; and a more powerful one still, by adding sulphuric acid (the super-sulphate of zinc).

### Zinci Valerianas. Valerianate of Zinc.

$ZnO$, $C^{10}$ $H^9$ $O^3$, or $Zn$ $(C_5$ $H_9$ $O_2)_2$.

Prepared by the action of valerianate of soda on sulphate of zinc. See Brit. Pharm.

*Charact.*—In brilliant, snow-white, pearly, tabular crystals, with a bitter, metallic, slightly astringent taste, and a slight odour of valerian; soluble in water, but requires to be rubbed in a mortar.

*Actions and uses.*—A powerful antispasmodic and tonic. It has been found of great service in hysteria and neuralgic affections, especially of the face and head; of benefit also, at times, in chorea and epilepsy. In the convulsive disorders of children, when these depend on worms, its use is also attended with benefit. Dose, gr. ss. to ij. in pill, with ext. tarax., twice or thrice a-day; for children, gr. $\frac{1}{4}$th, in a little scammony and aromatic powder.

*Incompatibles.*—The soluble carbonates, most metallic salts, the acids, and astringent infusions.

### Zincum. Zinc.

Zinc of commerce. Zincum Granulatum. Granulated zinc. Used to prepare liq. zinci chloridi; zinci chloridum, and zinci sulph.

### Zingiber. Ginger.

Zingiber Officinale (Amomum Zingiber). N. F. Zingiberaceæ. The rhizome, scraped and dried; from plants grown in the West Indies.

*Charact.*—Knotty, palmated, hard, decorticated pieces, three or four inches long, yellowish-white, with a mealy fracture, hot taste, and aromatic odour.

*Actions and uses.*—An aromatic stimulant, tonic, and carminative. It is popularly employed for flatulence, and as a condiment ; and in practice, very extensively, to give flavour to or to correct the griping tendency of other drugs. When chewed, it irritates the mouth, and increases the flow of saliva, and it has been used in paralysis of the tongue. It stimulates the digestion a little, but should not be used in irritable stomach ; and from its stimulant effect on the genito-urinary organs, it should be avoided in acute gonorrhœa, and where there is a tendency to stricture.

*Syrupus.*—Strong tincture of ginger f℈vj.; syrup f℥xix. Mix with agitation. Dose, f℥j.

*Tinctura Zingiberis.*—Ginger ℥ijss.; rect. spt. Oj. Proceed as usual. Dose, min. xv. to f℥j.

*Tinctura Zingiberis Fortior.*—Ginger, in fine powder, ℥x.; rect. spt. Oj. Prep. by percolation. Dose, min. v. to xx.

# PART II.

## MEDICINES ARRANGED ACCORDING TO THEIR ACTIONS.

### Antacids.

#### (Alkalines, Absorbents, Antilithics, Lithontriptics.)

Antacids are medicines which neutralize, by combining chemically with, any free acid existing in the stomach or intestines. Tonics should be given with them, in order to improve that feeble or perverted state of the digestive organs on which the acidity depends. If the acid exists in the gaseous condition, ammonia, from its volatility, will best combat it; if in the lower bowel, magnesia or lime are most suitable, as they withstand for a longer time the action of the intestinal juices. When the acidity is in the urinary organs, the alkalies are to be preferred, from their direct diuretic action. Ammonia is most suitable for the old and feeble, being most stimulating.

Ammoniæ Carbonas. Ammon Aq. Spiritus Ammoniæ Aromaticus. Calcis Liquor. Calcis Carbonas Præcipitata. Creta Præp. Lithiæ Carbonas. Lithiæ Citras. Magnesia Levis. Magnesiæ Carbonas. Magnesiæ Carbonas Levis. Potassæ Bicarbonas. Potassæ Carbonas. Potassæ Liquor. Sodæ Bicarbonas. Sodæ Carbonas.

### Anthelmintics. (Vermifuges.)

These are substances which destroy or extirpate worms located in the intestines; as a rule they should be given on an empty stomach. If the parasite exists in the large bowel, as is the case with the ascaris vermicularis, which is chiefly in the rectum, enemata will very readily deal with it, and they should be added to internal remedies.

Cusso. Filix Mas. Granati Radicis Cortex. Sabadilla. Santoninum. Terebinthinæ Oleum. Most of the cathartics also act as vermifuges.

### Antispasmodics.

These allay spasm, that is undue or irregular muscular contraction. There are the pure or direct, and the indirect; the former have a direct influence on spasmodic action; the latter (such as a purgative in chorea, where it depends on intestinal irritation, or a tonic in epilepsy arising from vascular atony) operate indirectly. The pure or direct are, Assafœtida, Castoreum, Galbanum, Moschus, Rutæ Oleum, Valeriana; and the salts of valerianic acid.

### Astringents. (Styptics. Constringents.)

Substances which arrest secretions and excretions; they do so by causing a condensation of contractile fibres, improving tone, and altering action.

Acetum. Acidum Carbolicum. Acidum Gallicum. Acidum Sulphuricum. Acidum Tannicum. Alumen. Belæ Fructus. Bismuthum Album. Borax. Catechu. Creasotum. Calcis. Carb. Præcip. Cupri Sulphas. Ergota. Ferri Sulphas. Ferri Perchlor. Tinct. Ferri Pernit Liquor. Galla. Hæmatoxyli Lignum. Kino. Krameria. Matico. Plumbi Acetas. Plumbi Carbonas. Plumb. Subacet. Liquor. Dil. Quercus. Rosa Gallica. Uva Ursi. Zinci Acetas. Zinci Carb. Zinci Oxidum. Zinci Sulphas.

### Cathartics. (Purgatives. Evacuants.)

Medicines which promote the evacuation of the intestinal contents. Mild ones are laxatives; stronger purgatives; and those are drastic which operate with painful energy. They vary in their mode of action; some rouse and increase the peristaltic action, others merely stimulate the mucous glands—inducing watery evacuations. Further, these medicines elect certain parts of the bowel on which to operate. Jalap deals with the small intestine chiefly; aloes and colocynth prefer the large bowel; while rhubarb embraces both.

Aloe. Cambogia. Cassia. Colocynthis. Crotonis Oleum. Elaterium. Hydrarg. cum Creta. Hydrarg. Subchlor. Jalapa. Jalapæ Resina. Magnesia. Magnes. Sulph. Manna. Mel. Olivæ Oleum. Podophylli Resina. Potass. Acet. Potass. Sulph. Potass. Tart. Acida. Prunum. Rhamni Succus. Rheum. Ricini Oleum. Scammoniæ Resina. Scammonium. Senna. Sodæ Phophas. Sodæ et Potass. Tart. Sulphur P. Sulphur Sub. Tamarindus. Terebinth. Oleum.

### Caustics. (Cauterants. Escharotics.)

Substances possessing the power of destroying living tissue. When they act powerfully, they produce an eschar, hence escharotic.

Acidum Aceticum. Acid. Arseniosum. Acid. Hydrochlor. Acid Nitric. Acid. Sulphuric. Ammon. Liq. Fortior. Antimon. Terchlor. Liquor. Argenti Nitras. Cupri Sulphas. Hydrarg. Nit. Liquor Acid. Hydrarg. Oxid Rub. Potassa Caustica. Zinci Chloridum. Zinci Sulphas.

### Diaphoretics. (Sudorifics.)

Remedies which increase the cutaneous transpiration. Some of them act by increasing the functional activity of the skin; some by quickening the circulation; others by lowering it where, as in fevers, increased vascular action is associated with a perversion of the cutaneous function. While using them, the surface of the body should be kept warm.

Ammon. Acet. Liquor. Antimon. Oxid. Antimon. Pulv. Antimon Sulphuratum. Antim. Tartaratum. Dulcamara. Guaiaci Lignum. Guaiaci Resina. Ipecac. Pulv. Cum Opio. Mezereum. Sarza. Sassafras. Sulphur.

### Disinfectants.

Substances which destroy by decomposition, foul effluvia, and infectious or putrescent emanations.

Carbo. Calx Chlorata. Cerevisiæ Fermentum. Chlori Liquor. Potassæ Permanganas. Sodæ Chlor. Liquor. Zinci Chlor. Liquor.

## Diuretics.

These promote the secretion and evacuation of urine, generally by stimulating the secreting vessels of the kidneys. Their operation is favoured by a cool skin, and that of some of them by not giving so much as would induce catharsis.

Ætheris Nitrosi Spiritus. Bucco. Cambogia. Cantharis. Digitalis. Juniperi Oleum. Pareira. Potass. Acetas. Potass. Nitras. Potass. Tart. Acid. Scilla. Scoparius. Terebinth. Canadensis. Terebinth. Oleum.

## Emetics. (Vomits.)

Medicines which occasion the emptying upwards of the contents of the stomach. There are the direct, topical, or irritant, producing vomiting by reflex action, and only when received into the stomach, and whose action is immediate; and the general, or specific, which act alike whether when introduced into the stomach, or any part of the vascular system (as, for instance, the veins), and whose operation is more tardy, a gradually deepening depression preceding it. The specifics are marked thus*.

*Antimonium Tartaratum. Cupri Sulphas. *Ipecacuanha. Sinapis. Sodii Chloridum. Zinci Sulphas.

## Emmenagogues.

Medicines which promote the menstrual discharge, by stimulating the uterus to increased action. Many so-called emmenagogues are merely cathartics, their influence on the rectum being reflected on the uterus. The following operate directly, and may be termed the true.
Borax. Ergota. Rutæ Oleum. Sabina.

## Emollients. (Demulcents. Relaxants.)

Substances which render the tissues softer and laxer, by lessening vital tone or cohesion; or which soften and protect the sensible surfaces of the body.

Acacia. Adeps Præp. Amygdala. Amygdal. Oleum. Amylum. Cera Alba. Cera Flava. Cataceum. Ficus. Gycerinum. Glycyrrhiza. Hemidesmus. Hordeum.

Lini Farinæ.  Lini Oleum.  Lini Semen.  Olivæ Oleum.
Saccharum.  Theriaca.  Tragacantha.  Uvæ.

**Epispastics.**  (Counterirritants.  Derivatives.  Rubefacients.
Revulsives.)

These redden, inflame, and vesicate the skin.

Acid. Carbolic.  Ammon. Liq. Fortior.  Antim. Tart.
Aqua Fervens.  Cantharis.  Capsicum.  Crotonis Oleum.
Mezereum.  Sabina.  Sinapis.  Terebinth. Oleum.

### Expectorants.

Medicines which increase pulmonary secretion, or promote its discharge.

Acid. Benzoicum.  Ammon. Benzoas.  Antim. Tart.
Bals. Peru.  Bals. Tolut.  Benzoinum.  Ammoniacum.
Ipecacuanha.  Lobelia.  Scilla.  Senega.

### Liquefacients.  (Deobstruants.  Alteratives.)

Medicines acting obscurely or specifically, and altering
morbid conditions of the system; others acting on the
lymphatic and capillary systems, accelerating the meta-
morphosis of tissue, and thus promoting the removal of
swellings, fluid and solid.

Acidum Arseniosum.  Hydrargyrum.  Hydr. Perchlor.
Hydr. Iodid. Rub.  Hydr. Iodid. Virid.  Hydr. Subchlor.
Iodum.  Morrhuæ Oleum.  Podopyhilli Resina.  Potassii
Bromidum.  Potassæ Chloras.  Potassii Iodidum.

### Narcotics.  (Hypnotics.  Soporifics.  Anodynes.)

Medicines which induce prostration of the vital powers
and sleep; this being preceded by a stimulating effect on
the brain and heart.  In large doses, the stimulant effect
is overborne, and they operate like sedatives.

Belladonna.  Cannabis Indica.  Hyoscyamus.  Lupulus.
Morphiæ Hydrochloras.  Opium.  Papaver. Rhœas.  Stramonii Folia et Semina.

### Refrigerants.

These act by diminishing the force of the circulation
when it is unduly or morbidly excited, thus reducing the

heat of the body, and giving rise to a sensation of coolness throughout the system. The most powerful are cold drinks, cold bath, cold air. Freezing mixtures.

Acetum. Acid. Citric. Acid. Sulph. Dil. Acid. Tart. Limonis Succus. Mori Succus. Potass. Chlor. Potass. Nit.

**Sedatives.** (Contra-Stimulants. Calmatives.)

Medicines which directly depress the vital powers, there being no antecedent excitement. In large doses, they give rise to delirium, whereas in the case of narcotics, the tendency is to apoplexy and coma.

Acidum Hydrocyanicum Dilutum. Aconitum. Aconiti Radix. Antimonium Tartaratum. Chloroformum. Conii Fructus. Conium. Creasotum. Digitalinum. Digitalis. Laurocerasus. Lobelia. Tabacum. Veratri Viridis Radix.

### Sialagogues.

Substances which excite the secretion of saliva by a topical, irritant, or stimulant action.

Armoracia. Caryophyllum. Mezereon. Pyrethri Radix. Senega. Zingiber.

### Stimulants. (Excitants. Hypersthenics.)

Remedies which excite the vital powers, and give an impulse to the circulation, by increasing the force and frequency of the heart's contractions. The most important are marked thus *.

*Æther. Ammoniacum. *Ammoniæ Carbonas. *Ammoniæ Liquor. *Ammon. Spt. Aromat. Anethum. Anisi Oleum. Armoracia. Arnica. Bals. Peruv. Cajuputi Oleum. *Calx Chlorata. *Camphora. Capsicum. Cardamomum. Carui. Caryophyllum. Cerevisiæ Fermentum. *Chlori Liquor. Cinnamomum. Coriandri Oleum. Elemi. Fœnicul. Fructus. Lavandulæ Oleum. Menth. Piperit. Oleum. Menth. Virid. Ol. Myristica. Pimentæ Oleum. Piper. Rosmarini Oleum. Serpentaria. Sinapis. *Sodæ. Chlor. Liq. Sodii Chloridum. *Terebinth. Oleum. Thus Americanum. *Vinum Xericum (and other alcoholic 'rinks). Zingiber.

### Tonics. (Corroborants.)

Medicines which impart firmness, vigour, and tone to the body when it is relaxed and debilitated. They are stimulants so far, inasmuch as they quicken the vital powers; but this result is brought about gradually, and is of a more lasting nature. Some act upon the nervous system only, others on the vascular, but our arrangement compels us to class them all together. The more important are marked thus *.

Acid. Hydrochlor. Dil. Acid. Nitric. Dil. Acid. Phosph. Dil. Acid. Sulph. Dil. Anthemis. *Argenti Nitras. Argent. Oxid. Aurantii Cortex. *Beberiæ Sulphas. *Bismuth. Subnit. *Calumba Radix. Cascarilla. Cetraria. Chirata. *Cinchona. *Cuspariæ Cortex. Fel. Bovinum Pur. *Ferri Carb. Sacch. Ferri et Ammon. Cit. *Ferri et Quin. Cit. *Ferri Iodidum. Ferri Perchlor. Tinct. *Ferri Pernit. Liq. Ferri Perox. Ferri Perox. Hydrat. Ferri Phosph. *Ferri Sulph. Ferrum Redact. Ferri Tart. *Gentiana. Myrrha. *Nux Vomica. *Quassia. *Quiniæ Sulphas. *Strychnia. Taraxacum. Ulmus. *Zinci Oxidum. *Zinci Sulph.

---

### The Natural Families, Classes, and Orders.

| N. F. | Class. | Order. |
|---|---|---|
| Apocynaceæ | Pentandria | Monogynia |
| Aurantiaceæ | Polyadelphia | Icosandria |
| Algæ | Cryptogamia | Algæ |
| Aristolochiaceæ | Gynandria | Hexandria |
| Caprifoliaceæ | Pentandria | Trygynia |
| Cichoraceæ | Syngenesia | Polygamia Æqualis |
| Colchicaceæ | Hexandria | Trigynia |
| Coniferæ | Monœcia | Monadelphia |
| Convolvulaceæ | Pentandria | Monogynia |
| Corylaceæ, *or* Cupuliferæ | Monœcia | Polyandria |
| Corymbiferæ | Syngenesia | Polygamia Superflua |
| Cruciferæ | Tetradynamia | Siliquosa |
| Cucurbitaceæ | Monœcia | Monadelphia |
| Ericaceæ | Decandria | Monogynia |
| Euphorbiaceæ | Monœcia | Monandria |
| Filices | Cryptogamia | Filices |
| Gentianaceæ | Pentandria | Digynia |
| Graminaceæ | Triandria | Digynia |
| Guttiferæ | Polygamia | Monœcia |

| N. F. | Class. | Order. |
|---|---|---|
| Iridaceæ | Triandria | Monogynia |
| Labiatæ | Diandria | Monogynia |
| Lauraceæ | Enneandria | Monogynia |
| Leguminosæ | Diadelphia | Decandria |
| Lichenes | Cryptogamia | Lichenes |
| Liliaceæ | Hexandria | Monogynia |
| Linaceæ | Pentandria | Pentagynia |
| Menispermaceæ | Diœcia | Hexandria |
| Myrtaceæ | Icosandria | Monogynia |
| Papaveraceæ | Polyandria | Monogynia |
| Piperaceæ | Diandria | Trigynia |
| Polygonaceæ | Octandria | Trigynia |
| Polygalaceæ | Diadelphia | Octandria |
| Ranunculaceæ | Polyandria | Polygnia |
| Rosaceæ | Icosandria | Polygnia |
| Rubiaceæ _or_ Cinchonaceæ | Tetrandria | Monogynia |
| Rutaceæ | Decandria | Monogynia |
| Scrofulariaceæ | Didynamia | Angiospermia |
| Smilaceæ | Diœcia | Hexandria |
| Solanaceæ | Pentandria | Monogynia |
| Terebinthaceæ | Octandria | Monogynia |
| Thymelaceæ | Octandria | Monogynia |
| Ulmaceæ | Pentandria | Digynia |
| Umbelliferæ | Pentandria | Digynia |
| Urticaceæ | Tetrandria | Monogynia |
| Valerianaceæ | Triandria | Monogynia |
| Zingiberaceæ | Monandria | Monogynia |

# PART III.

## ON PRESCRIPTION WRITING, AND CERTAIN POINTS WHICH SHOULD BE ATTENDED TO IN PRESCRIBING.

### 1. On Prescription Writing.

A prescription may often properly and preferably contain only one drug, as for example, Ergota, Acidum Gallicum, or Ferri Pernitratis Liquor : these (the one in uterine inaction, and the others for astringent purposes), it would be difficult to improve by the addition of others. This is exceptional, however, most other drugs being rendered either more active and pleasant by combination with others, or having objectionable properties neutralized or modified. For instance, scilla is the better of digitalis, and both (for diuretic purposes) of a little calomelas; colocynthis is improved by scammonium or jalapa; and aloe by ferri sulph. or extract. hyoscyam; while the acrid properties of elaterium, sabadilla, crotonis oleum, and cambogia, may be modified by judicious combinations. There are other drugs, again, which cannot be very safely given in substance, although they may not require to be united with others, such as Hydr. Corrosiv. Sub., Acid. Arsenious, &c. As a result of this, a medicinal formula is usually divided into several parts, and most commonly into four, viz., the Base, the Adjuvant, the Corrective, and the Excipient.

1. *The Base.* This is the active ingredient. 2. *The Adjuvant.* This is meant to promote the action of the base. 3. *The Corrective.* This is intended to neutralize, or modify, or diminish its hurtful or disagreeable properties. 4. *The Excipient.* This gives consistence and form.

Now let us take for example the Pilula Cambogiæ Co.

In this the gamboge is the base, the aloes and aromatic powder the adjunct and corrective, while the soap and syrup form the excipient.

When any officinal preparation (that is, one ordered in the pharmacopœia, and for which a formula is given), is prescribed, its officinal name is simply written; as for instance, Unguentum Atropiæ; Pilula Rhei Composita, &c.; but in extemporaneous formulæ, the medicines are placed in separate lines, the base going first. Incompatibles, though not always therapeutically inert or objectionable when combined, should, in general, be avoided: acid. sulph. dil. should not go along with potassii iodid. (as we have seen); acid. gallic. with the persalts of iron, nor ammonia with peruvian bark; and so on.

### 2. On certain points which demand the consideration of the Prescriber.

In prescribing, it should be borne in mind that the action of medicines is influenced by age, sex, temperament, and habit, by diet, condition of system, idiosyncrasy, and climate.

1. *Age.*—Children bear nearly as large a dose of calomel as an adult, but they are extremely susceptible of the action of opiates. Old people do not tolerate narcotics and sedatives so well as those of middle life.

2. *Sex.*—Females, as a rule, require rather smaller doses than males, and they are especially susceptible to the operation of drastic cathartics. The state of the uterine system always requires attention.

3. *Temperament.*—The phlegmatic tolerates stimulants and cathartics better than the sanguine.

4. *Habit.*—This is an important head. It is a well-known fact that the habitual use of many drugs, as for instance, opium, arsenic, and even such powerful cathartics as croton oil and colocynth, &c., begets a tolerance of them in gradually and greatly increased doses; so much so, that some individuals are in the habit of taking daily as much of any one of these as would certainly destroy those unac-

customed to their use. Many persons are known who daily take as much opium as would kill a dozen people, and we know an individual who can hardly obtain a motion from any of the drastic cathartics. Again, we know some who at one time had their neuralgic pains effectually allayed by ext. belladonnæ, who can now obtain no relief whatever from it; and many more examples might be multiplied.

5. *Diet, or condition of stomach.*—Anthelmintics, in general, operate most effectually on an empty stomach, while this condition is unfavourable in the case of iron, zinc, arsenic, &c., pain and nausea being more apt to follow when they come in contact with the mucous membrane of the stomach.

6. *Condition of system.*—If a disease is going on favourably, it is as well to consider whether improvement can be furthered by the administration of drugs, or whether, on the other hand, it may not be retarded. If a patient is suffering from intense pain, say in acute rheumatism, and the agony is aggravated by the least personal movement, we had better abstain from the use of cathartics, though called for by the state of the intestines, until the pain be lessened or allayed. Again, if the patient were suffering from an acute internal inflammation, it would be as well to know the state of the kidneys before resorting to mercury. The head, moreover, merits attention in a contemplated resort to narcotics, and the heart in connection with sedatives.

'7. *Circumstances of the patient.*—We should not give a diaphoretic to a man obliged to be in the open air, nor suppositories to those who could not command a good deal of rest in the recumbent posture, nor drugs in diabetes, where we could not thoroughly control the diet.

8. *Idiosyncrasy.*—We occasionally meet individuals (but the class is not a very large one) in whom the usual and common effects of certain drugs are either aggravated or lessened, inverted or absent. In one, a small dose of mercury will salivate intensely; in another, a purgative will constipate; and in a third, the smallest opiate will induce profound

sleep. There are others, again, whom an astringent will loosen, and some who are slowly acted upon by either opium or mercury. The explanation is not easily given, and it is as well to begin always with moderate doses of powerful drugs, until the patient's system is understood.

9. *Climate.*—Narcotics are better borne in hot climates than in cold, but the reverse is the case in general with mercurials.

10. *Peculiarities connected with certain drugs.*—Lead, digitalis, silver, and probably mercury and iodine, accumulate in the system; hence the doses should not follow each other too quickly, nor be administered for protracted periods without considerable breaks or intermissions.

The following Table represents the gradation of doses from infancy to manhood.

For an adult, supposing the dose to be 1, or gr. lx.

| | | | | |
|---|---|---|---|---|
| Under 1 year, will be | | . | . | $\frac{1}{12}$th or gr. v. |
| „ 2 „ | „ | . | . | $\frac{1}{8}$th or gr. vijss. |
| „ 3 „ | „ | . | . | $\frac{1}{6}$th or gr. x. |
| „ 4 „ | „ | . | . | $\frac{1}{4}$th or gr. xv. |
| „ 7 „ | „ | . | . | $\frac{1}{3}$rd or gr. xx. |
| „ 14 „ | „ | . | . | $\frac{1}{2}$ or gr. xxx. |
| „ 20 „ | „ | . | . | $\frac{2}{3}$ds or gr. xl. |

Above 21, the full dose.

„ 70, the dose should be diminished in the inverse ratio of the above.

There are some drugs which should be cautiously given to children, if given at all, such as Opium, including Morphia.

Crotonis Oleum, Elaterium, Strychnia, Digitalis, Acidum Arseniosum, Aconitum, Aconiti Radix, Stramonii Fol. et Sem., Veratria, demand caution in the adult.

There are some drugs never given internally either to the child or adult. They are: Aconitia, Antimonii Terchloridi Liquor, Atropia, Belladonnæ Radix, Elemi, Hydrarg. Nit. Liq. Acid. Hydrarg. Oxid. Rub. Hydrarg. Ammon. Lythargyrum. Plumb. Subacet. Liq. Potassa Caustica. Zinci Chloridum.

*Officinal Preparations containing Opium, with the Proportion.*

| | | | |
|---|---|---|---|
| Tinctura Opii | contains | gr. j. | in min. xiv. |
| Tinctura Opii Ammon | „ | gr. j. | in min. xcvj. |
| Tinctura Camphoræ cum Opio | „ | gr. j. | in fʒss. |
| Extractum Opii Liquidum | „ | gr. j. ext. | in min. xxij. |
| Vinum Opii | „ | gr. j. ext. | in min. xxjj. |
| Confectio Opii | „ | gr. j. | in gr. xl. |
| Pulv. Opii. Co. | „ | gr. j. | in gr. x. |
| Pilula Saponis Co. | „ | gr. j. | in gr. v. |
| Pilula Plumbi cum Opio | „ | gr. j. | in gr. viij. |
| Pulvis Cretæ Aromat. cum Opio | „ | gr. j. | in gr. xl. |
| Pulvis Ipecacuanhæ cum Opio | „ | gr. j. | in gr. x. |
| Pulvis Kino Co. | „ | gr. j. | in gr. xx. |
| Enema Opii | min. xv. tinct. or | gr. j. | in fʒj. |
| Emplastrum Opii | „ | 1 part | in 10 parts. |
| Linimentum Opii | „ | fʒij. tinct. | in fʒjv. |
| Unguentum Gallæ cum Opio | „ | gr. xxxij. | in oz. |
| Suppositor. Plumb. Co. | „ | gr. j. | in each. |

---

*Officinal Preparations containing Mercury, with the Proportion in each.*

| | | | |
|---|---|---|---|
| Hydrargyrum cum Creta | contains | gr. j. | in gr. iij. |
| Pilula Hydrargyri | „ | gr. j. | in gr. iij. |
| Unguentum Hydrargyri | „ | 1 part | in 2 parts. |
| Linimentum Hydrargyri | „ | 1 „ | in 3 „ |
| Emplastrum Hydrargyri | „ | 1 „ | in 3 „ |
| Emplastrum Ammoniaci cum Hydrardyro | „ | 1 „ | in 5 „ |
| Suppositoria Hydrargyri | about | gr. ij. | in each. |

---

*Preparations of Morphia, with the Proportion.*

| | | | |
|---|---|---|---|
| Morphiæ Acetat. Liquor | contains | gr. iv. | in fʒj. |
| Morph. Hydrochlor. Liq. | „ | gr. iv. | in fʒj. |
| Suppositor. Morph. | „ | gr. ⅓ | in each. |

## 224

*Preparations of Acidum Arseniosum, with the Proportion.*

Liquor Arsenicalis       contains gr. $\frac{1}{24}$th     in min. v.

Liq. Arsenici Hydrochlor.   ,,    gr. $\frac{1}{24}$th     in min. v.

------

*Preparation of Strychnia, with the Proportion.*

Liquor contains gr. $\frac{1}{24}$th in min. v.

------

*Preparation of Hydrarg. Perchlorid. with Proportion.*

Liquor contains gr. $\frac{1}{12}$th in f℥i.

# PART IV.

## ON PARTICULAR FORMS OF MEDICINES.

### Alkaloids.

These are the active principles of drugs, removed, in general, by the addition of alkalies, such as Lime, Potash, and Ammonia, to solutions in water or spt. Many of them are highly poisonous.

### Cataplasms. Poultices.

These are soft pultaceous preparations, for external use, and made extemporaneously. There are six in the Brit. Pharm :—the C. Carbonis (absorbent and disinfectant); C. Conii (anodyne); C. Fermenti (stimulant); C. Lini (emollient and suppurative); C. Sinapis (rubefacient); C. Sodæ Chloratæ (suppurative, stimulant, and disinfectant).

### Confections. Conserves. Electuaries.

These are preparations of the consistence of honey, composed of dry powders mixed with honey, sugar, syrup, or mucilage. They are a convenient form for covering the taste of disagreeable drugs, or diminishing the bulk of light powders, such as Guaiacum, Sulphur, &c.; and useful excipients for pill masses. There are eight in the Brit. Pharm., but none of them contain any very potent drugs, excepting the C. Opii.

### Decoctions.

Solutions of the active parts of vegetables, obtained by boiling in dist. water. They are generally a little stronger than infusions.

### Emulsions.

Preparations in which substances sparingly soluble in water, such as oils and resins, are suspended by means of mucilage, sugar, yolk of egg, &c.

### Enemas. Clysters.

Liquid preparations for injection by the rectum. If intended to promote the evacuation of the intestine, a pint or so should be used; but if to be retained, f℥ij. to f℥jv. is enough.

### Extracts.

These are prepared by evaporating the juices, infusions, or decoctions of vegetables, down to masses of the consistence of an electuary. They are rather stronger than the drugs from which they are prepared. Liquid extracts are not evaporated, and have, in general, a little spt. added.

### Infusions.

Aqueous solutions of vegetables, made by maceration either in hot or cold water. Many of them are now made with cold water, thus preserving principles liable to be dispelled by heat, and rendering them less liable to decay. They are not strong preparations, the dose of the great bulk of them being f℥j. to f℥ij.

### Liniments.

Liquid preparations for external use, and generally combinations of rather strong drugs with fluid and concrete oils; which latter render them of a somewhat emollient nature.

### Lotions. (Fomentations. Collyria. Gargles. Injections.)

Liquids for external use, not oily, and often watery. Fomentations are of the same nature, and are applied of various degrees of temperature. Collyria are those applied to the eye; and gargles those to the mouth and throat. Injections are for throwing up the various canals opening on the surface of the body.

### Mixtures

Are liquid preparations, consisting of combinations of different solids and fluids in water, syrup, mucilage, milk, &c. The dose of most of them is the same as the infusions.

### Ointments. (Cerates.)

Preparations for external use, of the consistence of butter, being combinations of lard or wax and resin (melted at a moderate heat), with various solid ingredients.

### Pessaries. (Not in the B. P.)

Preparations of about the consistence of suppositories, larger, and of a conical shape, for introduction into the vagina. They are made with lard and wax, or cacao butter. The following are the chief:—*Astringent*—Alum, acetate of lead, sulphate of iron, gallic acid, tannic acid. *Alterative*—Iodide of potass., iodide of lead, mercurial oint., bromide of potassium. *Sedative*—Atropine, belladonna, morphia, opium, conium. *Disinfectant*—Carbolic acid, carbolate of lime. *Caustic*—Sulphate of zinc, red oxide of mercury.

### Pills.

Masses of firmer consistence than the preceding, so that they may retain the globular form. They are usually combinations of active ingredients reduced to fine powder, and mixed with soap, syrup, confection, water, &c. They are a convenient form for the administration of disagreeable or acrid drugs. The usual size is 5 grains, which should not be exceeded; many now make them 4 gr. The usual dose is from one to two pills.

### Plasters.

Combinations of wax, resin, fats, or soap, with more active ingredients, of firmer consistence than ointments, and intended for application to the surface of the body. There are fourteen in the pharmacopœia. Three stimulant and resolvent, the emp. plumb. iod., emplast. ammon cum hydrarg.; four stimulant and protective, the emplast. ferri., emplast. galbani., emplast. resinæ, and emplast. picis; one vesicant, emplast. cantharidis; one rubefacient, emplast. calefaciens; two anodyne and sedative, the emplast. belladonnæ, and emplast. opii; the remaining three, emplast. lithargyri, emplast. saponis, and c. saponis, being employed for strapping, and to afford support to weak parts.

### Syrups.

Watery infusions, juices, solutions, and tinctures, combined with sugar.

### Suppositories.

Preparations of a rather harder consistence than ointments, of a conical shape, and about the diameter of the little finger, intended for introduction into the rectum. They.are made of various drugs, combined with wax and lard, or cacao butter.

### Tinctures.

Solutions of the active parts of vegetables in proof spt. (which consists of 5 parts of rect. spt., and 3 parts dist. water), or rect. spt. They are made either by maceration for 7 days, or 48 hours, in which case they also undergo the process of percolation. The dose of the great bulk of them is from half a drachm to two drachms. The exceptions are:—Tinct. Aconiti (min. v. to xv.); T. Belladonnæ (min. v. xx.); T. Cannabis Indicæ (m. v. to xx.); T. Cantharidis (m. v. to xx.); T. Capsici (m. x. to xx.); T. Chloroformi Co. (m. xx. to lx.); T. Colchici seminum (m. x. to xxx.); T. Conii (m. xx. to lx.); T. Digitalis (m. x. to. xxx.); T. Ferri Acetatis (m. v. to xxx.); T. Ferri Perchlor (m. x. to xxx.); T. Hyoscyami (m. xxx. to f3j.); T. Iodi (m. v. to xx.); T. Lobeliæ (m. x. to xxx.); T. Lobeliæ Ætherea (m. x. to xxx.); T. Nucis Vomicæ (m. x. to xx.); T. Opii (m. v. to xl.); Do. Ammon (m. xxx. to lx.); T. Sabinæ (m. xx. to lx.); T. Scillæ (m. x. to xxx.); T. Stramonii (m. x. to xxx.); T. Sumbul (m. x. to xxx.); T. Tolu (m. xx. to lx.); T. Veratri Viridis (m. v. to xx.); T. Zingiberis (m. xv. to lx.); T. Zingiberis Fortior (m. v. to xx.).

# APPENDIX.

## CONTRACTED TERMS IN COMMON USE.

*A.  Aa.  Ana.*  Of each ingredient.
*Ad libit.  Ad libitum.*  At pleasure.
*Adde, or, addantur.*  Add.
*Admov.  Admoveatur.*  Apply.
*Alternis horis.*  Every other hour.
*Alvo adstricto.*  When costive.
*Aqua bulliens.*  Boiling water.
*Aqua fervens.*  Boiling water.
*Bis indies.*  Twice a-day.
*Bulliat.*  It should boil.
*Balneum vaporis.*  A vapour bath.
*Capiat.*  Take.
*Capillitium abradatur.*  Let the head be shaved.
*Cras mane.*  To-morrow morning.
*Coch. amp.  Cochleare amplum.*  A table-spoon.
*Coch. mag.  Cochleare magnum.*  A table-spoon.
*Coch. med.  Cochleare mediocre.*  A dessert-spoon.
*Coch. parv.  Cochleare parvum.*  A tea-spoon.
*Col.  Colatus.*  Strained.
*Congius.*  A gallon.
*Cont. med.  Continuantur medicamenta.*  The medicines
    to be continued.
*Contr. Contritus.*  Finely powdered.
*Coq. Coque.*  Boil.
*Cras.  Crastinus.*  To-morrow.
*Cujus.*  Of which.
*Cyathus.*  A wine-glass.
*Dej. alvi.  Dejectiones alvi.*  Stools.
*Det.  Detur.*  It should be given.

*Diebus alternis.* Every other day.
*Diebus Tertiis.* Every third day.
*Dimidius.* One half.
*Donec alvus soluta fuerit.* Until a stool has been obtained.
*Extende super alutam.* Spread upon leather.
*Femoribus internis.* On the inner part of the thighs.
*Fiat venæsectio.* Bleed.
*Fist. arm. Fistula armata.* A clyster-pipe and bladder, fitted.
*Gr. Granum.* A grain.
*Gtt. Gutta.* A drop.
*Hor. decub. Hora decubitus.* At going to bed.
*Hora somni.* At bed-time, or the hour of sleep.
*Injiciatur enema.* An enema should be given.
*Lateri dolenti.* To the affected side.
*Lb. Libra.* A pound weight.
*M. Misce.* Mix.
*Manipulus.* A handful.
*Mane primo.* Early in the morning.
*Min. Minimum.* The 60th part of a drachm.
*Mitte.* Send.
*Mor. sol. More solito.* In the usual manner.
*O. Octarius.* A pint.
*Omni hora.* Every hour.
*Omni biduo.* Every two days.
*Omni bihorio.* Every two hours.
*Omni mane.* Every morning.
*Omni nocti.* Every night.
*Omni quadrante horæ.* Every quarter of an hour.
*Partitis vicibus.* In divided doses.
*Post singulas sedes liquidas.* After every loose stool.
*Pro re nata.* As occasion serves.
*Quantum sufficit.* As much as may suffice.
℞. *Recipe.* Take.
*Redactus in Pulverem.* Powdered.
*Repet. Repetatur.* It should be continued.
*Semihora.* Half-an-hour.
*Sesquihora.* An hour and a half.

*Si opus sit.*   If necessary.
*Signa* (*Signetur*).   Write (as follows, or the direction).
*Singulorum.*   Of each.
*S. V. R.   Spiritus vinosus rectificatus.*   Rectified spt.
*Temp. dext.   Tempori dextro.*   To the right temple.
*Ult. præscr.   Ultimo præscritus.*   The last ordered.
*V. O. S.   Vitello ovi solutus.*   Dissolved in the yolk of
   an egg.
*Vom. urg.   Vomitione urgente.*   When the vomiting
   begins.

---

## MEDICINES IN USE NOT IN THE BRITISH PHARMACOPŒIA.

### Actæa Racemosa.

*Tinctura.*—Root i., proof spt. iv., macerate 14 days.
Dose, min. xxx. to lx.   Given in rheumatism and neuralgia,
doing good in the former disease.

### Aloine.

Prepared from Barbadoes aloes.   In yellow crystals.
*Uses.*—An excellent cathartic.   Dose, gr. ½ to iij.

### Amyl Nitris.

A stimulant of unrivalled potency, and demanding
caution in its use.   A single drop inhaled raises the pulse
30 to 50 beats in a few seconds, and occasions singularly
bright flushing of the countenance.   Has been recommended
in angina pectoris.

### Calcis Hypophosphis.

*Uses.*—Tonic in debility and phthisis.   Dose, gr. iij.
to v.

### Carbon, Tetrachloride of.

Anæsthetic, but not so effectual as chloroform.

### Caulophyllin.   (Blue Cohosh.)

*Uses.*—A uterine stimulant, but not very efficacious.
Dose, gr. ¼ to gr. iij.

### Corydalin. (Turkey Pea Root.)

Tonic, and said to be anti-syphilitic.   Dose, gr. ⅛ to v.

### Chlorodyne.

Anodyne and sedative.   Dose, min. v. to xx.   Prepared as follows :—Chloroform fʒiv.; ether fʒi.; spt. rect. fʒiv.; treacle ʒiv.; ext. liquorice ʒij½.; hydrochlor. morph. gr. viij.; oil of peppt. min. xvj.; syrup ʒxvijss.; prussic acid (2 per cent. strength) ʒij.   Dissolve the morph. and the peppt. in the rect. spt.; mix the chlorof. and ether with the solution.   Dissolve the ext. liquorice in the syrup and add the treacle ; shake these two solutions together ; and finally add the prussic acid.

### Huile de Cade.   Juniper Tar.

A useful external stimulant in obstinate skin diseases.

### Iodoform.

In yellow crystals.   Given to alleviate the pain of cancer. Dose, gr. v., twice a-day, in mixture with mucilage.

### Iridin.   Blue Flag.

*Uses.*—Cathartic and diuretic.   Given in renal dropsy. Dose, gr. ⅛ to ij.

### Leptandrin.   Veronica Virginica.

Purgative and cholagogue.   Given in sluggish liver, and chronic constipation.   Dose, gr. ⅛ to jv.

### Methylene, Bichloride of.

Anæsthetic, but not so suitable as chloroform.

### Neurolyne.

A mixture of quiniæ, sulph. potass., iodid. potass., bromid, and iron.

*Uses.*—A powerful alterative, deobstruant, and tonic. Given with marked benefit in strumous disorders, syphilis, neuralgia, and rheumatism.   Dose, fʒi. to fʒij., in water, three or four times a-day.

### Pepsine.

The gastric juice obtained from the stomachs of the calf, sheep, or hog, killed fasting; purified, dried, and mixed with dry starch. Given to promote digestion, in cases of deficient secretion. Often fails. Dose, gr. xv. before meals.

### Rumicin. Yellow Dock.

Astringent, and a useful antiscorbutic. Dose, gr. ij. to v.

### St. Ignatius' Bean.

The seeds of ignatia amara from the Philippine Islands. They contain strychnia.

*Uses.*—Nerve-tonic. Dose, gr. ⅛ to j. in pill.

### Salicinum. Salicine.

Obtained from the bark of salix alba. In white silky crystals; bitter taste.

*Uses.*—A useful tonic in debility. Dose, gr. ᴠ. to x.

### Tar Capsules.

Five or six capsules a-day as a stimulant, and in leucorrhœa, and cystirrhœa.

---

PREPARATIONS—MIXTURES, ETC.—IN USE, NOT IN

THE BRITISH PHARMACOPŒIA.

### Brandish's Alkaline Solution.

Pearl ashes, quicklime, wood ashes, and water.

Given in glandular diseases .(strumous). Dose, fʒss. to ʒij., in milk.

### Caustic Points.

These are made by fusing potass. nit. with the nitrate of silver. They are convenient for oculists and others.

### Chelsea Pensioner.

Sulphur vi.; powd. guaiacum iii.; mustard vi.; rhubarb and nitrate of potash, of each, i¼. Mix. Then add treacle sufficient to make into an electuary.

This preparation has been long famous among " Tars " and sons of Mars as a remedy in rheumatism; and it is really a useful medicine. Dose, gr. xxx. to lx., or a teaspoonful every second night.

### Chemical Food. Parish's Syrupus Ferri Phosph. Co.

In every f℈i. there is gr. i. phosph. ferri, and gr. ij$\frac{1}{2}$. phosph. lime, besides soda and potass. Useful as a tonic in debility. Dose, f℈i. to f℈ij.

### Colloid Styptic (Dr Richardson's).

A saturated solution of tannic acid and xyloidine or gun cotton in absolute alcohol and pure ether, with a little benzoin. Used as a coating over wounds, and in erysipelas.

### De Valangin's Solution.

This contains gr. xxx. of arsenic, dissolved by min. xc. of hydrochloric acid, in ℥xx. of water. Dose, min. iij., gradually increased.

### Donovan's Solution.

A fluid drachm of this contains $\frac{1}{16}$th of a grain of arsenic; gr. $\frac{1}{4}$ mercury, and gr. $\frac{1}{2}$ of iodine. An excellent alterative preparation. Dose, min. x. to xxx.

### Muriate of Lime.

In crystals. Consists of equal parts by weight of water and dried chloride of calcium.

*Uses.*—This drug is of considerable service in glandular diseases, and in some cases of sickness and vomiting will do good when other remedies fail. Dose, gr. i. or ij. in water, often repeated in cases of sickness.

### Nepenthé.

A watery solution of opium. Dose, same as tincture of opium.

### Scheele's Prussic Acid.

This is fully twice the strength of the acid of the B. P. It is variable in strength, owing to its deteriorating when kept, and therefore not a very reliable preparation.

### Sinapine Paper.

Rubefacient, counterirritant. Its irritant property is due to capsicine.

## WEIGHTS AND MEASURES OF THE BRITISH PHARMACOPŒIA.

### *Weights.*

| 1 pound | lb. | = | 16 ounces | = | 7000 grains. |
| 1 ounce | oz. | = | | = | 437·5 grains. |
| 1 grain | gr. | = | | = | 1 grain |

### *Measures.*

| 1 gallon | C. | = | 8 pints . . | O. viij. |
| 1 pint | O. | = | 20 fluid ounces . | fl. oz. xx. |
| 1 fluid ounce fl. oz. | = | 8 fluid drachms | fl. drs. viij. |
| 1 fluid drachm fl. drm. = | 60 minims . | min. lx. |
| 1 minim | min. | = | 1 minim . | min. j. |

## POISONS, WITH THEIR ANTIDOTES AND TESTS.

### Acidum Arseniosum.

*Antidotes.*—Stomach-pump, or if not at hand, an emetic of zinc. sulph. or cupri sulph. Wash out stomach with tepid water, in which is suspended the humid peroxide of iron. This forms the inert sub-arseniate of protoxide of iron. Give largely also of light magnesia, and demulcent drinks.

*Test.*—Slowly sublimed it forms minute transparent octahedral crystals. Sprinkled on a hot iron it gives out an alliaceous odour. Solution gives, with ammonio-nitrate of silver, a canary-yellow precipitate, insoluble in water, but readily dissolved by ammonia, and by nitric acid.

### Acidum Hydrochloricum.

*Antidotes.*—Chalk, magnesia, and demulcent drinks.

*Test.*—Gives, with nitrate of silver, a curdy-white precipitate, soluble in excess of ammonia, insoluble in nitric acid.

### Acidum Hydrocyanicum Dilutum.

*Antidotes.*—Fresh air, vigorous cold affusion—water

being showered down head and neck—and artificial respiration. Newly precipitated oxide of iron with an alkaline carbonate.

*Test.*—Treated with a small quantity of a mixed solution of sulphate, and persulphate of iron, afterwards with potash, and finally acidulated with hydrochloric acid it forms prussian blue. Gives no precip. with chloride of barium; but with nitrate of silver it gives a white precip., entirely soluble in boiling concentrated nitric acid.

### Acidum Nitricum.

*Antidotes.*—Same as in acid. hydrochlor.

*Test.*—Poured over copper filings dense red vapours are immediately formed, but if the acid be mixed with an equal volume of water, and then added to the copper, it gives off a colourless gas, which acquires an orange-red colour, as it mixes with the air, and which, if introduced into a solution of ferri sulph., communicates to it a dark purple or brown colour.

### Acidum Oxalicum.

*Antidotes.*—Chalk, magnesia, or whiting, suspended in water, should be given if patient is early seen. Emetics, and stomach-pump also, if necessary.

### Acidum Sulphuricum.

*Antidotes.*—Magnesia and demulcent drinks.

*Test.*—Evolves heat on addition of water, and when thus diluted gives a copious precip., with chloride of barium.

### Aconiti Radix.    Aconiti Folia.

*Antidotes.*—Emetic of zinci sulph. or cupri sulph., internal and external stimulants.

### Antimonium Tartaratum.

*Antidotes.*—Tannin, catechu, and vegetable astringents.

*Test.*—Decrepitates and blackens upon the application of heat. Its solution in water gives, with hydrochloric acid, a white precip., soluble in excess, and which is not formed if tartaric acid be previously added. 20 grains dissolve without residue in f℥j. of aq. dest. at 60⁰, and the solution gives with sulphuretted hydrogen an orange precip., which when washed and dried at 212⁰ weighs 9.91 grains.

### Argenti Nitras.

*Antidote.*—Solution of common salt.

*Test.*—Solution gives with HCl a curdy-white precip., which darkens by exposure to light, and is soluble in solution of ammonia.

### Belladonnæ Folia et Radix.

*Antidotes.*—Emetic of zinc. sulph., cold to the head, ammonia internally and externally, other stimulants, and after a brisk purgative, probably careful doses of opium.

### Calx Chlorata.

*Antidotes.*—Emetics, albumen, milk, flour, demulcent drinks.

*Test.*—The solution evolves chlorine on adding oxalic acid, and deposits at the same time oxalate of lime.

### Cantharidis.

*Antidotes.*—Emetics, mucilaginous drinks, opium by the mouth, and by enema; blood letting if necessary.

### Chloroformum.

*Antidotes.*—Currents of fresh air, galvanism, artificial respiration, stimulants.

### Conii Folia et Fructus.

*Antidotes.*—Emetics, external and internal stimulants.

### Colchici Cormus et Semina.

*Antidotes.*—Emetics promptly, and demulcent drinks; and if coma has been induced give powerful stimulants, such as ammonia and brandy, with coffee. Tannin may be also given, as it forms an insoluble compound with the colchicia.

### Digitalis.

*Antidotes.*—Emetic of zinci sulph., internal and external stimulants, and especially the recumbent posture.

### Elaterium.

*Antidotes.*—Demulcent drinks, mucilaginous enemata, small and repeated doses of opium, and the warm bath.

### Ferri Perchloridi Liquor.

*Antidote.*—Same as for Hydrochloric Acid.

### Hydrargyri Perchloridum.

*Antidotes.*—Albumen, white of egg, flour, milk, protochloride of tin.

*N.B.*—Too much white of egg should not be given, in case of re-dissolving the albuminate. About the white of one egg is enough for gr. iv. of the poison.

*Test.*—Solution (in water) gives a yellow precip. with caustic potash; a white precip. with ammonia; and a curdy white precip. with nitrate of silver. Heated, it sublimes without decomposing, and without leaving any residue.

### Hyoseyami Folia.

*Antidotes.*—Emetics, stomach pump, stimulants, lemon juice.

### Liquor Ammoniæ Fortior.

*Antidotes.*—Vinegar, lemon juice, tartaric acid, demulcents.

### Lobelia.

*Antidotes.*—Internal and external stimulants.

### Morphiæ Hydrochloras.

*Antidotes.*—Same as opium.

*Test.*—Aqueous solution gives a white curdy precip. with nitrate of silver, and a white one with potash, which is re-dissolved when an excess of the alkali is added; moistened with strong nitric acid it becomes orange-red, and with solut. of perchloride of iron, greenish-blue.

### Nux Vomica.

*Antidotes.*—Tobacco, in the form of the B. P. enema.

### Oleum Crotonis.

*Antidotes.*—Emetic, if seen early; demulcent drinks and opium.

### Opium.

*Antidotes.*—Emetic of zinci sulph., stomach pump, external stimulants (such as ammonia to nostrils), artificial respiration, and enforced exertion.

### Phosphorus.

*Antidotes.*—Demulcent drinks, and small doses of opium.

### Plumbi Acetas.

*Antidotes.*—Phosphates of soda and magnesia, sulphate of magnesia, laxatives, and afterwards opium, and the warm bath.

*Test.*—Solution gives a yellow precip. with iodide of potassium, and is precipitated white by sulphuric acid—acetic acid being set free. Solution in dist. water has a slight milkiness, which disappears on the addition of acetic acid.

### Potassæ Caustica.

*Antidotes.*—Dilute acetic acid, citric acid, fixed oils, demulcents, lemon juice.

### Sabinæ Cacumina.

*Antidotes.*—Emetics, demulcents, and opiates.

### Stramonii Folia et Semina.

*Antidotes.*—Same as for Belladonna.

### Strychnia.

*Antidotes.*—Chloroform, tinct. aconiti. belladonna. A little tinct. belladonnæ or aconiti should be given, the patient being afterwards put under chloroform. A case of recovery after three grains.

*Test.*—Sparingly soluble in water, but communicating to it its intensely bitter taste ; soluble in boiling rectified spt. and in chloroform, but not in absolute alcohol or ether. Pure sulphuric acid forms with it a colourless solution, which, on the addition of bichromate of potash, acquires an intensely violet hue, quickly passing through red to yellow. Not coloured by nitric acid.

**Veratria.**

*Antidotes.*—Same as in colchicum.

---

### QUESTIONS IN MATERIA MEDICA.

The following questions are inserted in order to afford an indication of the style and scope of examinations on the subject of Materia Medica :—

Actions, poisonous and medicinal, of the preparations of lead ; doses of the acetate, and the chief diseases in which it is employed.

The distinctive characters of sulphureous thermal springs, the chief ones in Europe, and the maladies in which they are employed.

General external characters of digitalis, aconite, and hyoscyamus.

Prescriptions.—A chalybeate tonic in the form of pill. An emetic in narcotic poisoning. An astringent and sedative in chronic diarrhœa.

The preparations of iron in which it exists simply as an oxide, characters, doses, and manner of administration.

The poisonous and medicinal actions of squill, and the diseases in which it is given.

Prescriptions.—An aperient in habitual constipation, when there is a tendency to hæmorrhoids. Nitric acid and uva-ursi, in chronic inflammation of the bladder. A purgative in a case of lead colic.

Distinguishing characters of ergot in the entire state and in powder.

Composition and distinguishing marks of calomel, corrosive sublimate, white precipitate and red precipitate.

Actions, poisonous and medicinal of cantharides.

Nature, proximate composition, and actions, poisonous and medicinal, of gamboge.

Treatment, medicinal and dietetic, of uric gravel.

What is elaterium ?  Give its botanical name, and natural order of the plant yielding it ; its action, and dose for adult.

Prescription.—A lotion with acid. hydrocyan. for allaying the irritation of a cutaneous eruption.

Prescription for a course of powders with rheum., sodæ bicarb., and calumba, in dyspepsia.—Oxide of zinc in pill.

Formula for nit. argent., and name the diseases in which it is employed.

*Aconite.*—Its actions poisonous and medicinal.  Ordinary officinal form.  Dose.  Frequency of administration.  Effect of overdose, and treatment of same.  Principal diseases wherein it is used.

*Colchicum.*—Poisonous and medicinal actions.  Officinal forms.  Doses.  Frequency of administration.  Effect, and treatment of overmuch.  Principal diseases treated by it.

*Hemlock.*—Name of plant.  Family.  Habitat.  Odour. Odour disengaged by trituration with potash solution. External marks of the plant and root.

Prescriptions.—A diuretic pill containing iron and squill, and state at what intervals it is to be administered.

Prescription for a blister 6 in. long and 4 broad to be applied to the chest.

Prescription for a gargle of alum in infusion of roses.

Prescribe strychnia in solution as a remedy in nervous diseases.

From what plants and natural orders are the following drugs obtained :—Ipecacuanha, Jalap, Scammony, Croton Oil, Elaterium?

What are the physiological actions of Gamboge? with what objects, in what doses, and with what precautions is it usually prescribed?

What are the chief mineral and vegetable vermifuge substances?

Tartar emetic ; its physiological actions ; and how should it be administered in order to induce its various therapeutic actions?

*Colocynth.*—Botanical source, natural family. Chief pharmaceutic preparation, and its medicinal dose and action. Its inconveniences, and how these are prevented. Is it ever a poison?

*Ether.*—Characters, density. In what shape administered. Action when swallowed. Medicinal dose. Action when inhaled. Quantity required in this way. Is it ever a poison?

Prescriptions.—Aconite for external use. Belladonna for internal use. A tonic and sedative in dyspepsia. Quinine in solution for a case of tertian ague. Sulphate of zinc in a case of poisoning with laudanum. An astringent and anodyne ointment for a case of piles. A bitter infusion along with a mineral acid. Veratria for external use. An emmenagogue pill with directions. An expectorant mixture with directions.

*Nitric Acid.*—Characters. Odour. Effect on Skin. Action in poisonous doses. On the lips and mouth, gullet, stomach, bowels. Treatment of these effects. Action in medicinal doses on the stomach, liver, and urine. Uses in fevers. In dyspepsia. In gravel. The urinary diathesis in which it is serviceable. Theory of its action in this. Pharmaceutic form of use, and its dose. How to cover its acid taste, and how to prevent its action on the teeth.

*Nitrate of Silver.*—Characters. Effect on the skin. Action internally in large doses. Any remote action. Antidote. Actions in medicinal doses. Special uses. Form for giving it, and dose. Inconvenient effect which may arise, and in what circumstances. Precautions for avoiding it. Is it avoidable by substituting another preparation of silver? Action externally when concentrated. Examples in the case of certain ulcers. Of acute inflammation. Of chronic inflammation. Action in diluted solution. Examples.

*Spirit of Nitrous Ether.*—Characters. Actions in large and in medicinal doses. Special uses in disease. Dose.

*Belladonna.*—Characters and family of the plant. Preparations of it. Source of activity. Nature and constitution of that substance. Actions of Belladonna in large doses. Actions in medicinal doses internally on the nervous system. On the intestinal canal. Topical actions. Doses of the chief preparations internally. Forms for external use.

*Chlorinated Lime.*—Constitution. Characters. Form. Odour. Taste. Actions in large doses internally. Topical effects in ordinary quantity. Special uses as a topical remedy. Form for use.

Prescriptions.—A colchicum mixture in gout. Oil of maleshield fern for tapeworm. Corrosive sublimate in solution as an alterative. An astringent mixture in chronic diarrhœa.

*Ipecacuanha.*— External characters. Natural family. Sources of its activity. Nature of its active principle. Its various actions. Some diseases in which these are applied in practice. Its principal preparations. Doses, according to its varied actions. The several modes of using it in dysentery.

*Nux Vomica.*—Natural family. Country. Part used. Form, texture, and taste. Source of its activity. The chief galenical preparation, and its dose. Chemical test for the active principle. Action of the principle as a poison. Action in medicinal doses. Diseases in which it is used. Doses and frequency.

*Carbonate of Lead.*—Characters. How formed naturally on lead. Composition. Action in continued small doses. How counteracted.

Prescriptions.—Columba, Sodæ Bicarb., and Aloes in powder for disorder of stomach and sluggish bowels. Nitrate of silver in pill, to be taken every eight hours. Epsom Salts and Tartar Emetic in solution, in a febrile attack.

*Gallic Acid.*—Its form, taste, solubility, test, elementary composition. Action. Diseases in which it is given. Doses, and frequency. Forms for administration.

*Hydrochlorate of Morphia.*—Form, taste, solubility, composition. Physiological action on stomach, bowels, mucous membrane, skin. Its occasional inconvenient effects on the nervous system, the stomach, and skin.   Modes of administration in acute dysentery, with the best forms and doses; also in acute bronchitis, and obstruction of the bowels.   Its chief pharmaceutic forms and their doses.

Prescriptions.—Pills with strychnia in paraplegia.   A diaphoretic mixture containing acetate of ammonia and tartar emetic.   A diuretic mixture containing squill, sweet spirit of nitre, and fox-glove.   Remedies applicable in a case of painters' colic.   An acid mixture for a case of oxaluria.

*Assafœtida.*—Whence obtained.   Natural family.   How known by sensible properties.   Its active part.   Actions on the body.   Chief uses in diseases.   How given by the mouth and anus.

*Chalybeate Mineral Waters.*—The two forms of iron in them.   Examples in Britain, or on the Continent.   Actions of a simple chalybeate spring.   Diseases chiefly treated by them.   Any precautions necessary.

*Charcoal.*—Define it.   Two kinds employed in medicine. Their composition respectively.   Uses as disinfectants. Chemical action as such.   Which preferable.

*Cantharides.*—Ordinary actions in medicinal doses on the urine.   On the mucous membranes.   In large doses on the alimentary canal.   On the kidneys.   On the genital organs. Usual form for internal use.   Dose and frequency of this preparation.   Action of cantharides externally : the several local changes occasioned according to the length of its application : in certain constitutional states such as typhus : occasional inconveniences through absorption by the skin : treatment of these.

Mention a remedy for destruction of vermin on the skin, and the form for use.

Prescriptions.—Nux vomica and phosphate of zinc, in pill, for paraplegia.   A carminative for an infant of six months.   Egot of rye, in feeble action of the uterus.   A dose of calomel and jalap for an adult.   Nitrate of silver as a collyrium in chronic ophthalmia.   Tannic acid and opium, in pill, for diarrhœa.

# INDEX.